101 SCI-FI MOVIES

YOU MUST SEE BEFORE YOU DIE

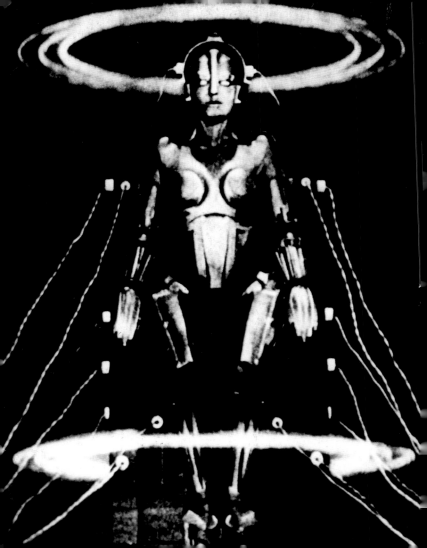

101 SCI-FI MOVIES
YOU MUST SEE BEFORE YOU DIE

GENERAL EDITOR
STEVEN JAY SCHNEIDER

A Quint**essence** Book

First edition for the United States and Canada
published in 2009 by Barron's Educational Series, Inc.

ISBN-13: 978-0-7641-4125-6
ISBN-10: 0-7641-4125-2
QSS.MBSF

All inquiries should be addressed to:
Barron's Educational Series, Inc.
250 Wireless Boulevard
Hauppauge, NY 11788
www.barronseduc.com

This book was designed and produced by:
Quint**essence**
226 City Road
London EC1V 2TT

Project Editor	Chrissy Williams
Editor	James Harrison
Editorial Assistant	Helena Baser
Designer	Nick Withers
Editorial Director	Jane Laing
Publisher	Tristan de Lancey

Color reproduction in Singapore by Pica Digital Pte Ltd.
Printed in China by SNP Leefung Printers Ltd.
9 8 7 6 5 4 3 2 1

CONTENTS

INTRODUCTION Steven Jay Schneider, General Editor

Science fiction is the genre where fantasy and reality coexist—or collide—to portray alternative visions of our planet and far-flung worlds. Sometimes daydreams and sometimes nightmares, they invariably play out the practical and ethical implications of new technologies. As grounded scientist and gifted sci-fi author Arthur C. Clarke put it, "There's no real objection to escapism, in the right places… But science fiction is often very far from escapism, in fact you might say that science fiction is escape into reality… It's a fiction which does concern itself with real issues: the origin of man; our future."

If the relationship between science fiction and film feels so intimate, so essential, that is undoubtedly due to the fact that cinema itself is science fiction. Many of the first moving pictures ever screened were set in the future or on distant planets, and included unbelievable camera tricks, special effects, costumes, and makeup for audiences then. Today we've grown up with fantastic advancements in cinema technologies, whether at the level of effects, editing, cinematography, or exhibition. The moviegoing experience is all about escapism, and science fiction is its ultimate expression.

But no matter how many years in the past or the future, no matter how many millions of light years from home, no matter how bleak the future or barren the landscape, no matter how epic the galactic war, what makes the films discussed within *101 Sci-Fi Movies You Must See Before You Die* is the inescapable truth that they all— somehow— resonate with our reality. In the words of The Twilight Zone host, Rod Serling, "Fantasy is the impossible made probable. Science fiction is the improbable made possible."

Steven J. Schneider

Hollywood, U.S.A.

LE VOYAGE
DANS LA LUNE

VOYAGE TO THE MOON 1902 (FRANCE)

Director Georges Méliès **Producer** Georges Méliès **Screenplay** Georges Méliès
(loosely based on *From the Earth to the Moon* by Jules Verne and *The First Men in the
Moon* by H. G. Wells) **Cinematography** Michaut, Lucien Tainguy **Cast** Georges
Méliès, Bleuette Bernon, Victor André, Depierre, Brunnet, Farjaux, Kelm, Jeanne d'Alcy

French cinema is not best known for its science-fiction films, but
France has a great claim to fame in this genre's history. Thanks
to this country—and the magical work of Georges Méliès
over 100 years ago—the sci-fi movie genre was launched. A
magician by trade, Méliès constantly sought to improve upon
his tricks, and in 1902, borrowing elements from Jules Verne's
From the Earth to the Moon (1865) and H. G. Wells's *First Men in
the Moon* (1901), he showed even greater ambition.

Voyage to the Moon (a.k.a. *Le Voyage dans la lune*) tells the
story of an expedition, led by Professor Barbenfouillis (Méliès),
that flies to the moon in a shell fired by a giant cannon. It's not
long before they are captured by the moon's inhabitants, the
Selenites, and brought before their king. They finally manage to
escape, get back to the shell, and *fall* back to Earth. Barbenfouillis
and his companions are received with all the honors, while a
Selenite, who has clung to the rocket, is shown to the public.

Voyage to the Moon is symptomatic of both an early stage of
cinema and the new possibilities it could foresee. Composed of
about twenty shots, mostly static, it doesn't let verisimilitude
get in its way and at times even seems to ignore the basic

◄
This image, that
shows the instant
the lunar capsule
lands in the eye of
the moon, is one
of the best
known sights in
cinematic history.

laws of perspective. However, using elaborate scenery with removable parts, cuts, dissolves, and double exposures, Méliès is able to bring life to a world of pure fantasy. Acrobats, music hall singers, and dancers appear in front of the camera at a time when respectable actors wouldn't compromise themselves in what was not then a recognized art form. For various filmmakers, including American Edwin S. Porter,

"IN CINEMATOGRAPHY IT IS TODAY POSSIBLE TO REALIZE THE MOST IMPROBABLE THINGS." GEORGES MÉLIÈS

Méliès's improbable adventure quickly became a model to imitate from a technical, narrative, and aesthetic standpoint. Even today, the brief shot that shows the shell landing in the eye of the moon face remains famous and retains at least some of its poetical as well as comical attraction.

Méliès's foray into space is reported to last around 20 minutes (although surviving prints are much shorter), a most unusual length for the period. Since films were still sold by the meter, *Voyage to the Moon* was an extremely expensive picture and, at first, the director's clients (fairground people) refused to invest so much money. However, after a triumphant public screening, orders quickly began to flow in. The film's success was international, but all the money won didn't go straight into Méliès's pocket as bootleg copies were widely distributed in the United States. Some things never change. **FL**

► The cannon operators were all dancers from the famous Châtelet ballet in Paris.

A TRIP TO MARS 1918 (DENMARK)

Director Holger-Madsen **Producer** Holger-Madsen **Screenplay** Ole Olsen, Sophus Michaelis (from the novel by Sophus Michaelis) **Cinematography** Frederik Fuglsang, Louis Larsen **Cast** Nils Asther, Philip Bech, Frederik Jacobsen, Lilly Jacobson, Alf Blutecher, Svend Kornbech, Nicolai Neiiendam, Alfred Osmund

Though told in images at times startling and often beautifully composed by director Holger-Madsen, *A Trip to Mars* (a.k.a. *Himmelskibet,* or "heaven ship") is not primarily an exercise in special effects, still less a fanciful evocation of alien worlds along the lines of Georges Méliès's *Voyage to the Moon*. Rather, it uses the idea of Mars almost as a metaphor, as part of a thoughtful meditation on the notion of the ideal human society, somewhat akin to Thomas More's *Utopia*. Though largely forgotten now, it was a major and expensive production in Denmark at the time, boasting some massive and amazing sets, with Martian exteriors filmed in a rock quarry near to Copenhagen.

Modern viewers may be surprised to discover that the Earth travelers are welcomed by the people of Mars, who are pacifists and vegetarians, and long past their guests' uncivilized and warlike stage of evolution. The leader of the Earth mission falls in love with beautiful Martian Lily Jacobsen, and they return to Earth to promote the advanced ideas of tolerance and peace.

Despite the often grandiose production design, there is no effort to make anything unusual of the Martian landscape or the Martians themselves. This is deliberate: The aliens are

◄
The spaceship in the poster reflects the fascination with the relatively new technology of aviation: The spaceship has wings and a propeller.

different from the voyagers purely by virtue of their moral superiority. Accordingly, their world is classically styled: They wear togas and the social hierarchy conforms to something like the Platonic ideal—the leaders all sages and philosophers.

Several writers have pointed out the film's many logical errors and absurdities: for example the fact that the sun is the same relative size to the Martian landscape as it is to

> ## "PERHAPS THE LEAST ANTAGONISTIC MEETING OF MARTIANS AND EARTHLINGS IN SCREEN HISTORY."

► **Actor Nils Asther, prominent among the Martians, later moved to Hollywood and enjoyed a brief career in major romantic leads in the early 1930s, and a longer one in B-movie supporting roles through the late 1930s and 1940s.**

Earth; the Martians' globe of planet Earth with the North Pole at the top; the airship-style rocket with propellers and a horizontal trajectory; and doubtless many more. It was conceived, of course, long before many of the realities of space and space travel we now take for granted were generally known, such as variations in atmospheric density and differing gravitational pressures.

Nevertheless, *A Trip to Mars* was produced at a time when the First World War was showing little sign of ending, and in this respect the film cannot fail to impress when seen as a plea for compassion and tolerance, featuring as it does perhaps the least antagonistic meeting of Martians and Earthlings in screen history. That it is also among the very first of alien-Earthling screen encounters makes it seem even more downright tragic. **MC**

AELITA 1924 (U.S.S.R.)

Director Yakov Protazanov **Screenplay** Aleksei Fajko, Fyodor Otsep (from the novel by Aleksei Tolstoy) **Cinematography** Emil Schünemann, Yuri Zhelyabuzhsky **Music** Sergei Prokofiev **Cast** Nikolai Tsereteli, Yuliya Solntseva, Igor Ilyinsky, Nikolai Batalov, Vera Orlova, Valentina Kuindzh, Pavel Pol, Konstantin Eggert, Yuri Zavadsky

The Marxist struggle reaches outer space in this Russian science-fiction film from the silent period. Based on the novel by Alexsei Tolstoy, the picture follows a Soviet engineer, Los (Tsereteli), who dreams of traveling to other worlds and that a beautiful woman named Aelita (Solntseva) awaits him on his travels. Upon receiving a mysterious radio message from Mars, he decides to pose as a rocket scientist, build a spaceship, and embark on the first ever voyage to the planet. When he arrives, he finds that Aelita does, in fact, exist and is Queen there (the film was also released as *Aelita: Queen of Mars*). However, the petty political struggles that Los left behind on Earth still exist on Mars; the Martian proletariat are attempting to rise up and take power. Los, once again, finds himself standing between the ruling leadership and the workers attempting to take control of their own lives.

Aelita is acclaimed as the world's first space travel melodrama as well as the Soviet's first science-fiction film. The scenes of common workers revolting against the ruling class would be repeated similarly in Universal's *Flash Gordon* serials of the 1930s. However, *Aelita* is much more valuable as a daringly

◄
This film became such a hit in the Soviet Union that many new parents named their baby girls "Aelita."

objective look at city life under socialization and communism. Life on Mars mimics life on Earth, and before long the Martian Union of Soviet Socialist Republics stages a major revolution against the upper class and all hell breaks loose. The film takes a political stance even in its depiction of the former

"A SOCIALIST SCIENCE-FICTION SPECTACLE WITH . . . CONSTRUCTIVIST AND CUBIST MOTIFS." JAMES NEWMAN (WRITER)

aristocrats coping in a Soviet community—they are portrayed negatively albeit with a touch of sympathy.

Most notable from the film's production are its set and costume designs for the Martian sequences. The art design is incredibly complicated for its time: Pokes radiate from the Queen's hat, doors open like camera apertures, staircases start in one direction and then twist back in other directions, and Aelita's maid wears a spiral-shaped hat that seems to radiate from her forehead and sweep around her head. This highly stylized form of design helps to suggest much more than what actually appears on screen. Ultimately, *Aelita* sets the tone for future Soviet sci-fi films by using the genre as a metaphor to visualize more psychological and down-to-earth issues. Moviegoers certainly enjoyed it at the time, as many reputedly named their little girls "Aelita" after seeing it. **CK**

▶
The futuristic Martian locations and costumes by Alexandra Ekster and Isaak Rabinovich are still visually effective, to say the least.

THE CRAZY RAY

THE WHOLE WORLD STOPPED IN TIME!

PARIS ASLEEP 1925 (FRANCE)

Director René Clair **Producer** Henri Diamant-Berger **Screenplay** René Clair
Cinematography Maurice Desfassiaux, Paul Guichard (with Art Direction by Claude
Autant-Lara) **Music** Jean Wiener **Cast** Henri Rollan, Albert Préjean, Antoine
Stacquet, Marcel Vallée, Louis Pré Fils, Martinelli, Madeleine Rodrigue, Myla Seller

The night watchman at the Eiffel Tower awakens one morning
to discover that all life and movement in the City of Light has
been frozen in time. Only he and a small company of airplane
passengers he soon hooks up with appear unaffected. Roaming
freely about the slumbering city, they all proceed to make the
most of it, and cheerfully relieve the cataleptic Parisians of their
possessions. Bonding and solidarity, however, eventually go
awry as boredom sets in and male rivalry (for the only female
in the group) takes over. The chaos is interrupted by a wireless
radio message eventually leading to a mad scientist who has
devised a powerful freezing ray. The protagonists coerce him
into setting the world back into motion, and after a number of
burlesque derailments the lead couple finds refuge at the top of
the Tower where they exchange vows with a ring that seems to
attest to the reality of the events they have just lived through.

An early experimental opus, René Clair's directorial debut
Paris Asleep (a.k.a. *Paris qui Dort*) is often wrongly claimed to be
the first sci-fi movie, as many were then unaware of Georges
Méliès's *Voyage to the Moon* (1902). *Paris Asleep* is rightly thought
of, however, as one of the landmarks of French silent cinema.

◄
**Also known in
America as both
The Crazy Ray (as
shown here) and
At 3:25, a 35-
minute version
was put together
by the director
in 1971 after
recovering
material from
earlier work. It is
now included in
the DVD release
of *Under the Roofs
of Paris* (1930).**

Reportedly based on one of Clair's daydreams, it is no doubt best described as a comic fantasy short, revolving around a "survivors-in-a-lifeless-environment" situation (subsequently developed and diversified by the post-apocalyptic sub-genre). More important perhaps the film is an ode—not so much to Paris as a showcase for technological innovation (automobile, aviation, and above all the Eiffel Tower as a formidable beacon

"I DON'T KNOW WHERE THE HELL THAT CAME FROM." RENÉ CLAIR, WHILE WATCHING A COPY OF HIS FILM, GROSSLY PADDED BY FOREIGN DISTRIBUTORS

of progress) as to a modernity born in, and with, the invention of cinema. Not only are the two founding ends of the cinematic spectrum here reconciled (the realism of the Lumière brothers and the magic of Méliès), but Clair implicitly pays homage to other great pioneers like Louis Feuillade and his serial films (the urban, dreamlike poetry of *Fantômas* and *Les Vampires*) as well as Mack Sennett and his madcap comedies (with their zany chases and slapstick fist fights).

▶
René Clair employed dizzying vertical tracking shots under the steel skirt of the Eiffel Tower to showcase the power of cinema.

While shaped by a set of proliferating divisions (utopia vs. dystopia, stasis vs. motion, still Cinematography vs. cinema, etc.) and demonstrating the power of cinema (the on/off lever and the magic ray of the scientist's device as analogues for the filmic process), the narrative is not overly "knowing," and the socio-political subtext (anarchy vs. monetary society) is kept in check by the comic shenanigans.   **PM**

METROPOLIS 1927 (GERMANY)

Director Fritz Lang **Producer** Erich Pommer **Screenplay** Thea von Harbou, Fritz Lang **Cinematography** Karl Freund, Günther Rittau **Music** Original release score composed by Gottfried Huppertz **Cast** Alfred Abel, Gustav Fröhlich, Brigitte Helm, Rudolf Klein-Rogge, Fritz Rasp, Theodor Loos, Erwin Biswanger, Heinrich George

Fritz Lang's *Metropolis* is crowded with startling images and flashes of brilliant technique that transcend all other considerations (such as its often risibly naïve parable of the struggle between capital and labor) and warrant its inclusion in any comprehensive list of screen classics.

Within the tangled narrative, muddled further by many cuts and existing in several versions of differing lengths and degrees of completeness, Lang posits a future where technology rules and an army of workers living underground slave on the orders of a small ruling elite. Into this hidden realm stumbles Freder (Fröhlich), son of the city's Master. Moved by the workers' plight and the purity of Maria (Helm), a serenely beautiful young woman who ministers to them and cares for their children, he decides to improve their lot. Meanwhile, Rotwang (Klein-Rogge), a crazed inventor, has created a "Maschinenmensch," an android slave capable of assuming human form. He kidnaps Maria and transforms the robot in her image before using it, for reasons of his own, to stir the workers to revolt. At the end, order is restored and Maria and Freder reconcile the two strata. In later years, Lang himself dismissed the plot as "a fairytale, definitely,"

◄ **Brigitte Helm's doppelganger robot in its gold-painted, pre-humanized incarnation remains the defining visual signature of *Metropolis*.**

and it seems clear that he paid little attention to it. The pictures are the thing: In a succession of beautifully composed images, Lang vividly depicts a dehumanizing underworld in which identically dressed workers toil before and within vast banks of (surely impractical) art deco machinery, illuminated by billowing jets of smoke and electric sparks. These scenes have influenced countless subsequent sci-fi filmmakers, and

"I DIDN'T LIKE THE PICTURE— I THOUGHT IT WAS SILLY AND STUPID"

FRITZ LANG

now form part of the standard repository of images by which futuristic architecture is identified.

The film's final quarter, in which the workers rise up and destroy the city, is its startling highlight, combining mammoth sets with seamlessly integrated model shots, gallons of flooding water and a surging crowd comprised of many thousands of extras in an astounding feat of direction, construction, editing, and special effects. Lang also makes impressive use of montage in a number of sequences, notably in Freder's fevered vision of the fake Maria's erotic dance before a crowd of leering men, with the screen at one point becoming a tangled mass of staring eyes. The human element of *Metropolis* is as incidental to its importance as its narrative, but Brigitte Helm's performance as both the saintly Maria and her bewitching, gyrating robot doppelganger has become justly iconic. **MC**

►
Gustav Fröhlich (playing Freder, right) had been an editor and journalist before taking up acting. Starring in many films and plays in the mid-1920s, *Metropolis* was his big break.

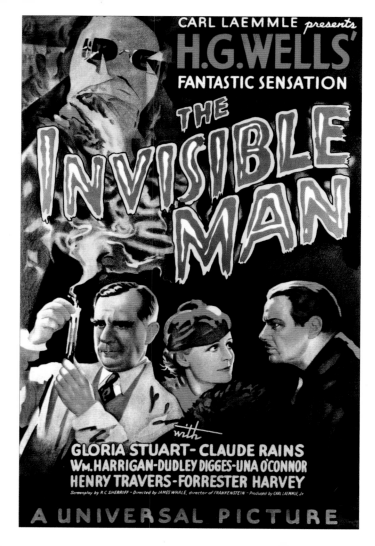

THE INVISIBLE MAN 1933 (U.S.)

Director James Whale **Producer** Carl Laemmle, Jr. **Screenplay** R. C. Sherriff
(from the novel by H. G. Wells) **Cinematography** Arthur Edeson **Music** Heinz
Roemheld **Cast** Claude Rains, Gloria Stuart, William Harrigan, Henry Travers, Una
O'Connor, E. E. Clive, Dwight Frye, Forrester Harvey, Holmes Herbert, Dudley Digges

Released the same year as *King Kong*, *The Invisible Man* was
a similar milestone in screen fantasy and special effects.
Director James Whale's keen eye for telling images and
odd juxtapositions, seen in such celebrated images as the
mysterious scientist Dr. Griffin (Rains) unraveling the bandages
around his head to reveal only empty space beneath, a terrified
man being swung around by unseen hands, and a pair of
trousers chasing a screaming woman down a country lane,
created a sensation and has since entered movie legend.

The script by R. C. Sherriff retained the outline of H. G.
Wells's original novel while modernizing (and simplifying)
the concepts behind it. None of the myriad earlier treatments
that Whale was handed had actually referred to the book,
which was out of print in America at the time. The problem,
carefully explained in a typical bit of 1930s weird science by
kindly elder scientist Henry Travers (later the angelic Clarence
in *It's a Wonderful Life*), is a substance called Monocaine, which
"draws color from everything it touches." We are told that it was
used for bleaching cloth before being abandoned because "it
destroyed the material" and that next, mysteriously, "they tried

◄

"Fantastic
Sensation" says
the poster. The
effects work in the
film is exceptional,
especially for the
time. Bicycles
ride on their own,
lines of shoeprints
appear in the snow,
cigarettes are
lit, and smoke is
puffed in mid-air.

it on a dog," intending who knows what, but "it turned it dead white and sent it raving mad." In ignorance of the insanity side-effect, but soon to fall foul of it, Griffin has injected the drug into himself for reasons that are hard to imagine: Certainly from the first time we meet him he is ranting about its potential to hold governments ransom, enslave the world, "rob, rape, and kill." No misunderstood, well-intentioned

"WE'LL NEVER CATCH HIM IN A THOUSAND YEARS . . . HOW CAN I 'ANDCUFF A BLOOMIN' SHIRT?" P.C. JAFFERS

▶

Although the actor under the bandages was usually Claude Rains, often it was a double (shown here). You can tell the double apart from the real Rains because he is taller and has a nose so prominent that it is visible even through the bandages.

Frankenstein, he derives mischievous delight, rather than grim satisfaction, from the mayhem he unleashes.

The melodious voice, receiving its first screen exposure, belongs to Claude Rains. He inherited the role from Boris Karloff who was unhappy at the prospect of playing a character seen only for a few seconds at the end. Ironically, Griffin's appearance throughout in bandages, dark glasses, and false nose, became iconic in its own right. The invisibility effects were achieved via a complicated matte process that required Rains to wear a tight-fitting black velvet body covering, and then filming him against a black background, so that when combined with film of the location only his clothes were visible. It is often claimed that the film errs in showing shoeprints, rather than footprints, as the naked Griffin flees his pursuers through the snow, but the tracks are indefinite and could surely be either. **MC**

H.G.WELLS'

Things to come

A LONDON FILM PRODUCTION   **DIRECTED BY WILLIAM CAMERON MENZIES.**
PRODUCED BY ALEXANDER KORDA.
DISTRIBUTED BY ··· UNITED ARTISTS

THINGS TO COME 1936 (U.K.)

Director William Cameron Menzies **Producer** Alexander Korda **Screenplay** H. G. Wells, from *The Shape of Things To Come* **Cinematography** Georges Perinal **Music** Arthur Bliss **Cast** Raymond Massey, Edward Chapman, Ralph Richardson, Margaretta Scott, Cedric Hardwicke, Maurice Braddell, Sophie Stewart, Derrick de Marney, Ann Todd

An epic saga, unique in scope and outlook, imaginatively and ingeniously staged, *Things to Come* remains almost wilfully uncommercial in content. It is also the most eccentric product of producer Alexander Korda's drive to make Britain a center of "prestige" film production to rival Hollywood in the 1930s.

The screenplay is by H. G. Wells, who was enjoying a brief flirtation with British cinema at the time: He also wrote the delightful fantasy *The Man Who Could Work Miracles* the same year. But whereas the latter was playful in tone, mixing some philosophical speculation with a lot of whimsy, this is an exercise in solemn prophecy trading solely in ideas. More an illustrated lecture than a drama, none of the characters are given dramatic life (save, perhaps, Ralph Richardson's pompous warlord, and that is more thanks to performance than script).

Yet for all its coldness and earnestness, we can still admire the sheer ambition of the film's central concept: an attempt to predict mankind's course over the next century. Wells begins uncannily with another World War in 1940, but one that lasts for 30 years, by which time the world is a ruined shell and human society has reverted to tribalism. Rescue comes in

◄

Wells's ultimate image of humankind, once again divided into two warring factions (progressives and reactionaries), may yet prove to be his most important prophecy.

the form of a new scientific elite who cure disease and unite warring factions in the name of progress, building enormous cities underground and finally launching the first rocket to the moon in 2036.

For a major British production of the 1930s, the film is brazenly pessimistic, setting characters we meet only in passing on a course of devastating war, ensuing plague, and

"MAKE AN END TO PROGRESS NOW! LET THIS BE THE LAST DAY OF THE SCIENTIFIC AGE!" *THEOTOCOPULOS*

regression to barbarism. Even the ending, with a re-civilized meritocracy preparing to explore outer space, is darkened by the prospect of failure and the threat of sabotage from Cedric Hardwicke's futuristic Luddite agitator.

▶
The film's final speech—"All the universe or nothingness? Which shall it be…?"—is one of the most visionary speeches in all of sci-fi cinema, espousing the view that the whole of the universe can be ours for the taking.

Of course the film is best remembered for its innovative effects and set designs, and these do not disappoint. Director William Cameron Menzies, a brilliant Hollywood art director noted for his lowering skylines in *Gone With the Wind*, has produced a visually striking panorama, enhanced immeasurably by the stirring music of Arthur Bliss. Among the most lingering images are the first shot of "Everytown," a jumble of English landmarks, the exploding cinema, the burrowing machine and subterranean city, the "space gun" that ejects lunar rockets like bullets, and not least, the accurate prediction of World War II. **MC**

INVADERS FROM MARS 1953 (U.S.)

Director William Cameron Menzies **Producer** Edward L. Alperson **Screenplay** Richard Blake (from a story by John Tucker Battle) **Cinematography** John F. Seitz **Music** Raoul Kraushaar, Mort Glickman **Cast** Helena Carter, Arthur Franz, Jimmy Hunt, Leif Erickson, Hillary Brooke, Morris Ankrum, Max Wagner, Milburn Stone

Superficially, *Invaders from Mars* now looks distinctly hammy: A Martian brain that is patently human gets carried around in a goldfish bowl by mutants who are hefty extras in pajamas, with special effects and decor straight out of Poverty Row. Yet after repeated viewings, more than the uncanny music remains unsettling.

By 1953 the Cold War turned hot when Communist North Korea invaded the South. Paranoia about alien Reds and the Atom Bomb quickly found its way into a large number of anti-Communist movies, and science fiction proved the perfect way to designate Communists as radically "other," devoted solely to domination and turning people into brain-washed automata. The characters taken over in the film become sinister zombies devoid of personal thought and action, obeying orders thanks to a device planted in their necks. We are also treated to endless shots of trains transporting American soldiers off to combat the aliens, with tanks galore on display.

And yet, the film's most positive character is an open-minded astronomer who brings grist to the liberal mill. America has constructed a rocket that will lead to space stations armed with

◄

In one scene, Dr. Kelston refers to the "Lubbock Lights." This was a real-life UFO event that created a nationwide sensation in its day.

nuclear weapons ready to destroy any enemy. He interprets this situation not just as self-defense but as a threat to the Martians whose race is thus endangered. *Invaders from Mars* echoes the liberal content of *The Day the Earth Stood Still* (1951) and also the hysterical one of *Invasion U.S.A.* (1952). An openly anti-Soviet message, complete with the need for security, coexists uneasily here with a call for understanding.

"HE SAYS HE SAW A BRIGHT LIGHT OR SOMETHING. HE'S NOT [A] BOY GIVEN TO IMAGINING THINGS." GEORGE MACLEAN

The film turns out to be a dream, but even this is open to two radically different interpretations. Given that the dreamer is a little boy (at the origin of the alert concerning invaders from Mars), we could argue that this is proof that even youngsters are aware of the dangers of a Communist takeover. But his parents are among the first victims of the Martians: They change from being loving and caring to brutal and repressive.

▶
An allegory of 1950s suburban America, *Invaders from Mars* suggests its imposed order and harmony were prone to an imminent collapse.

Most interesting of all is how the boy finds substitute parents (the astronomer and his fiancée) and a surrogate father: A Colonel, representative of authority in every sense. The film unconsciously reflects the function of the home and family life in the 1950s and the determination on the part of the ruling elite to reinforce these values. The little hero's nightmare therefore indicates that all was not well in America's suburbia at that time. **RH**

IT CAME FROM OUTER SPACE 1953 (U.S.)

Director Jack Arnold **Producer** William Alland **Screenplay** Harry Essex (from the story by Ray Bradbury) **Cinematography** Clifford Stine **Music** Irving Gertz, Henry Mancini, Herman Stein **Cast** Richard Carlson, Barbara Rush, Charles Drake, Joe Sawyer, Russell Johnson, Alan Dexter, Kathleen Hughes, Ralph Brooks, Budd Buster

When a ball of fire crashes in the middle of the desert, everyone thinks it's only a meteor, except star-gazer John Putnam (Carlson), who is able to identify it as a spaceship. But Putnam finds it hard to convince his fellow citizens. In spite of this apparently conventional premise for a 1950s science-fiction film, Jack Arnold's first entry in the genre has been labeled left-wing since it does not sing the usual paranoiac chorus.

If the visitors from outer space take human shapes, complete with hollow voices and robotic manners, in order to move freely among us, they don't intend to invade Earth: They only need time and equipment to repair their means of transport. Not unlike Robert Wise's *The Day the Earth Stood Still* (1951), they are well aware of humans' aggressiveness and fear of difference, but here they don't want to interact with them yet. Criticizing cold war mentality—and, beyond that, human nature—the film demonstrates that, endowed with superior knowledge and power, aliens have wisdom to share.

The desert setting, to which Arnold would later successfully return in *Tarantula* (1955), is described as a dangerously alien place and stands as a metaphor of the vast, unknown world

◄
A seminal sci-fi film in many ways, this was Ray Bradbury's first produced screenplay (though he only contributed a treatment) and also saw the directorial debut of Jack Arnold.

that surrounds us and threatens not only our lives but also our way of thinking. The main character remains one of its major assets. Living at the edge of town, mocked by its inhabitants before the spaceship's arrival, John appears to be an outsider, and so he is quite logically chosen by the aliens to serve as a middleman. Whereas the town is said to be certain of its future, John's childlike behavior leaves him open to new possibilities.

"SPIELBERG SAID . . . CLOSE ENCOUNTERS COULDN'T HAVE EXISTED IF HE HADN'T SEEN OUTER SPACE." *RAY BRADBURY*

In each case, the visitors' actions are revealing: They even turn Ellen (Rush), the tame schoolteacher, into a kind of vamp.

The aliens' presence is made palpable and frightening by an eerie musical theme that uses a theremin, an electronic instrument that was already at this time associated with the genre. Their physical appearance seems to have been a major concern of the production, and it is handled in several ways. They can be invisible, take human shape, or allow us to glimpse their extremely monstrous bodies, but *It Came from Outer Space* also resorts, strangely enough, to the point of view of creatures that have only one eye. This trick turns out to be quite effective in indicating the moment when they revert to their original form. Here, however, the film's pacific message also shows its limitations: One more time, the aliens are terrifying predators. **FL**

▶
The Universal Studios makeup department created two different designs for the aliens. One was used here, while the other was later picked up for the Mutant in *This Island Earth* (1955).

THE WAR OF THE WORLDS 1953 (U.S.)

Director Byron Haskin **Producer** George Pal **Screenplay** Barré Lyndon (from the eponymous novel by H. G. Wells) **Cinematography** George Barnes **Music** Leith Stevens **Cast** Gene Barry, Ann Robinson, Les Tremayne, Robert Cornthwaite, Sandro Giglio, Lewis Martin, Houseley Stevenson Jr., Paul Frees, William Phipps, Vernon Rich

The first screen version of H. G. Wells's pioneering novel of Martian invasion, this may on the surface seem a quintessential Hollywood travesty. The drive-in characterization and casting, the one-man viewpoint, and the meticulous detail of the novel are abandoned in favor of large-scale mayhem, and its setting is updated from Victorian London to 1950s California. However, *War of the Worlds* is largely successful on its own terms, and a high point of the 1950s alien invasion cycle.

The driving force of the film is its enterprising producer, George Pal (later both producer and director of the 1960 adaptation of Wells's *The Time Machine*), who commissioned a screenplay by the distinguished Barré Lyndon, fresh from DeMille's *The Greatest Show On Earth*, the big Oscar winner for 1952. Taking care to begin slowly and suspensefully, before giving way to well-staged action sequences, the film stages a few key moments of the novel well, notably when the Martian cylinder slowly unscrews to reveal its lethal contents to the dumbstruck onlookers. What first emerges, however, is disappointingly metallic compared to the repulsively organic creatures that, says Wells, "glistened like wet leather,"

◄
This film is perhaps the most cynical and anti-science of all 1950s sci-fi movies. Not only is scientific advance, as usual, the threat (though this time not manmade but in the form of the technologically superior alien hardware), it also proves impotent as a solution.

while the aliens themselves, when finally glimpsed, are sadly unimpressive, E. T.-like creatures with electric-light eyes.

By some miracle Lyndon has also been permitted to retain the superbly ironic ending, in which, after all the guns and bombs have failed, the invaders are destroyed by what Wells calls "the humblest things that God, in his wisdom, has put upon this earth"—common airborne germs against which

> ## "IF THEY'RE MORTAL, THEY MUST HAVE MORTAL WEAKNESSES. THEY'LL BE STOPPED, SOMEHOW." *FORRESTER*

the Martian immune system has no defense. Whether it is the designs of God (in his wisdom) that save Earth (as Cedric Hardwicke's narration would like to have it), or sheer luck, it's certainly not the atom bomb.

What most impresses about the film is its documentary-like vividness and pace, with real footage of bombed towns, displaced citizens, and military action effectively intercut with impressively choreographed scenes of alien attacks, public pandemonium, and good model shots of the burning and destroyed cities. Impressive, too, are the looming Martian fighting machines, designed in conscious avoidance of the traditional "flying saucer" image, and the doom-laden finale in a disintegrating church, all very efficiently handled by director Byron Haskin, a distinguished graduate of the Warner Bros. special effects department. **MC**

► **The documentary style edginess combined with the dynamically different alien craft won the movie an Oscar for Best Special Effects.**

THEM! 1954 (U.S.)

Director Gordon Douglas **Producer** David Weisbart **Screenplay** Russell Hughes, Ted Sherdeman (from a story by George Worthing Yates) **Cinematography** Sid Hickox **Music** Bronislau Kaper **Cast** James Whitmore, Edmund Gwenn, Joan Weldon, James Arness, Onslow Stevens, Sean McClory, Chris Drake, Sandy Descher

Warner Bros. and director Gordon Douglas had already produced the most scurrilous film in the anti-Red cycle: *I Was a Communist for the FBI* (1951). Here the credits give the game away, albeit retroactively: The title is in red, but the film itself is in black-and-white. Red equals both ants and Communists; the former symbolize the latter, with their sense of organization and their penchant for waging war.

The brilliance of *Them!* lies in its ability to exploit natural locations (the deserts of New Mexico, the storm drains of Los Angeles), create suspense, highlight nuclear experiments as being responsible for the monstrous mutations that are the giant ants, and show that men have something to learn from a female scientist. Like *The Day the Earth Stood Still* (1951) and *Invaders from Mars* (1953), *Them!* is a film racked by contradiction. Scientists are in charge of nuclear experiments, yet they are somehow to be feared. Women exist basically to be looked at, yet the film's leading female character is a scientist able to impose her opinions and her presence on those around her. Faced with the benighted FBI agent, played by James Arness, who had already distinguished himself as the alien in *The Thing*

◄

The moral message of *Them!* is shouted loud and clear, exemplified by the fact that the FBI agent joins the soldiers in burning out the ants' nest—eloquent testimony to how the Cold War prepared America for future warfare.

from Another World (1951), Patricia (Weldon) adds another dimension to the anti-Communist and anti-intellectual movie.

Them! is a profoundly anti-democratic movie: It propounds an extreme situation which justifies martial law, a sign that the average American cannot be trusted. However, shots showing the military invading the streets of Los Angeles while the population stands and watches can be interpreted

"THE ANTENNAE! SHOOT THE ANTENNAE, SHOOT THE ANTENNAE!"

DR. HAROLD MEDFORD

as the abrogation of freedom without discussion. It is through the narrative and representation of certain male and female characters that the film's reactionary message becomes clear. The hero is a uniformed policeman who discovers a little girl wandering in the desert, which leads to the revelation concerning the mutant ants. The heroine is the above-mentioned scientist. Yet both are eliminated at the end of the film. The policeman dies trying to save the boys trapped in the storm drains, while the scientist marries the FBI agent and prepares to be a housewife and mother, like the boys' mother whom she befriends. As the cop's death is unnecessary from a narrative standpoint, he has become symbolically a "'foreign body." America needs a couple representing a new order based on the secrecy and surveillance necessary to protect America from alien forces, ants, or Communists. **RH**

▶
***Them!* was originally meant to be shot in 3-D. Some of the 3-D elements remain, such as the extreme close-ups on the ants, having been deemed effective enough to keep in the final cut.**

GOJIRA 1954 (JAPAN)

Director Ishiro Honda **Producer** Tomoyuki Tanaka **Screenplay** Ishiro Honda, Shigeru Kayama, Takeo Murata **Cinematography** Masao Tamei **Music** Akira Ifukube **Cast** Takashi Shimura, Akira Takarada, Momoko Kochi, Akihiko Hirata, Sachio Sakai, Fuyuki Murakami, Toranosuke Ogawa, Ren Yamamoto, Miki Hayashi

Inspired by the successful rerelease of *King Kong* (1952), and by the success of *The Beast from 20,000 Fathoms* (1953), director Ishiro Honda and his cowriters Shigeru Kayama and Takeo Murata set out to create a giant prehistoric dinosaur that was to become a staple not just of Japanese but of global pop culture. Cranky from being awakened by the blast of an atomic test and leaving a trail of poisonous radiation in his wake, Gojira island-hops from a fishing village across Tokyo Bay right into Tokyo's most modern central district, the Ginza.

While massive military mobilization and high-tech electrified fences around the city provide visual thrills to an enraptured audience, they do little to stop Gojira. Only the personal sacrifice of a slightly sinister scientist (who is revealed, however, as the model of modern scientific ethics) makes it possible to defeat the monster. Its demise—by way of a terrible weapon that, used just once, perishes together with its inventor—leaves survivors pondering the heavy burdens of the atomic age: Will humankind ever learn? This didactic turn at the film's ending also reveals another source of inspiration, the Lucky Dragon Number Five, a Japanese fishing boat

◀

This poster is taken from the Japanese release. In the U.S., the title was *Godzilla, King of the Monsters!* (1956) and the main difference was the use of an actor in a rubber costume playing Gojira, rather than miniature stop motion effects.

exposed accidentally to radiation after a U.S. nuclear test on March 1, 1954. In the opening scene of *Gojira* several boats are mysteriously lost at sea, a few survivors washing ashore days later. While this incident, ripped from the headlines, and other clues established it as a key text in the history of Cold War science fiction, Honda and his coauthors enriched the nuclear theme with imagery that, for its original Japanese audience,

"AWAKENED BY THE A-BOMB . . . GOJIRA BECAME A KIND OF BAROMETER OF THE POLITICAL MOOD." DONALD RICHIE (WRITER)

hearkens back to more complex historical trauma: The long special-effects sequence of Gojira stomping through Tokyo evokes both the trauma of the catastrophic Kanto earthquake of 1923 and, more urgently, the dropping of the atomic bombs on Hiroshima and Nagasaki, and the repeated firebombing of Tokyo by the U.S. Air Force in 1945.

Partly because of a weirdly reedited American version, featuring an actor in a rubber monster suit, and its increasingly tongue-in-cheek sequels, *Gojira* went on to acquire a reputation as pure camp among audiences who, for the most part, had never seen the original. Measured against this undeserved reputation, the film is surprisingly serious in tone, competent in its special effects, and convincing in its performances. It is certainly not the film with "the guy in the rubber suit" many take it for. It warrants serious viewing. **SH**

▶

The characteristic sound of Gojira's roar, which is very rarely heard in the first film, was created by recording a contrabass and then distorting it electronically.

THE MIGHTIEST MOTION PICTURE OF THEM ALL!
Walt Disney
presents
20,000
Leagues
UNDER
THE
Sea
Starring
KIRK DOUGLAS · JAMES MASON
PAUL LUKAS · PETER LORRE
TECHNICOLOR
Jules Verne
RICHARD FLEISCHER
EARL FELTON
CINEMASCOPE

20,000 LEAGUES UNDER THE SEA

1954 (U.S.)

Director Richard Fleischer **Producer** Walt Disney **Screenplay** Earl Felton
(based on the novel by Jules Verne) **Cinematography** Franz Planer **Music** Paul
Smith **Cast** Kirk Douglas, James Mason, Paul Lukas, Peter Lorre, Robert J. Wilke,
Ted Cooper, Carleton Young, Ted de Corsia, J. M. Kerrigan, Percy Helton, John Daheim

You can't go wrong with a movie whose first few minutes
include a ship-shattering sea monster. *20,000 Leagues* then
quickly builds into the story of innocent men taken captive by a
mad genius bent on destruction. Disney's colorful production
of Jules Verne's classic novel (first filmed as a silent in 1916) is
essentially a story of the need to escape, one that is itself a
purely escapist piece of entertainment—an amusement park
of a film that is enchanting for adults and children alike.

The Oscar-winning special effects and art direction may
seem a bit dated today, but viewers will long remember the
images of Captain Nemo's (Mason) mysteriously powered
Nautilus creeping through the ocean depths, especially when
a gargantuan squid attacks the submarine in a climactic battle.
In addition, the documentary-like underwater photography
effectively balances spell-binding scenes of pure fantasy with
realistic shots of marine life. Underlying the grand adventure
and dazzling spectacle, however, is a story that is close to
Greek tragedy. It is the tale of hubristic techno-wizard Nemo,
who attempts to transcend the conventional realm of human

◄

**Although the film's
best-loved icons
are the giant squid
and the Nautilus
itself, the poster
chose to emphasize
the human element
under the sea,
with the Nautilus
a dim shape in
the background.**

civilization, only to suffer a downfall due to his obsessive pursuit of revenge, not to mention his quest for the divinelike knowledge that will make this vengeance possible. The story centers in many ways around the dangers that an excessive desire for knowledge and power can engender, and it also reminds us that compassion and conscience are what make us truly human. When Nemo is saved from an otherwise certain

"I HAVE DONE WITH SOCIETY FOR REASONS THAT SEEM GOOD TO ME. I DO NOT OBEY ITS LAWS." CAPTAIN NEMO

death by one of his own captives, he stares uncomprehendingly at this feat of humane sacrifice. And toward the end of the film, Professor Aronnax (Lukas) scolds Nemo for his lack of dignity, a lack that results from his loss of faith in humanity. The central moral lesson here is that Nemo has gradually dehumanized himself because he has learned to do this to others. Although Nemo claims to have a humane cause for which he fights, and although he dreams of a more perfect world, he is a clear example of a dogmatic idealist gone wrong, especially since he finds it impossible to live with others in this imperfect world.

The real jewel in this cinematic treasure chest is the hilarious teaming of Kirk Douglas, who plays a barrel-chested and guitar-playing harpooner with heroic charisma, and Peter Lorre, who portrays the professor's bumbling assistant with comic precision. **KS**

▶
The main performances are fittingly cartoonlike at times, but the actors clearly relished the opportunity to play up their roles. James Mason is splendidly diabolical and yet debonair; a fusion of Ahab and Prospero.

WALTER WANGER CREATES THE ULTIMATE IN SCIENCE-FICTION!
INVASION OF THE BODY SNATCHERS
COLLIER'S MAGAZINE called it "THE NIGHTMARE THAT THREATENS THE WORLD"
AN ALLIED ARTISTS PICTURE
starring
KEVIN McCARTHY · DANA WYNTER
with LARRY GATES · KING DONOVAN · CAROLYN JONES · JEAN WILLES · RALPH DUMKE
Directed by DON SIEGEL · Screenplay by DANIEL MAINWARING · Based on the COLLIER'S MAGAZINE Serial by JACK FINNEY
FILMED IN
SUPERSCOPE

INVASION OF THE
BODY SNATCHERS 1956 (U.S.)

Director Don Siegel **Producer** Walter Wanger **Screenplay** Daniel Mainwaring (based on the story by Jack Finney) **Cinematography** Ellsworth Fredericks **Music** Carmen Dragon **Cast** Kevin McCarthy, Dana Wynter, Larry Gates, King Donovan, Carolyn Jones, Jean Willes, Ralph Dumke, Virginia Christine, Tom Fadden

When are human beings at their most vulnerable? Some genre directors, like Alfred Hitchcock, would argue that taking a shower isn't always such a good idea; while others, Wes Craven included, might advise us never to fall asleep. Belonging to the second category, Don Siegel's *Invasion of the Body Snatchers* tells the story of Dr. Miles Bennell (McCarthy), who discovers that the apparently quiet Californian town in which he lives is being taken over by identical duplicates grown in seedpods.

The film's studio-imposed flashback structure slightly softens the impact of the original downbeat ending (by leading us to think the invasion can indeed be stopped); nevertheless, the highly contrasted black-and-white cinematography with oblique camera angles, claustrophobic compositions, and carefully planned movements convey a disturbing sense of pervasive dread. It also seems to question what makes us human beings in the first place. Is it merely the shape of our body, the memories we share, or the little something that is missing in the victims' eyes, such as true feelings like love?

◄

The movie's enduring popularity saw it remade three times, as *Invasion of the Body Snatchers* (1978), *Body Snatchers* (1993) and *The Invasion* (2007). It also inspired the 1998 film *The Faculty*.

Central to this B-movie jewel is obviously a strong feeling of paranoia that it shares with a lot of narratives from the same period, although Jack Finney, the author of the original story, always pretended he didn't have any political agenda when writing it. The "extraterrestrials" also promise to bring some kind of happiness (albeit a numb, brainwashed life, free of all trouble) to their "'followers" so there is "sect" paranoia too.

> ## "PEOPLE GLANCED WORRIEDLY AT THOSE SEATED ON EITHER SIDE OF THEM. WERE THEY PODS TOO?" DON SIEGEL

The fast-moving invasion it depicts is a very insidious disease as it first affects close family members in the comfort of their own homes. So, on the one hand, *Invasion* has often been interpreted as an anti-Communist movie that enacts Senator Joseph McCarthy's ideology of tracking down the enemy from within. However, Siegel's only entry in the science-fiction genre can be seen as tackling the growing pressure toward conformity and standardization present in modern-day America: As evidenced by a handful of frightening shots, each body snatcher is nothing more than a single cell, a small part of a bigger, single-minded corpse. One could also argue that *Invasion*, a film in which the alien has a vegetal origin like the creature of *The Thing from Another World* (1951), has yet another "message" in tune with serious contemporary concerns over some agricultural practices: Keep watching the fields! **FL**

▶
Kevin McCarthy and Dana Wynter are shown here on the run from alien doppelgangers. Although both had extensive and successful careers, *Invasion of the Body Snatchers* remains the most famous outing for both.

FORBIDDEN PLANET 1956 (U.S.)

Director Fred M.Wilcox **Producer** Nicholas Nayfack **Screenplay** Cyril Hume
Cinematography George J. Folseyx **Music** Louis & Bebe Barron **Cast** Walter
Pidgeon, Anne Francis, Leslie Nielsen, Warren Stevens, Jack Kelly, Earl Holliman,
James Drury, Richard Anderson, George Wallace, Robert Dix, Robby the Robot

Shakespeare and Sigmund Freud make common cause in
Forbidden Planet, whose central theme is man's divided nature
and capacity for self-deception and destruction.

A crew in search of the long-missing *Bellerophon* expedition
travels to the planet Altair IV, where they find the only
survivors of an attack by a mysterious "planetary force."
Dr. Edward Morbius (Pidgeon) has ensconced himself and his
beautiful daughter, Altaira (Francis), in a futuristic residence
with amenities provided by a robot chef-cum-chauffeur named
Robby (a 1950s sci-fi icon if there ever was one) who simulates
human speech (in the rich tones of actor Marvin Miller) and can
synthesize anything from diamonds to Kansas City bourbon.

Morbius takes Commander John J. Adams (Nielsen) and Lt.
"Doc" Ostrow (Stevens) on a tour of the elaborate subterranean
laboratory built by the Krell, a long-vanished advanced
civilization who devised a '"plastic educator" that allowed them
to permanently boost their intelligence and generate three-
dimensional images from their own thoughts. Morbius himself
has had such a brain boost, doubling his I.Q. and making it
possible for him to begin to reconstruct the vast body of Krell

◄

Forbidden Planet's
**Oscar-nominated
special effects
(the likes of
which predate
both *Star Trek* and
Star Wars) make
it a science-fiction
film landmark.**

knowledge recorded in a script that he has been patiently deciphering for two decades. While Adams pursues the lovely Altaira, his crew settles in for what becomes a horrific mission as the powerful force turns up, visible only as a crimson outline in the disintegration beams of their security perimeter and resistant to their most advanced weaponry as it tears crew members limb from limb. Adams rushes to Morbius's home

"IT WAS A SERIOUS ATTEMPT TO REPRESENT A COMPLETELY UNIQUE WORLD." JOHN DYKSTRA (SPECIAL EFFECTS)

to evacuate the scientist and his daughter while Ostrow gets an I.Q. boost at the Krell lab, thus enabling him to understand that the "dark, terrible, incomprehensible force" is a construct of the *id*, the primitive aspect of Morbius's own mind. It is a metaphor for *Forbidden Planet*'s insight, as Adams tells Altaira, that "we're all part monsters in our subconscious, so we have laws and religion."

In a harrowing climax, Morbius, Altaira, and Adams seek shelter in the underground laboratory as the monster from the *id* burns its way through layer upon layer of 26-inch Krell steel until it destroys Morbius. These memorable scenes make the most of Louis and Bebe Barron's soundtrack, considered controversial in its day because it consisted entirely of electronic tones but actually perfectly suited to this visually stylish, highly influential special effects movie. **SS**

▶
Star Trek creator Gene Roddenberry has been quoted as saying that *Forbidden Planet* was a major inspiration for the series, which began in 1966, ten years after the movie's release.

A FASCINATING ADVENTURE INTO THE UNKNOWN!

THE INCREDIBLE

SHRINKING MAN

A UNIVERSAL-INTERNATIONAL PICTURE STARRING

GRANT WILLIAMS · RANDY STUART

with APRIL KENT · PAUL LANGTON · RAYMOND BAILEY

DIRECTED BY JACK ARNOLD · SCREENPLAY BY RICHARD MATHESON · PRODUCED BY ALBERT ZUGSMITH

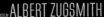

THE INCREDIBLE SHRINKING MAN
1957 (U.S.)

Director Jack Arnold **Producer** Albert Zugsmith **Screenplay** Richard Matheson (from his eponymous novel) **Cinematography** Ellis W. Carter **Music** Irving Gertz, Elliot Lawrence, Hans J. Salter, Herman Stein **Cast** Grant Williams, Randy Stuart, April Kent, Paul Langton, Raymond Bailey, William Schallert, Frank J. Scannell

A paranoia fantasy that exploits masculine insecurity for its effects, *The Incredible Shrinking Man* is the strangest, the most ambitious (both conceptually and technically), and perhaps the finest of Jack Arnold's era-defining sci-fi movies.

It is best remembered, of course, for its special effects and suspense sequences as the miniature Scott Carey (Williams) battles spiders, mousetraps, and other enlarged household perils; but the film is artfully structured and written (by Richard Matheson, from his novel) so that the mayhem only begins after a cerebral first half that slowly and clinically details Williams's mounting anguish as his condition becomes apparent.

Despite his wife's continued affection, he is unable to accept her unconditional support; this leads to an unexpected subplot in which he begins a chaste relationship with Clarice, a midget employed as a sideshow attraction (played by actress April Kent on enlarged sets). Her optimistic nature briefly reconciles him to his condition, but even her empathy proves insufficient the moment he discovers that he has become a little smaller than she. These sequences play artfully on male fears of

◄
None other than Orson Welles did the narration for the trailer for *The Incredible Shrinking Man*. He was at Universal working on *Touch of Evil* (1958) at the time.

emasculation and the preoccupation with physical stature: Williams is the same man (the shrinking does not affect his mental capabilities or personality), but his notion of masculine status denies him the ability to come to terms with what he has become: "The incredible shrinking freak . . . one more joke for the world to laugh at!" Even today, the audience laughter that greets the first scenes of him perched on seat cushions

"I RESOLVED THAT, AS MAN HAD DOMINATED THE WORLD OF THE SUN, I WOULD DOMINATE MY WORLD." CAREY

or struggling to lift the telephone receiver with both hands is most likely to be of the nervous variety. It is at this point that Matheson and Arnold turn the screw, and Williams's nightmare moves from the conceptual to the physical, commencing with the superb image of him opening his dolls' house front door to the massive, squealing face of the family cat, and continuing to a series of perils culminating in a nail-biting life or death struggle with a marauding spider.

> ► **The Incredible Shrinking Man was the screen debut of legendary writer Richard Matheson. With much of the screenplay playing to comedy, it successfully then changes mood to make the climactic spider fight truly horrible.**

The film's biggest surprise is its cosmic finale, in which Williams, suddenly free of fear and hunger, shrinks from microscopic to atomic, dissipating into the atmosphere, still conscious but with no physical dimensions, his narration concluding: "and in that moment I knew the answer to the riddle of the infinite . . . that existence begins and ends in man's conception, not nature's." **MC**

20th
Century-Fox
presents

JULES VERNE'S

JOURNEY TO THE CENTER OF THE EARTH

STARRING

PAT BOONE · JAMES MASON

ARLENE DAHL · DIANE BAKER

CINEMASCOPE   COLOR by DE LUXE

PRODUCED BY   DIRECTED BY   SCREENPLAY BY
CHARLES BRACKETT · HENRY LEVIN · WALTER REISCH and CHARLES BRACKETT

JOURNEY TO THE CENTER OF THE EARTH 1959 (U.S.)

Director Henry Levin **Producer** Charles Brackett **Screenplay** Walter Reisch, Charles Brackett (based on the novel by Jules Verne) **Cinematography** Leo Tover **Music** Bernard Herrman **Cast** James Mason, Arlene Dahl, Pat Boone, Diane Baker, Thayer David, Peter Ronson, Robert Adler, Alan Napier, Gertrude the Duck

Less inhibited by scientific rigor than the fantasies of H. G. Wells, Jules Verne's adventures make a virtue of their almost childlike sense of wonder and enchantment, and this beguilingly good-natured yarn remains the most successful translation of their spirit to the more literal medium of cinema. The tone is somewhat akin to a Disney live-action film of the period, especially *20,000 Leagues Under the Sea* (1954), another Verne adaptation in which James Mason also starred. In a not overly inspiring cast—uncertainly accented pop singer Pat Boone is top-billed—Mason emerges clearly as the film's strongest suit. He is wonderful as Professor Lindenbrook, the crotchety Edinburgh scientist whose single-minded devotion to his quest never overshadows a commitment to social proprieties: "Let us have tea with a double ration of raisins; ladies on the left, gentlemen on the right," he says at one point, roughly halfway to the center of Earth.

The film is steadily paced, with much scene setting and intrigue before the expedition begins, and frequent digressions

◄
Fox greenlit this big-budget CinemaScope production partially on the basis of the success of the recent Jules Verne adaptations, *20,000 Leagues Under the Sea* (1954) and *Around the World in Eighty Days* (1956).

thereafter. We stop for love interest and comic battle-of-the-sexes bickering, a couple of songs, and some cute business with a pet duck that, surprisingly, ends up being eaten by the film's chief villain. Once underground, the *Boy's Own* adventures move up a gear, as the expedition is beset by falls, floods, and sabotage before a rip-roaring last act in which our heroes fight off the carnivorous attentions of amusingly magnified lizards.

"SINCE THE BEGINNING OF TIME ALL WOMEN HAVE HEARD FOOTSTEPS 'UP THERE.'" LINDENBROOK

Then in the gleefully absurd film finale, the voyagers burst back through Earth's crust on a geyser of molten lava.

A lot of suspension of disbelief is required, not least the concept of a massive ocean (beneath a limitless open sky) at Earth's core. Despite this, there is also something delightful about the sheer madness of it all. Likewise, though the effects now seem charmingly dated, and many of the cavernous sets are obviously studio-bound, the artificiality of the production seems somehow very in keeping with the very Victorian imagination animating it. At no point is it in the business of trying to convince us, as Wells's works try to do, through the accumulation of realistic detail; rather, it is a grand eruption of the 19th-century imagination, painted in the broadest strokes. It is a tribute to the film to suggest that Jules Verne and Georges Méliès may well have enjoyed it equally. **MC**

▶
Successful pop star-turned-actor Pat Boone has largely retained his well-groomed, clean-cut image, despite some backlash over some of his political statements.

THE TIME MACHINE 1960 (U.S.)

Director George Pal **Producer** George Pal **Screenplay** David Duncan (based on the novel by H. G. Wells) **Cinematography** Paul C. Vogel **Editor** George Tomasini **Music** Russell Garcia **Cast** Rod Taylor, Yvette Mimieux, Alan Young, Sebastian Cabot, Tom Helmore, Whit Bissell, Doris Lloyd, Bob Barran, Wah Chang

Having graduated from animated children's programs in the 1940s, Hungarian-born producer, writer, and director George Pal was the creative mind behind a number of special-effects driven films that set the scene for American science-fiction cinema in the 1950s and 1960s (and were irrevocably left behind after the quantum leap of Stanley Kubrick's *2001* in 1968). Besides the 1953 version of *War of the Worlds*, it is Pal's second adaptation of an H. G. Wells novel, *The Time Machine*, for which he is remembered most fondly.

Given the popularity of Wells's 1895 novel, Pal's film stays close to the original's basic plot. But despite its melancholic evocation of late-Victorian London, the warm glow of its patented Metrocolor palette, the steam-punkish quaintness of its models and miniatures, and its time-lapse and stop-motion special effects, Pal's movie is not an exercise in nostalgia. Rewritten for U.S. audiences at the height of the Cold War, it is anchored firmly in the global politics of the time. Where Wells's novel features a scene of dark cosmic grandeur in which two feeble cretaceous descendants of humankind struggle mutely toward each other, in a distant future beneath an entropic sun,

◀

Many writers have used H. G. Wells's novel as a basis for sequels and alternate histories, and the film itself was remade by Wells's great-grandson in 2002, starring Guy Pierce, and Jeremy Irons as the "Über-Morlock."

Pal takes us through a 20th century of perpetually escalating warfare, culminating in the annihilation of London by an atomic satellite that triggers natural disasters on an unprecedented scale. As in the earlier *War of the Worlds* (1953), some of the most spectacular scenes in *The Time Machine* revel in howling air-raid sirens, urban crowds fleeing into public shelters, and destruction on a massive scale.

"A MILLION YEARS OF SENSITIVE MEN DYING FOR THEIR DREAMS, FOR WHAT? SO YOU CAN . . . DANCE AND PLAY." GEORGE

Pal, however, transforms Wells's potent metaphor for the British class system—segregated into effete Eloi and predatory Morlocks—into a subtext about the need for global American imperialism in direct competition with its sinister Cold War enemies. Since social class is hardly an urgent fear for an America priding itself on being a classless society, Pal instead evokes the Eloi as a preindustrial Third World culture, colonized and exploited by the technologically superior Morlocks. While Wells's time traveler recognizes a weak trace of their former humanity even in the Morlocks, Pal's protagonist (Taylor) is appalled and incensed by their inhumanity. He is sympathetic to the Elois' essential goodness, and their helplessness against their inhuman exploiters, and accepts as an ethical imperative the task of liberating them from their utopian indolence and advancing them to hard work and technological progress. **SH**

► The Morlocks' sensitivity to light proves to be their downfall, although ultimately it is the time machine itself which helps in whisking George away to safety.

ХУДОЖЕСТВЕННЫЙ ФИЛЬМ
По мотивам одноименного романа А. БЕЛЯЕВА
Постановка Г. КАЗАНСКОГО, В. ЧЕБОТАРЕВА
Главный оператор Э. РОЗОВСКИЙ
В ролях:
В. КОРЕНЕВ, А. ВЕРТИНСКАЯ, М. КОЗАКОВ, Н. СИМОНОВ, А. СМИРАНИН, В. ДАВЫДОВ
ЧЕЛОВЕК-АМФИБИЯ
ПРОИЗВОДСТВО КИНОСТУДИИ „ЛЕНФИЛЬМ“

THE AMPHIBIAN MAN 1962 (U.S.S.R.)

Directors Vladimir Chebotaryov, Gennadi Kazansky **Screenplay** Akiba Golburt, Aleksei Kapler, Aleksandr Ksenofontov (from the novel by Aleksandr Belyaev) **Cinematography** Eduard Rozovsky **Music** Andrei Petrov **Cast** Anastasiya Vertinskaya, Nikolai Simonov, Mikhail Kozakov, Vladimir Korenev, Vladlen Davydov

A virtually unclassifiable nautical reverie, *The Amphibian Man* (a.k.a. *Chelovek-Amfibiya*) combines seafaring adventure, romance, monstrous fantasy, water choreography, and tragedy into a strange, beguiling dream of a motion picture. A likely influence on Luc Besson's *The Big Blue* (1988), with which it shares several nearly identical sequences and a similar story arc, this film by directing team Vladimir Chebotaryov and Gennadi Kazansky is an excellent place to start for newcomers to Russian *cinema fantastique*.

Based on Aleksandr Belyaev's popular 1928 sci-fi novel of the same name, the film is set among sailors and fishermen of a remote Spanish town (it was actually filmed on the Crimean coast) who are sent into a panic when divers spot a glittering man, a "sea beast," lurking beneath the depths. However, the creature's nature is more benevolent than expected when he comes to the rescue of young Gutiere Baltazar (Vertinskaya), who unfortunately becomes betrothed to the unscrupulous sea captain Don Pedro (Kozakov). This amphibious denizen of the deep reveals himself by emerging into the town, where he turns out to be Ichthyander Salvator (Korenev), the blond son

◄

Set, somewhat incongruously for a Soviet film, in a Spanish fishing village, the production values for *The Amphibian Man* (a.k.a. *Chelovek-Amfibiya*) are commendably high, particularly for the 1960s.

of a local professor (Simonov) who saved his ailing son's life by transplanting shark's gills to his lungs. Ichthyander's (the word is Greek for "fish man") love for Gutiere eventually forces him to confront some of the less than receptive villagers, who make life difficult indeed for the aquatic outcast.

On its release in the U.S.S.R., a reputed 65 million ticket sales were churned out—making it something of a smash Soviet hit.

"A DIZZY MORPH FROM . . . THE BLACK LAGOON *TO A FORECAST OF* EDWARD SCISSORHANDS." *MICHAEL ATKINSON (FILM CRITIC)*

With attractive actors, stunning effects and photography, and memorable music and songs, Russians flocked to the screenings. However, until its recent DVD release, *The Amphibian Man* was rarely seen in anything resembling its intended form thanks to dubbed, muddy bootleg video and TV prints, and so had largely been consigned to oddball fringe status by American viewers, though apparently its reputation flourished in Europe.

The fantasy and science-fiction elements are well-integrated into the period setting, coupled with a haunting music score and exquisite color photography (MGM could have easily remade this). Of course, an American studio would have most likely vetoed the unexpected ending, so it is probably best that this Soviet gem remains a quiet little treasure to be discovered by adventurous viewers. **NT**

► Nikolai Simonov gave a superb performance as the Professor. He was awarded the Order of Lenin three times to celebrate his achievements as an actor.

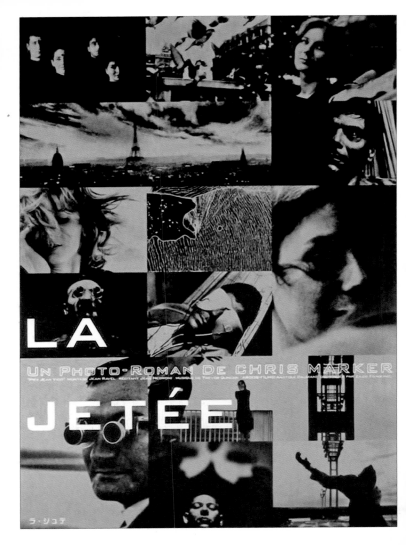

LA

UN PHOTO-ROMAN DE CHRIS MARKER

JETÉE

ラ・ジュテ

LA JETÉE 1962 (FRANCE)

Director Chris Marker **Producer** Anatole Dauman **Screenplay** Chris Marker
Cinematography Jean Chiabaut, Chris Marker **Music** Trevor Duncan **Cast** Jean
Négroni, Hélène Chatelain, Davos Hanich, Jacques Ledoux, André Heinrich, Jacques
Branchu, Pierre Joffroy, Étienne Becker, Philbert von Lifchitz, Janine Klein, William Klein

Conveyed almost entirely through a series of still images, Chris
Marker's *La Jetée* defies categorization. On one level, it is a sci-fi
film about a soldier (Hanich) from a post-apocalyptic future who
time-travels into the past. His mission: to bring back provisions
and, if possible, discover information that could be used to
reverse the suffering of those living in the future. The soldier
is selected because of his vivid memory, his ability to retain an
emotionally charged, if initially baffling, mental picture from his
youth. As the film's narrator informs us very early on: "This is the
story of a man marked by an image from his childhood."

However, to reduce *La Jetée* to a simple genre exercise is
to overlook the extent to which Marker's brilliant new-wave
experiment intersects with a myriad of cinematic forms and
modes of expression, as well as the socio-political tenor of
the historical moment in which it was filmed. In addition to
conforming to conventions frequently attributed to science-
fiction narratives, *La Jetée* also mobilizes conceits of the essay
film, documentary cinema, experimental/avant-garde movies,
and, save for one two-second sequence, the literary tradition
known as the photonovella. Filmed during the height of the

◄

**La Jetée was
initially released
on a double-bill
with Jean-Luc
Godard's *Alphaville*
because of its
length (only 28
minutes). This
poster is from
its later solo
Japanese release.**

Cold War, *La Jetée* also foregrounds anxieties surrounding the threat of atomic warfare and ecological devastation.

Loosely remade in 1996 by Terry Gilliam as *Twelve Monkeys*, a big-budget thriller starring Bruce Willis, Madeleine Stowe, and Brad Pitt, *La Jetée* is itself a reworking of an earlier film: Alfred Hitchcock's 1958 masterpiece, *Vertigo*. Like *Vertigo*, *La Jetée* examines the power of memory on the human imagination

"A PEACETIME BEDROOM. REAL CHILDREN. REAL BIRDS. REAL CATS. REAL GRAVES." NARRATOR (JEAN NÉGRONI)

and the impulse to recapture an always illusory and intangible past. What's more, in a gesture that anticipates his 1983 film *Sans Soleil* (a more sustained veneration of Hitchcock's highly influential psychological thriller), Marker includes several overt references, both visual and narratological, to *Vertigo*. For example, Marker's use of conspicuous close-ups of The Woman's (Chatelain) profile deliberately echoes Hitchcock's similar framing of Kim Novak in her incarnation as both Madeleine Elster and Judy Barton. Similarly, while visiting the ringed cross-section of a large redwood tree covered with dates, the time-traveling soldier, trying to explain to The Woman the time from which he has traveled, points a gloved hand toward a space beyond the tree's perimeter. His posture and explanation recalls a similar sequence between James Stewart and Novak in *Vertigo*. **MC**

► The film is comprised entirely of still-shot photography, except for a shot of The Woman (Chatelain) opening and blinking her eyes.

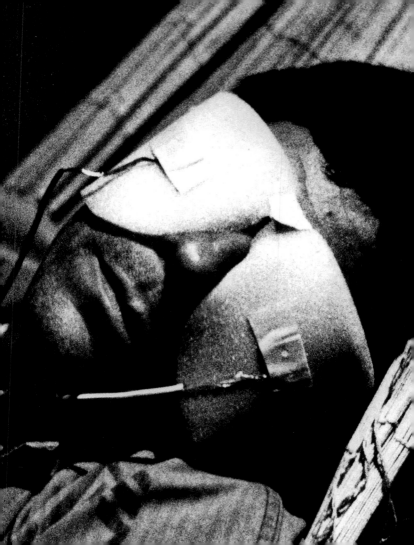

ROBINSON CRUSOE ON MARS
1964 (U.S.)

Director Byron Haskin **Producer** Aubrey Schenck **Screenplay** John C. Higgins,
Ib Melchior (idea taken from the novel *Robinson Crusoe* written by Daniel Defoe)
Cinematography Winton C. Hoch (with art direction by Arthur Lonergan, Al Nozaki
and Hal Pereira) **Music** Van Cleave **Cast** Adam West, Paul Mantee, Victor Lundin

This inventive sci-fi adaptation of the classic survivalist novel
by Daniel Defoe tells the story of Commander Christopher "Kit"
Draper (Mantee) and Colonel Dan McReady (West) and their
quest to reach Mars. Just as the crew of the *Mars Gravity Probe 1*
are set to reach their target, they are forced to burn up their
remaining fuel to avoid a collision with a meteor. The two men
are forced to exit the spacecraft and are subsequently stranded
on Mars. McReady is killed during the landing, and Draper is
left with only a monkey, Mona, for company. The majority of
the picture focuses on Draper's struggle for survival, and just
like the titular Robinson Crusoe he is forced to rely on his wits
and ingenuity. Draper and Mona are eventually joined by a
humanoid slave of an alien race—a futurist Man Friday.

    This film captures society's desire to send a man to Mars and
conveys a sense of excitement at the discovery of being on
another planet. Comedic relief is provided through the monkey,
as Mona is able to decipher situations before her seemingly
superior human companion. At one point, Mona discovers a
cave that supplies an alien fish-life, which provides a source of

◄
**This sci-fi retelling
of Daniel Defoe's
classic novel was
only released on
DVD for the first
time in 2007.**

both nourishment and oxygen. Perhaps this suggests that in a time of human ignorance or obliviousness, a more simple-minded creature might actually have the answer to life, the universe, and everything. Director Bryon Haskin keeps close to Defoe's original classic treatment on survival and loneliness in extreme conditions and the nature of friendship in a master-servant relationship without ever being sentimental or

"FRIDAY, YOU'RE GONNA LEARN ENGLISH IF I HAVE TO SIT ON YOUR CHEST FOR TWO MONTHS." DRAPER

overblown—as when Commander Kit Draper shouts out in frustration, "Mr. Echo, go to hell!"

Special effects extraordinaire and genre master Bryon Haskin, also known for his work on the 1953 version of *The War of the Worlds*, continues to captivate fantasy lovers everywhere with this graphically designed masterpiece into the unknown. The hostile landscape of Mars was fittingly supplied by the location filming in California's Death Valley National Park at the suitably lifeless Zabriskie Point. The superb photography coupled with Albert Whitlock's matte art combine for one of the best looking Martian landscapes ever conceived, all raw colors and horrifically stark dust-blown vistas. Using the photographic techniques of vast Techniscope and Technicolor, the film is an imaginative as well as aesthetically stimulating technical marvel of classic science fiction cinema. **CK**

► **Most of the Martian surface scenes were shot at Zabriskie Point in Death Valley, California, which was also the location for the album cover shoot for U2's *The Joshua Tree*.**

ANDRÉ MICHELIN présente

EDDIE CONSTANTINE

dans

ALPHAVILLE

UNE ÉTRANGE AVENTURE DE LEMMY CAUTION

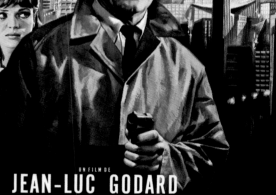

UN FILM DE

JEAN-LUC GODARD

ANNA KARINA

AKIM TAMIROFF

MUSIQUE DE PAUL MISRAKI

ATHOS FILMS
DISTRIBUTION

ALPHAVILLE 1965 (FRANCE)

Director Jean-Luc Godard **Producer** André Michelin **Screenplay** Jean-Luc Godard **Cinematography** Raoul Coutard **Music** Paul Misraki **Cast** Eddie Constantine, Anna Karina, Akim Tamiroff, Howard Vernon, Valérie Boisgel, Michel Delahaye, Jean-Louis Comolli, Jean-André Fieschi, Christa Lang, Jean-Pierre Léaud

In a move that anticipates the gritty, rain-soaked urban technoscape of Ridley Scott's *Blade Runner* (1982), Jean-Luc Godard's *Alphaville, A Strange Adventure of Lemmy Caution* (its full English title) fuses science fiction with *film noir* to tell the tale of an aptly named private detective, Lemmy Caution (Constantine). A character that has seemingly stepped out of the pages of a hard-boiled pulp novel, Caution travels from the United States to the mysterious Alphaville, where emotion and creative expression have been criminalized. His goal is to find Henri Dickson (Tamiroff), an agent who has disappeared, and assassinate the nefarious scientist, Professor Leonard Nosferatu, a.k.a. Von Braun (Vernon), creator of the powerful and loquacious Alpha 60 computer. In the course of his mission, he encounters Natacha Von Braun (Karina), the evil professor's beautiful daughter, with whom he falls in love. Indeed it is love—and the ability to express it with words—that ultimately allows humans to escape from Alphaville and its fascist repression of sentiment and hope.

Of course, by 1965 Godard had established himself as a director for whom the conflation of genres was not so much

◄

This poster from the French release shows the full original French title, *Alphaville, Une Étrange Aventure de Lemmy Caution*, and was designed by Jean Mascii.

a stylistic device as a critical avenue for launching cultural and aesthetic inquiries into cinema itself. Consequently, *Alphaville*'s plot provides the scaffolding around which Godard crafts a multilayered and profoundly insightful work. For example, in addition to its action-packed narrative, *Alphaville* functions as an homage to many of film's greatest auteurs, from F. W. Murnau and Jean Cocteau to Fritz Lang and Howard Hawks.

"I REFUSE TO BECOME WHAT YOU CALL NORMAL. I BELIEVE IN THE INSPIRATIONS OF CONSCIENCE." *CAUTION*

Additionally, *Alphaville* serves as a platform for placing multiple discourses on the structure of time and the value of the human imagination into a dialogue designed to provide as many questions as potential answers. Furthermore, Godard's film critiques the dehumanizing potential of modernist architecture, as well as the political dangers of censorship. Though the city of Alphaville is described as a futuristic metropolis on another planet, the setting is intentionally and unmistakably 1965 Paris. Acknowledging this strategy is essential to understanding the film's embedded messages.

▶

Eddie Constantine was used to playing suave detectives, although audiences were used to seeing him in more conventional parts.

Godard is a filmmaker concerned with the present, often carefully loading his works with references to contemporary events and political concerns. In this sense Godard's *Alphaville* conforms to sci-fi doyen Ursula K. Le Guin's observation that "science fiction is not predictive, it is descriptive." **MR**

THE TENTH VICTIM 1965 (ITALY · FRANCE)

Director Elio Petri **Producer** Carlo Ponti **Screenplay** Tonino Guerra, Giorgio Salvioni, Ennio Flaiano, Elio Petri (taken from the story by Robert Sheckley) **Cinematography** Gianni di Venanzo **Music** Piero Piccioni **Cast** Marcello Mastroianni, Ursula Andress, Elsa Martinelli, Salvo Randone, Massimo Serato

Always ready to make the most of a potentially profitable genre, Italian cinema has produced over the years a fair share of science-fiction films, sometimes even predating some of America's biggest successes (such as Mario Bava's *Planet of the Vampires* [1965]). However, Elio Petri, who won an Oscar in 1971 for a controversial *giallo* entitled *Investigation of a Citizen Above Suspicion*, didn't belong to the exploitation brand of genre directors: He always aimed at socially and politically challenging Italian society through the use of fiction—something he was frequently criticized for at the time.

In the 21st century, murder has been in part legalized as a money-winning game so that violence and births can be controlled. *The Tenth Victim* (a.k.a. *La Decima Vittima*) focuses on Marcello Polletti (Mastroianni) and Caroline Meredith (Andress), who are engaged in one of them, as a victim and a hunter, respectively. This most satirical film tackles the voyeurism of the media and shows death treated as a commodity in order to promote consumer goods. Despite, or thanks to, its futuristic setting, it refers to various topical subject matters, including a then-hot debate about divorce.

◄

The Tenth Victim is an adaptation of Robert Sheckley's 1953 novella *The Seventh Victim*—three victims were added to the title, presumably so as not to confuse the movie with the Val Lewton witchcraft thriller *The Seventh Victim* (1943).

The Tenth Victim's near-future world is constructed in relation to various Roman antique settings—which link the fiction to the environment of contemporary Italian viewers—and modern art, in particular the pop art movement. Roy Lichtenstein, Joe Tilson, and George Segal are among the numerous artists quoted or imitated by the director, while costumes of ballet dancers are clearly inspired by André Courrèges's "space-age"

"DOING FILMS DEVOID OF ANY SPECTACULAR EFFICIENCY IS ALMOST POINTLESS." *ELIO PETRI (DIRECTOR)*

look. Petri also often resorts to monochromatic photography and reflections that divide the screen like images taken from a comic book. That generic bias leads to a comical and completely absurd series of different endings that play with conventions and, in an interesting way, seem to provide the spectators with every possible alternative.

However, the cat and mouse game between the two main characters also emphasizes important gender issues. With strange peroxide hair, Mastroianni plays a male figure in crisis who doesn't correspond at all to the Latin lover type. *The Tenth Victim* deals with a recurring problem that plagues a lot of its counterparts in Italian cinema: Society approves of the male being a seducer, but once he has settled down he is constantly harassed by the women of his life—whether spouse or mistress. **FL**

► **Caroline (Andress), who played the part of victim in the original short story by Robert Sheckley, is the hunter here, and ultimately forces Marcello (Mastroianni) to marry her.**

Julie Christie - Oskar Werner
DANS UN FILM DE
François Truffaut
Fahrenheit 451
TECHNICOLOR®
UNE PRODUCTION
VINEYARD FILMS Ltd
DISTRIBUÉE PAR
UNIVERSAL
Universal International
AVEC
CYRIL CUSACK · ANTON DIFFRING · JEREMY SPENSER · ALEX SCOTT
SCÉNARIO DE FRANÇOIS TRUFFAUT et JEAN-LOUIS RICHARD D'APRÈS LE ROMAN DE RAY BRADBURY MISE EN SCÈNE DE FRANÇOIS TRUFFAUT PRODUCTEUR LEWIS M. ALLEN

FAHRENHEIT 451 1966 (U.K.)

Director François Truffaut **Producer** Lewis Allen **Screenplay** François Truffaut, Jean-Louis Richard (based upon the eponymous novel written by Ray Bradbury) **Cinematography** Nicolas Roeg **Music** Bernard Herrmann **Cast** Oskar Werner, Julie Christie, Cyrill Cusack, Anton Diffring, Jeremy Spenser, Bee Duffell, Alex Scott

When man in the 1960s returned from his brave voyage to outer space back to Mother Earth, what he found was a dystopian landscape: In science fiction, politics often turns to totalitarianism, our planet doesn't have much of a chance, the near future is bleak. The genre itself was redefined during this period from an anticipation of what will happen to observations of what already is happening. This dystopian trajectory leads from idealized concepts to a realization of the constitutive errors in all variations of human societies.

In François Truffaut's *Fahrenheit 451*, the rhetoric of negative Utopia is achieved through a fundamental prohibition: that of books. In the past, civilizations were founded upon a (Holy) Scripture; now the current political regime wants to "correct" all past mistakes when it comes to organizing a social universe. The entirety of poetical, philosophical, and cultural knowledge is erased in order to create a truly democratic system in which all subjects will be equal, because what is eliminated is that troublesome existential and aesthetic thinking which only brings sorrow and disappointment to citizens—that which makes a difference between persons. However, freedom is

◀

The title is taken from the original novel, and is given as the temperature at which paper (and books) will supposedly catch fire. The exact temperature is in reality slightly lower.

only possible because texts are structurally unstable—that is, because they are open to many interpretations, there is always an irreducible excess of meaning in them. In one essential way, books are always "out of order," so democracy in *Fahrenheit 451* is actually the ideal for all totalitarian regimes, and the burning of books is a metaphor for all political restrictions.

"WHAT TRAITORS BOOKS CAN BE! YOU THINK THEY'RE BACKING YOU UP, AND THEY TURN ON YOU." *RAY BRADBURY*

Truffaut, stylistically at his most Hitchcockian here, follows a fireman hero (Werner) in his transformation from burner of books to reader, from enforcer of suppression to preserver of tradition. The director's melodramatic imagination finds its perfect expression in the fact that, in the end, renegades from the law of prohibition must completely interiorize knowledge: they are "on fire"; they learn various books by heart.

But is this really a happy ending, or is there still some unresolved irony in this supposedly optimistic conclusion? Is this act of human defiance sufficient? There is a question over the identity of the book people: Who are they now? Did they lose themselves in this absorption? And then, what about the exactness of future transfers of knowledge? Once knowledge is dislocated from books to mere memory, its fragility becomes palpable, more vulnerable than ever. **AB**

▶
One of the books that the firemen burn shows a picture from *À bout de souffle* (1960), also by Truffaut.

Who are SECONDS?

The answer is almost too terrifying for words. From the bold, bizarre bestseller. The story of a man who buys for himself a totally new life. A man who lives the age-old dream—*If only I could live my life all over again.*

ROCK HUDSON

In an astonishing change of pace as a Second in

THE JOHN FRANKENHEIMER FILM

SECONDS

A JOEL PRODUCTIONS, INC PRESENTATION

CO-STARRING SALOME JENS · WILL GEER · SCREENPLAY BY **LEWIS JOHN CARLINO** · BASED ON THE NOVEL BY **DAVID ELY**

PRODUCED BY **EDWARD LEWIS** · DIRECTED BY **JOHN FRANKENHEIMER**

Music—Jerry Goldsmith
Produced in Association with Gibraltar Productions, Inc.

PARAMOUNT PICTURE

SECONDS 1966 (U.S.)

Director John Frankenheimer **Producer** John Frankenheimer, Edward Lewis
Screenplay Lewis John Carlino (from David Ely's novel) **Cinematography** James
Wong Howe **Music** Jerry Goldsmith **Cast** Rock Hudson, Jeff Corey, Will Geer, John
Randolph, Richard Anderson, Salome Jens, Karl Swenson, Khigh Dhiegh, Dodie Heath

Of all the gritty, paranoid rantings that exist from 1960s
American cinema, John Frankenheimer's fabulously uneasy
Seconds (1966)—standing now as a kind of Johnson-era
companion piece to the Dealey Plaza prophecy of *The
Manchurian Candidate* (1962)—has the vicious chill of a bad
dream endured facedown in your pillow. Science fiction with
a scratchy straitjacket on, post-*noir* with a junkie's nervous
twitch, *Seconds* presents a bureaucratic nightmare that is as
Kafkaesque as it is ruthlessly capitalistic.

Seconds is a pre-*Stepford*, post-*Body Snatchers* conundrum:
Middle-aged bank executive John Randolph, haunted by
mystery men following him through Grand Central, by the
phone call he got the night before from a dead friend, and by
his own affluent but empty existence, is seduced by a secret
corporation to scrap his old life and physical identity for this
year's model. His death is faked, his signature altered, and his
face remodeled into Rock Hudson's. He begins life anew as a
swinging Malibu bachelor. But this is an America trapped in
a self-loathing seizure: Randolph/Hudson's personnel odyssey
into the marrow of American restlessness is doomed, and as

◄

**The film received
an overwhelmingly
negative response
from critics upon
its premiere. It has
continued to gain
acclaim over the
years however,
and is now justly
recognized as
one of John
Frankenheimer's
masterpieces.**

the constrictions of being a "second" tighten around him, he quickly makes a shambles out of this life, too, finally returning to Company headquarters demanding to be recycled again. Once he's on the assembly line, however, he can't get off.

Seconds certainly doesn't spare the rod on either hedonistic youth culture or the discontented bourgeois that envied it so furiously in the era of flower power, hippies, psychedelia, and

> # "THE QUESTION OF DEATH SELECTION MAY BE THE MOST IMPORTANT DECISION IN YOUR LIFE." MR. RUBY

'Nam; both are self-destructing bad trips. James Wong Howe's blood-freezingly grim black and white cinematography, lending uncanny resonance to the fish-eye lens, is a major visceral factor in the film's bite.

But, since science fiction hones its hardest blades on social critique, in the end Frankenheimer's movie may be the most terrifying indictment of corporate service culture ever produced in the United States. It is certainly downbeat, which might account for its lack of success (like the aforementioned *Manchurian Candidate*), but perhaps audiences were also unwilling to see a Rock Hudson movie this edgy. He had, after all, carved his cinematic career as a romantic Hollywood leading man. Ultimately, Hollywood could have only burped out this bleak moment in the last remaining days before merchandizing tie-ins. **MA**

► *Seconds* is an astonishingly bleak film with terrifying relevations, and it has one of the grimmest endings ever seen on screen.

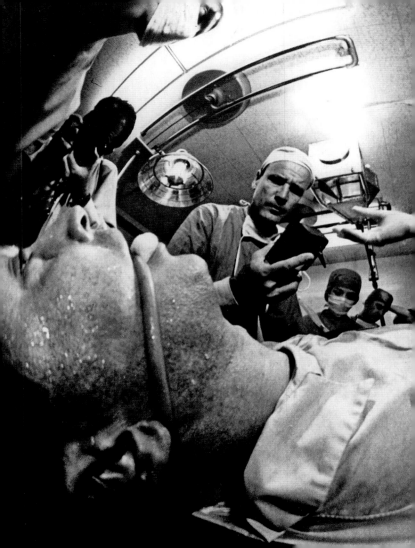

A FANTASTIC AND SPECTACULAR VOYAGE...
THROUGH THE HUMAN BODY...INTO THE BRAIN.

fantastic voyage

STARRING

Stephen Boyd, Raquel Welch, Edmond O'Brien, Donald Pleasence, Arthur O'Connell, William Redfield and Arthur Kennedy, Produced by Saul David, Directed by Richard Fleischer, Screenplay by Harry Kleiner, Adaptation by David Duncan, Music by Leonard Rosenman, CinemaScope, Color by DeLuxe.

20th
CENTURY-FOX

FANTASTIC VOYAGE 1966 (U.S.)

Director Richard Fleischer **Producer** Saul David **Screenplay** Harry Kleiner, David Duncan (from a story by Otto Klement and Jerome Bixby) **Cinematography** Ernest Laszlo **Music** Leonard Rosenman **Cast** Stephen Boyd, Raquel Welch, Edmond O'Brien, Donald Pleasance, William Redfield, Arthur Kennedy, Arthur O'Connell

It might not have had the "kapow!", "bam!", or "Holy Polaris" of *Batman* (1966), with which it featured in some places as a theatrical double bill release, but *Fantastic Voyage* was totally riveting (at least after the first five minutes of completely dialogue-free credits), and not just because of the image of Raquel Welch in a wetsuit. Watching the film decades later, although the special effects may have become dated and the story is still preposterous, *Fantastic Voyage* remains an utterly compelling piece of Hollywood science-fiction cinema.

The film's central conceit is that, in addition to the arms race, Russian and American scientists have also been experimenting with miniaturization—being able to shrink an entire army to fit inside a bottle cap. The fly in the ointment is that neither side can maintain this process for longer than an hour. Dr. Jan Benes (Del Val), however, has worked out how to prolong this miniaturization indefinitely, but before he can pass this information on to the American military, an assassination attempt is made on his life, and the scientist is put into a coma. A crew of doctors and military specialists miniaturize in a special submarine and are injected into the bloodstream of

◄

The team, listed prominently on the poster, scooped Oscars for Best Art Direction/Set Decoration and Best Special Effects. The movie was also nominated for Best Sound Editing, Best (Color) Cinematography and Best Editing.

the defecting Czech scientist to remove an inoperable blood clot in his brain and, ironically, hopefully save the secret to stabilizing this miniaturization process.

In 1966 most moviegoers were more than familiar with science fiction as "outer space" (this was before *Star Wars* changed sci-fi cinema forever), so what absolutely grabbed the audiences' imagination was this film's exploration of

> ## "WE STAND IN THE MIDDLE OF INFINITY BETWEEN OUTER AND INNER SPACE. THERE'S NO LIMIT TO EITHER." DR. DUVAL

"inner" space—of traveling in a spaceshiplike vessel through the human body. Of course, the *Fantastic Voyage* idea has been followed up in films like Joe Dante's *InnerSpace* (1987) and *Osmosis Jones* (The Farrelley Brothers, 2001); but actually the subgenre remains a surprisingly small oeuvre even though the idea of traveling and learning about the human body from within, and via a fictional adventure story, was—and remains—a "fantastic" device. Another interesting aspect of the film was that it is more or less filmed in real time, the process where the timeline of the action corresponds to the film's own running time. There is little doubt that director Richard Fleisher (son of the animator who gave us Betty Boop), had upped the ante since his escapist Disney offering, *20,000 Leagues under the Sea* (1954). He later added to his sci-fi oeuvre with the much bleaker sci-fi classic *Soylent Green* (1973). **MK**

► Director Richard Fleisher was a pre-med student for a time while in college, experience which served him well working on *Fantastic Voyage*.

WHO KILLED JESSIE? 1966 (CZECHOSLOVAKIA)

Director Václav Vorlícek **Producer** Bedrich Kubala, Ladislav Novotny
Screenplay Milos Macourek, Václav Vorlícek **Cinematography** Jan Nemecek
Music Svatopluk Havelka **Cast** Dana Medrická, Jirí Sovák, Olga Schoberová,
Juraj Visny, Karel Effa, Vladimír Mensík, Karel Houska, Ilja Racek, Bedrich Prokos

An outrageously inventive mix of science fiction, cartoon
fantasy, and zany comedy, *Who Killed Jessie?* (a.k.a. *Kdo chce
zabít Jessii?* and *Who Would Kill Jessie?*) remains mired in
obscurity even to this day. This is a terrible shame given the way
it anticipates, both narratively and stylistically, the much more
famous works of household-name filmmakers such as Sam
Raimi, Tim Burton, Charlie Kaufman, and Jean-Pierre Jeunet.

The brilliantly maddening plot actually starts off rather tame,
showing the daily grind of an unsatisfying marriage between
an overbearing wife, scientist Ruzenka "Rosie" Beránková
(Medrická) and her escapist husband, college professor Jindrich
"Henry" Beránek (Sovák). But things take off when Rosie
reveals her groundbreaking invention: "somnioreparation." By
connecting a special headset from a sleeping person to a video
screen, Rosie's machine is able to project the sleeper's psyche
to an audience of onlookers; it also has the ability to transform
nightmares into sweet dreams.

Following in the mad scientist tradition so familiar to
(and beloved by) fans of sci-fi and horror cinema, Rosie's
technological reach exceeds her grasp as it turns out that

◄
**The sexy
super-heroine
Jessie (*Playboy*
cover model Olga
Schoberová) is the
object of Henry's
dreamtime desire,
her comic origins
rendered in color
on the poster.**

somnioreparation allows for the elements in a person's dream to materialize and run amok in the real world (or at least 1960s Prague). And of course that's precisely what happens when Rosie uses her invention to see what exactly is going on in her poor hubby's head when the lights go out. It turns out Henry is fixated on the sexy super-heroine Jessie (Playboy cover model Olga Schoberová) featured in a black-and-white

"THE MISSING LINK BETWEEN EAST EUROPEAN SCI-FI AND QUINE'S HOW TO MURDER YOUR WIFE." *J ROSENBAUM (FILM CRITIC)*

comic strip entitled *Who Wants to Kill Jessie?*. As busty as she is brilliant, Jessie is herself an inventor of, among other things, "anti-gravity gloves," which give ordinary men the strength of Superman. Rosie's jealousy backfires when Jessie shows up in her apartment—to Henry's delight. Unfortunately, however, her arrival is accompanied by a pair of Jessie's arch-enemies: a superhero-costumed wrestler dude and his creepy cowboy sidekick, both of whom want the secret of the gloves for themselves. Mayhem, hi-jinks, and hilarity ensue.

▶ The three-dimensional cartoon-dialogue bubbles are a surreal treat, one of which has to be physically turned around so that it can be read by another character.

Rosie is eventually assigned the task of doing away with Jessie and her pals, and not surprisingly complications arise from her attempts to destroy fictional beings. As things heat up, Henry and Jessie begin to fall in love, allowing a surprisingly uplifting finale as the audience gets to see the put-upon protagonist's dreams (and fantasies) literally come true. **CK**

QUATERMASS AND THE PIT 1967 (U.K.)

Director Roy Ward Baker **Producer** Anthony Nelson Keys **Screenplay** Nigel Kneale (story and screenplay) **Cinematography** Arthur Grant **Music** Tristram Cary **Cast** Andrew Keir, Barbara Shelley, James Donald, Julian Glover, Grant Taylor, Duncan Lamont, Bryan Marshall, Peter Copley, Edwin Richfield, Maurice Good

Imagine an alien artifact that appears at the dawn of man with the precise impact of boot-strapping human evolution and transforming apes into men. Sound familiar? Of course, it's the central conceit of the far more famous sci-fi classic *2001: A Space Odyssey* (1968). But it is equally the core conceit of *Quatermass and the Pit* (a.k.a. *Five Million Years to Earth*). The difference, however, is in how that conceit plays out.

Having kicked our hairy ancestral butts up the evolutionary ladder, the alien intelligence in *2001* proceeds without us ever doubting that they are leading humanity up—to the moon, to the stars, and beyond. But in Kneale's atavistic vision, the alien intelligence behind this evolutionary effect was actually looking for slaves to harvest—and inadvertently bequeathed an evolutionary leap to our ancestors—along with some nasty, violent impulses.

Instead of the cool minimalist black slate of Kubrick's monolith, Kneale's artifact is a piece of gothic tech, a ship containing alien corpses. At the center of Kneale's vision is not a glowing fetal star child, but large, desiccated, and strangely fetal-like grasshoppers. And instead of leading humankind

◄

As shown on this poster, the movie was known as *Five Million Years to Earth* in northern America; *Quatermass and the Pit* was the original U.K. title.

up the ladder of progress from the invention of tools, to the exploration of space, into the depths of individual and collective consciousness, Kneale's malignant Jiminy Crickets are responsible not for humankind's greatest achievements but for all his darkest impulses. All of which is to say that *Quatermass and the Pit*, and all the *Quatermass* serials and features, and in fact Kneale's entire oeuvre, stand precisely

"... WE OWE OUR HUMAN CONDITION HERE TO THE INTERVENTION OF INSECTS?" MINISTER OF DEFENSE

at the dark crossroads of two genres: Science fiction, with its fundamental belief in the improvability of human beings in an ultimately orderly universe whose cold logic may yet destroy us (but without malice), and horror, in which the nature of the universe itself is inherently flawed, if not downright rotten, and humankind doomed to ignorance, madness, slavery, or death.

▶
All of Kneale's work is in a sense science fiction, but it is not astronomy, physics, biology or computer science; rather, it is "psycho-geography." The grasshopper-aliens here may be the origin of this idea, as well as Kneale's image of the Devil.

From the machine that captures the "memory" of death contained in walls of stone and makes ghosts out of them in his brilliant *The Stone Tape* (1972) to the alien discovery made in the subway station in *Quatermass and the Pit*—Kneale's work uses science only to uncover the dark realities embedded all around us. But equally *Quatermass and the Pit* is fundamentally horror, though one which locates its horror not in the supernatural but in a dark revelation about the horrific truth of nature itself—especially human nature. **AS**

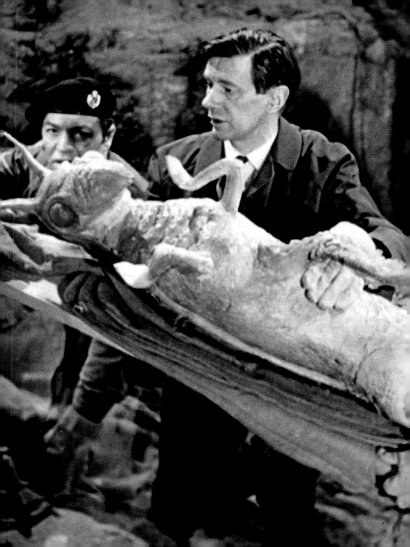

PLANET OF THE APES 1968 (U.S.)

Director Franklin J. Schaffner **Producer** Arthur P. Jacobs **Screenplay** Michael Wilson, Rod Serling (based on the novel *La Planète des singes* written by Pierre Boulle) **Cinematography** Leon Shamroy **Music** Jerry Goldsmith **Cast** Charlton Heston, Roddy McDowall, Kim Hunter, Maurice Evans, Linda Harrison, James Whitmore

Planet of the Apes is based on Pierre Boulle's 1963 novel *La planète des singes* (a.k.a. *Monkey Planet*), a tale of three 26th-century French explorers, led by Ulysse Mérou, who land their craft on a planet inhabited by mute humans of low intelligence and ruled by apes. These apes are militaristic gorillas, scholarly chimpanzees, and conservative orangutans running a society not unlike the one left behind on Earth.

The film version, developed from a draft screenplay by *Twilight Zone* creator, Rod Serling, introduces a number of significant transformations. *Planet of the Apes* replaces the explorers with American astronauts—Taylor (Heston) and crew—who travel two thousand years into the future, and crash-land on an alien planet. As in the book, they encounter a society in which apes have reached evolutionary ascendancy. From here, Taylor's adventure roughly parallels that of Mérou: He is captured along with his native mate Nova (Harrison), wins the confidence of chimpanzees Zira (Hunter) and Cornelius (McDowall), incurs the anger of the elder Zaius (Evans), and becomes aware that human civilization preceded that of the apes. The ending of *Planet of the Apes* is but one—albeit, the

◄

This was one of the first films to have large-scale merchandising tie-ins. This included toys and collectibles, action figures, picture and story books, trading-card sets, books, records, comics, and a series of graphic novels from Marvel Comics.

most famous—element in the film's (and film series') larger interest in apocalyptic images of catastrophic race wars and global nuclear devastation. Unlike the convivial Mérou, who comes to respect the dominant species, the anti-hero Taylor (as filtered through Heston's hubristic screen persona) has only hatred and contempt for his captors, as evinced in his signature line: "Get your stinking paws off me, you damned dirty ape!"

" . . . A POLITICAL FILM, WITH A CERTAIN AMOUNT OF SWIFTIAN SATIRE, AND . . . SCIENCE FICTION LAST." FRANKLIN J. SCHAFFNER

Set among American social and political events of the 1960s (civil rights movement, Vietnam-war protests), Schaffner's film has often been read as a liberal allegory of racial conflict and Western colonialism, but its political message was never meant to overwhelm its schlock sci-fi, entertainment value. Although the ending seemed to leave little room for a sequel, outstanding box-office returns prompted the producers to commission ideas for follow-ups, including (abandoned) treatments from Boulle and Serling.

► The revelation of the film's unique ending was nothing less than shocking, and despite numerous parodies over the years, it remains strikingly effective.

The sequel, *Beneath the Planet of the Apes* (1970), launched the franchise into the 1970s and was followed by three further features, television series, comic books, and serialized adaptations. The endless recycling of *Apes* iconography culminated in the big-budget (but inferior) 2001 Tim Burton remake with Mark Wahlberg in Heston's role. **CV**

An epic drama of adventure and exploration

Space Station One: your first step in an Odyssey that will take you to the Moon, the planets and the distant stars.

2001: a space odyssey

STANLEY KUBRICK'S

STARRING KEIR DULLEA · GARY LOCKWOOD · STANLEY KUBRICK AND ARTHUR C. CLARKE
SCREENPLAY BY
PRODUCED AND STANLEY KUBRICK · IN SUPER PANAVISION® · METROCOLOR
DIRECTED BY

GENERAL AUDIENCES
All Ages Admitted

MGM United Artists
A Transamerica Company

2001: A SPACE ODYSSEY 1968 (U.K. • U.S.)

Director Stanley Kubrick **Producer** Stanley Kubrick **Screenplay** Stanley Kubrick, Arthur C. Clarke **Cinematography** Geoffrey Unsworth **Music** Richard Strauss, György Ligeti, Aram Khachaturyan **Cast** Keir Dullea, Gary Lockwood, William Sylvester, Daniel Richter, Leonard Rossiter, Douglas Rain (voice of HAL 9000)

Stanley Kubrick's epic *2001: A Space Odyssey* boasts a formidable reputation, not just as one of the greatest of all science-fiction films but also as an important milestone in the development of film art. Seen solely in terms of its technique, it remains breathtaking. Its special effects still convince, its innovative use of classical music still impresses, and the breadth of its imagination and its extraordinary ambition are, if anything, even more evident now than they were at the time of the film's original release when, like many experimental works, it was widely misunderstood.

2001's narrative turns out, like so much else in the film, to be opaque. An alien monolith appears on prehistoric Earth and by some unspecified method enhances the intelligence of ape men who will later evolve into humans. Millions of years later, the monolith is discovered on the moon. It transmits a signal in the direction of Jupiter, and a manned spaceship is sent to investigate. The film ends with the sole survivor of the mission being transformed into a "Star-Child" and returning to Earth.

Anyone expecting a conventional story involving first contact with aliens will be disappointed by *2001*. No aliens

◄

Unlike any sci-fi film before it, and indeed after, *2001* was a complete (and Oscar award-winning) audio-visual experience, aided by Cinerama, and a sumptuous, and at times "difficult" classical score. Exiting cinemagoers scratched their heads en massse.

appear at all, and the purpose of the monolith is never fully explained. As co-screenwriter and author of the original book Arthur C. Clarke stated, "If you understand *2001* completely, we failed." One gets the impression that Kubrick himself was not interested in such matters anyway, for instead he sets out to combine some visually stunning images of deep space with what for him was a characteristically jaundiced view of

"HE'S RIGHT ABOUT THE 9000 SERIES HAVING A PERFECT OPERATIONAL RECORD. THEY DO." DAVE

the human race. For Kubrick, human evolution is inextricably linked to violence, with the initial fights between the ape men eventually becoming the Cold War tensions and secrecies that permeate the latter part of the film.

► Dr. Dave Bowman (Dullea) has a chesslike life-or-death struggle with HAL 9000, the ship's onboard computer. Go forward one letter in the alphabet for each letter of HAL's name to get the in-joke of the time.

Advanced technology might be a source of wonder, but there is no escape from human nature via this technology, as is demonstrated by the fact that the film's most humane and personable character turns out to be HAL, a shipboard computer that ends up murdering all but one of the ship's crewmen. From this perspective, the "Star-Child" itself is a considerably more disturbing figure than has sometimes been supposed. It might well be a source of hope for humankind, but seeing the film in terms of Kubrick's pessimism offers another possibility, namely that its appearance is just a sign that things are going to get worse. **PH**

CHARGING INSTRUCTION

Being the adventures of a young man
whose principal interests are rape,
ultra-violence and Beethoven.

STANLEY KUBRICK'S

A Stanley Kubrick Production "A CLOCKWORK ORANGE" Starring Malcolm McDowell · Patrick Magee · Adrienne Corri
and Miriam Karlin · Screenplay by Stanley Kubrick · Based on the novel by Anthony Burgess · Produced and
Directed by Stanley Kubrick · Executive Producers Max L. Raab and Si Litvinoff · From Warner Bros. A Kinney Company

Exciting original soundtrack available on Warner Bros. Records.

72/30

A CLOCKWORK ORANGE 1971 (U.K.)

Director Stanley Kubrick **Producer** Stanley Kubrick **Screenplay** Stanley Kubrick (from the eponymous novel by Anthony Burgess) **Cinematography** John Alcott **Music** Electronic arrangments by Walter Carlos, also Beethoven, Purcel, Rossini, and others **Cast** Malcolm McDowell, Patrick Magee, Anthony Sharp, Michael Bates

The human condition is a labyrinth without an exit: Wherever we go, we ultimately face a dead end. Stanley Kubrick's adaptation of Anthony Burgess's novel *A Clockwork Orange* dramatizes this notion in spectacular fashion, as an orgy of destruction and a cycle of aggression. Alex (McDowell) is both the subject and object of violence, both doer and sufferer: In a house bearing the sign "HOME" at the beginning of the film he is a bully and a brutal rapist, and near the end he is first a helpless victim of the terror of state-funded legal institutions (prison and police) and subsequently of political opposition and personal revenge. There is no breaking away from the circle of violence.

Alex is forced to learn—by watching movies, where colors seem more real than in reality—that violence and even sex are not acceptable, and his basic instincts are transformed into a reflex of disgust by a new conditioning technique. Kubrick's vision is satiric: This is not only a brainwashing instrument of a totalitarian state with the intent to produce an obedient and loyal member of society but also the fundamental process of civilization's sublimation of chaotic and destructive

◄

This poster design, by British artist Philip Castle, was used worldwide with very few alterations. The sculpted figure, here covered up, appeared naked on posters in Germany, Denmark and Argentina.

libidinal energies. After Alex's fall through the window (the cinematic equivalent of a frame) when he tries to commit suicide, he is back at the starting point, on the path of total recovery. He is reformed because he has retained the shape of his former self; he restores his penetrative and deadly gaze, which opens *A Clockwork Orange*. Thus, repression turns into expression. And once again Alex finds a proper "screen"

"PERHAPS IN OUR UNCONSCIOUS WE ARE ALL POTENTIAL ALEXES."

STANLEY KUBRICK

(here in his mind's eye) for the projection of his violent imagination: a scene of celebratory sex in front of almost Victorian-looking representatives.

Kubrick is a director of dark anthropological pessimism, both in his conclusions and his cold, stylistic perfection. He is, in other words, a radical ironic humanist: Human nature in the end is triumphant precisely because it is inherently corruptible, because it cannot be rehabilitated, because there is no cure for it. Kubrick's take on the dystopian inclination of science fiction is the most profound: Even more dangerous than a dehumanized society is an individual who is all-too-human, who absolutely follows his drives and desires. Rousseau's noble savage is actually a Sadeian libertine. The parthenogenetic "Star-Child" from *2001: A Space Odyssey* is here replaced with the son of Mother Nature herself. **AB**

► The crux of the film lies in the scenes of the so-called Ludovico Treatment, when science, with its most "advanced" tools, intervenes in human affairs.

The Future is here.
THX 1138

Warner Bros. presents THX 1138 · An American Zoetrope Production · Starring Robert Duvall and Donald Pleasence · with Don Pedro Colley, Maggie McOmie and Ian Wolfe · Technicolor® · Techniscope® · Executive Producer, Francis Ford Coppola · Screenplay by George Lucas and Walter Murch · Story by George Lucas Produced by Lawrence Sturhahn · Directed by George Lucas · Music by Lalo Schifrin

From Warner bros.
A Kinney company **GP**

THX 1138 1971 (U.S.)

Director George Lucas **Producers** Larry Stuhrmann, Francis Ford Coppola
Screenplay George Lucas, Walter Murch **Cinematography** Albert Kihn, David
Myers **Music** Lalo Schifrin **Cast** Robert Duvall, Donald Pleasence, Maggie McOmie,
Don Pedro Colley, Ian Wolfe, Marshall Efron, John Pearce, Irene Forrest, Gary Marsh

As difficult as it may seem after the *Star Wars* prequels, George
Lucas was once considered the greatest filmmaking talent of
his generation. Notable peers and fellow "film brats" Francis
Ford Coppola, Walter Murch, John Milius, and Martin Scorsese
knew Lucas from film school, where he had developed an image
of shy, aloof brilliance. When Coppola established American
Zoetrope, his doomed attempt to create an independent
studio run by idealistic filmmakers, it was no surprise that the
first picture on its release schedule would be directed by his
old friend George Lucas.

Expanding on a well-received student film of his, Lucas
set out to create an avant-garde science-fiction movie that
would form a dystopian mirror image of consumer society. It's
a *1984*, state-suppressed, drug-controlled future in which the
eponymous "hero" (Duvall) discovers desire and is hounded by
android cops. Rather than compromising with concerns voiced
by distributor Warner Bros., Lucas remained adamant that every
aspect of his debut feature would represent his full artistic
vision: from the Schönbergian atonal score and alienating
sound design through to its mannered, remote performances.

◄

The social critique
may be dated,
but the polished
cinematography
and innovative
sound design give
THX 1138 a unique
appeal that makes
one wish Lucas
would return to
this experimental
mode one day.

The experience would be a formative one for Lucas in many ways: After seeing the film wrested from his control and reedited by the distributing studio maintaining its right of final cut, he saw what was supposed to be the fledgling studio's flagship feature only barely released to poor reviews and zero box office. Disillusioned by his first filmmaking experience, the introverted director vowed never to relinquish artistic

"EVERYTHING WILL BE ALL RIGHT . . . I AM HERE TO PROTECT YOU. YOU HAVE NOWHERE TO GO." *CHROME ROBOT*

control again, severing his ties to American Zoetrope in the process. Lucas has, of course, since established his LucasFilm empire as a completely self-sufficient and independent filmmaking unit outside the studio system. The irony remains that his wealth has been built on the success of the movies that ultimately drove the independents back out of Hollywood.

Although this financially disastrous first entry on the flannel-clad director's résumé isn't likely to convince any doubters that Lucas is a great, or even an especially good director, the film does have enough about it that is worth recommending. It may be bleak, humorless, weakly structured, and inexpressively acted, but that's all part and parcel to this strangely hypnotic "film from the future," as Lucas likes to describe it. Like a protracted student film, but with better production values, the whole thing remains self-consciously experimental.   **DF**

▶
Android cops carry off a prisoner in Lucas's earnest and unemotional box-office flop *THX 1138* —a touching act of protest against the then-Hollywood production factory.

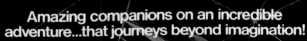

Amazing companions on an incredible adventure...that journeys beyond imagination!

"silent running"

starring

Bruce Dern · with Cliff Potts · Ron Rifkin · Jesse Vint

Original Songs Sung by JOAN BAEZ · Original Music Composed and Conducted by PETER SCHICKELE · Written by DERIC WASHBURN & MIKE CIMINO and STEVE BOCHCO · Directed by DOUGLAS TRUMBULL

Produced by MICHAEL GRUSKOFF · A MICHAEL GRUSKOFF / DOUGLAS TRUMBULL PRODUCTION

A UNIVERSAL RELEASE · TECHNICOLOR® · [G] GENERAL AUDIENCES · ORIGINAL SOUNDTRACK ALBUM NOW AVAILABLE EXCLUSIVELY ON DECCA RECORDS

SILENT RUNNING 1972 (U.S.)

Director Douglas Trumbull **Producers** Michael Gruskoff, Douglas Trumbull **Screenplay** Deric Washburn, Michael "Mike" Cimino, Steven Bochco **Cinematography** Charles F. Wheeler **Music** Peter Schickele **Cast** Bruce Dern, Cliff Potts, Ron Rifkin, Jesse Vint, Mark Persons, Steven Brown, Larry Whisenhunt

By the early 1970s, the social turmoil and protests of the previous decade had turned away from the subject of war and began manifesting in everyday life in numerous other channels. Chief among these was a growing concern about mankind's self-inflicted damage to Earth's ecology (very much on issue-agenda politics today). The conservation movement proved to be a surprisingly appropriate fit with the science-fiction genre, and films with environmental messages began to appear, including *No Blade of Grass* (1970) and *Z.P.G.* (1972). The most ambitious of this group, *Silent Running*, was the directorial debut of special effects maestro Douglas Trumbull, who started his career with the eye-popping space sequences in *2001: A Space Odyssey* (1968) and *Candy* (1968), with subsequent credits including his award-winning work on *Close Encounters of the Third Kind* (1977) and *Blade Runner* (1982).

Unlike most films nowadays trying to appeal to an environmentally aware audience, *Silent Running* never offers a message as simple as "hug a tree," opting instead to present viewers with a mature and complex sense of morality. The main character, Freeman Lowell (Dern), belongs to a space

◄
The name of the co-writer, given on the poster as "Mike" Cimino, is better known as Michael Cimino, who went on to write and direct *The Deer Hunter* in 1978.

crew entrusted with the last remains of Earth's natural forest resource. When superiors demand the abandonment of this cargo for a return home, he responds with great internal conflict by killing his uncomprehending fellow crew members in order to salvage what remains of Mother Nature. As a result, he becomes a man on the run with only a trio of robots to accompany him into the depths of space.

"THERE ARE NO PASSENGERS ON SPACESHIP EARTH. WE ARE ALL CREW."

MARSHALL MCLUHAN

▶
The three robots, nicknamed Huey (shown right, playing poker), Dewey, and Louie appear increasingly humanized as their programming is rewritten. Their movements, operated by multiple-amputee actors, also make them more human than robotic.

While some elements of *Silent Running* are dated (notably the sparing but hard-to-ignore presence of Joan Baez on the soundtrack), the film still packs a powerful emotional punch; in particular, the devastating final scene is one of the most heart-wrenching in the entire science-fiction canon. The casting of Dern is perceptive, as the actor was already familiar to audiences as someone able to maneuver believably between charm and insanity. His behavior offers a challenging moral question that the movie leaves up to audiences; however, modern viewers who respond to the first act by simply labeling him as either a hippie or a terrorist, and then judging the film by those terms, will certainly have difficulty with everything that follows.

Alongside the message, *Silent Running* remains a sci-fi film with stunning visuals: the work of a large effects team including Trumbull himself and John Dykstra. **NT**

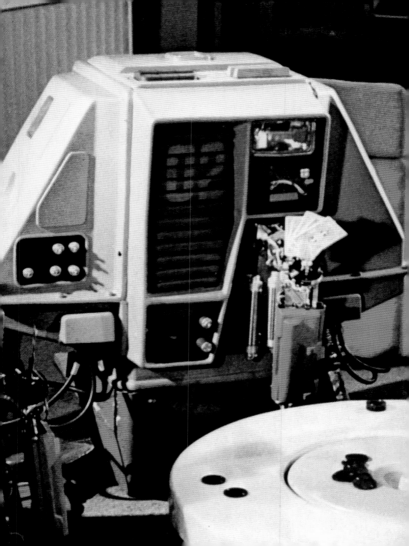

WINNER 1972 CANNES FILM FESTIVAL JURY PRIZE AWARD

Only American Film to be so Honored

SLAUGHTERHOUSE·FIVE

Billy
Pilgrim
lives
from time
to time
to time...

A GEORGE ROY HILL·PAUL MONASH PRODUCTION

SLAUGHTERHOUSE·FIVE

"One of the most daring, original, and totally fascinating pictures ever made."
Rex Reed.
N.Y. Daily News

starring MICHAEL SACKS · RON LEIBMAN · VALERIE PERRINE

Based on the novel by KURT VONNEGUT, Jr. · Screenplay by Stephen Geller · Directed by George Roy Hill · Produced by Paul Monash

R RESTRICTED
Under 17 requires accompanying
Parent or Adult Guardian

Music by Glenn Gould · A Universal Picture ·TECHNICOLOR®

SLAUGHTERHOUSE-FIVE 1972 (U.S.)

Director George Roy Hill **Producer** Paul Monash **Screenplay** Stephen Geller
(based on the novel by Kurt Vonnegut) **Cinematography** Miroslav Ondrícek
Music Glenn Gould **Cast** Michael Sacks, Ron Liebman, Valerie Perrine, Holly Near,
Eugene Roche, Perry King, Kevin Conway, Sharon Gans, Nick Belle, Sorrell Booke

Based on one of the most unfilmable novels ever written, this
adaptation of Kurt Vonnegut's *Slaughterhouse-Five* marked a
radical departure in the filmic treatment of time travel, which
had previously been the domain of filmmakers like George Pal
(*The Time Machine*) and Irwin Allen (*Lost In Space*). The source
material was derived from Vonnegut's own experiences as a
Dresden prisoner of war and channeled into the character of
Billy Pilgrim (Sacks), an American soldier captured by Germans
after surviving a Battle of the Bulge air raid. Throughout the
story he becomes what he refers to as "unstuck in time,"
traversing different locations and time periods of his own life
either in reality or internally. When not derailed by bizarre and
darkly humorous twists of fate (with deaths both major and
small accompanied by the oft-quoted refrain, "So it goes"),
he endures a chilly marriage to Valencia Merble (Gans), has
two children of varying virtues, and winds up in the hands
of the Tralfamadorians, an alien race who instruct him under
observation with a lusty porn star, Montana Wildhack (Perrine).

Critical response to the film version often seems more
relieved than laudatory, with the choice of George Roy Hill

◄

**The bones of
the story come
from Vonnegut's
own wartime
experiences as
a P.O.W. when he
witnessed the
destruction of
Dresden in the
1945 Allied
fire bombing.**

(in between 1969's *Butch Cassidy and the Sundance Kid* and 1973's *The Sting*) seeming as strange as anything Vonnegut could imagine. However, the decision to adapt Vonnegut's prose into a cinematic equivalent with unorthodox choices in pacing, camera placement, and visual humor provides enormous rewards, as does the decision to forgo name stars in favor of character actors suitable to their roles. The Bach-

"I CACKLE EVERY TIME . . . BECAUSE IT IS SO HARMONIOUS WITH WHAT I FELT WHEN I WROTE THE BOOK." VONNEGUT

heavy classical score by pianist Glenn Gould adds an austere, Kubrickian sense of wry melancholy to the entire production, even during the outrageous alien sequences that provide the film with its utterly mad, unforgettable closing moments.

The only possible comparable cinematic equivalent before it might be Chris Marker's *La Jetée* (1962), though ironically Terry Gilliam's *Twelve Monkeys* (1995) owes far more to this film than its accredited source. Cult favorite *Donnie Darko* (2001) nods more than a tip of the hat to all three. What still sets Hill's film apart from its peers (and from other "unadaptable" films like 1970's *Catch-22*) is its slippery but rewarding decision to leave all interpretations up to the viewer despite the rigid first-person narrative. Though we walk in Billy's shoes for nearly two hours, the meaning of the entire experience still feels as unknowable as any single moment of our everyday lives. **NT**

► The trials and tribulations of Billy Pilgrim are no less resonant just because he can time-travel away from them.

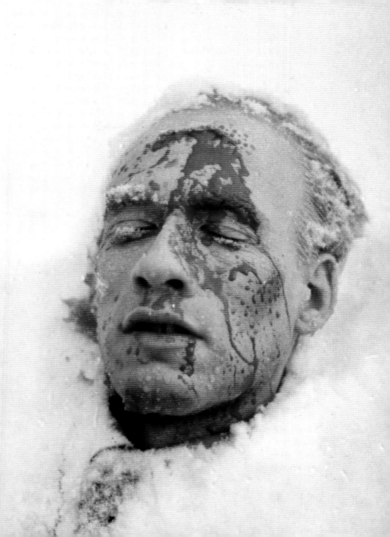

SOVĚTSKÝ FILM VYZNAMENANÝ ZVLÁŠTNÍ CENOU POROTY XXVI. MFF V CANNES.
FILMOVÉ ZPRACOVÁNÍ UTOPICKÉHO ROMÁNU STANISLAVA LEMA. REŽIE: ANDREJ TARKOVSKIJ
SOLARIS
Tlač: ZT-42 Bratislava

SOLARIS 1972 (U.S.S.R.)

Director Andrei Tarkovsky **Producer** Viacheslav Tarasov **Screenplay** Fridrikh Gorenshtein, Andrei Tarkovsky (based on the eponymous novel by Stanislaw Lem) **Cinematography** Vadim Yusov **Music** Vadim Yusov **Cast** Donatas Banionis, Natalya Bondarchuk, Jüri Järvet, Anatoli Solonitsyn, Sos Sargsyan, Nikolai Grinko

Although Andrei Tarkovsky considered it the least favorite of his films, *Solaris* (a.k.a. *Solyaris*) remains one of the director's most popular works among Western audiences. Based on the 1968 novel by Polish science-fiction writer Stanislaw Lem, *Solaris* features many of the aesthetic conceits, visual motifs, and prominent themes that characterized Tarkovsky's work from his student film, *The Steamroller and the Violin* (1962), to his final work, *The Sacrifice* (1986). Through a series of slow, graceful tracking shots and meticulously composed long takes, *Solaris* transports its viewers from the lush, natural beauty of an agrarian Russian landscape through the congested traffic of a concrete urban sprawl to, finally, a dilapidated space station orbiting the distant planet Solaris.

It is in this deep-space research station that the film's central protagonist, Kris Kelvin (Banionis), must discern exactly what has happened to its three remaining residents, one of whom, we soon learn, has recently committed suicide. What Kelvin discovers, however, is that Solaris's ocean not only is sentient but has been in constant contact with the scientists in the form of visitors. These visitors are apparently living

◄

In 2002 *Solaris* was remade in a manner that retained many of the 1972 version's more thoughtful components while streamlining the narrative for contemporary U.S. audiences. This poster is from the original release.

recreations of individuals who preoccupy the researchers' memories in the form of powerful emotions like grief or guilt. Before long, Kelvin encounters a visitor of his own when he awakens to find himself confronted by a perfect recreation of his wife, Hari (Bondarchuk), who had committed suicide several years earlier. Although frightened and resistant at first, Kelvin soon finds himself overwhelmingly drawn to this

"WE LOOK RIDICULOUS PURSUING A GOAL WE FEAR AND THAT WE REALLY DON'T NEED. MAN NEEDS MAN!" DR. SNAUT

uncanny guest and the chances for redemption and solace, no matter how illusory, that her presence represents.

Posited upon its U.S. release as a Soviet response to *2001* (1968), *Solaris* bears little resemblance to Kubrick's classic. Indeed, Tarkovsky went to great lengths to avoid miring his work with special effects, science jargon, and other genre trappings. Rather, he used Lem's novel as the foundation for tackling complex philosophical concerns, such as the power of nostalgia and memory, the pronounced connection between human beings and their environment, and the importance of love, forgiveness, and reconciliation. Audiences expecting scenes of space travel and futuristic sets were therefore disappointed by Tarkovsky's low-tech approach. However, time has been kind to *Solaris*, and it is now considered one of the most provocative science-fiction films ever made. **MR**

▶
Donatas Banionis is best known for his parts in Russian-speaking films, and is also a popular theater actor in Lithuania.

ROGER CORMAN
PRESENTS
A NEW WORLD PICTURE

FANTASTIC PLANET

WINNER
GRAND
PRIX
CANNES FILM FESTIVAL
1973

DIRECTED by RENE LALOUX · SCREENPLAY by ROLAND TOPOR · RENE LALOUX

BASED ON THE NOVEL by STEVEN WUL · MUSIC by ALAIN GORAGUER · METROCOLOR · LES FILMS ARMORIAL

PG PARENTAL GUIDANCE SUGGESTED

FANTASTIC PLANET
1973 (FRANCE • CZECHOSLOVAKIA)

Director René Laloux **Producers** Simon Damiani, Anatole Dauman, André Valio-Cavaglione **Screenplay** René Laloux, Roland Topor (based on the novel written by Stefan Wul) **Cinematography** Boris Baromykin, Lubomir Rejthar **Music** Alain Goraguer **Cast** (Voices) Jennifer Drake, Eric Baugin, Jean Topart, Jean Valmont

Fantastic Planet (a.k.a. *La Planète Sauvage*) takes place on a strange planet dominated by the Draags, giant blue-skinned humanoids who seem to spend most of their time meditating. Tiva, the daughter of the Draag prime minister, finds a baby wild Om (human being, from the French *hommes*), whom she raises as a pet and names Terr (*terre*, in French, is Earth). The tiny Oms, miniscule in comparison to the Draggs, are either domesticated rodentlike pets, or feral and wild. Draag children seem to spend their days having their Oms fight each other, often to the death. Terr grows up quickly, and as Tiva likes holding him while she receives her lessons through a pair of earphones, Terr too is quickly impregnated with the totality of the Draag education. Now educated on par with any Draag, Terr escapes his pet captivity, steals the earphones, and searches out the feral Oms in the hope of organizing them and bestowing them, Prometheuslike, with the fire of Draag knowledge.

The animated landscape Laloux creates for the Draag world is surreal, bizarre, beautiful, and profoundly disturbing. As Terr makes his way to the feral Oms, he experiences a variety of

◄

Although the film was first shown at the Cannes Film Festival in May 1973, where it won the Grand Prix, this poster is from the movie's first theater release in America that December.

strange living organisms, seemingly drawn from drug-induced nightmares. The nightmare landscape has strong echoes of the animation George Dunning created for *Yellow Submarine* (1968) in that world of Pepperland and Blue Meanies.

The opening sequence of the infant Terr watching his mother's death and seeing her body poked by curious Draag children, as any children would a dead animal they came

"THAT WHICH SUGGESTS IS SUPERIOR TO THAT WHICH SHOWS. WHAT WE NEED IS SCHIZOPHRENIC CINEMA." LALOUX

across, is profoundly disturbing. Because the Draags are the stuff of animated nightmares, we cannot identify with them, at least not in the same way we can with the pathetic Oms and the strong verisimilitude in which they are rendered.

While Terr attempts, Moses-like, to organize a mass exodus of Om-kind to find some kind of promised land where they can live in peace and safety, the Draags begin a program of mass extermination of all Oms in the park they'd been calling home. Evoking strong images of the Holocaust, particularly with the poisoned gas mass-exterminations and the collaborating Oms, wearing gas masks, running through the park on leashes searching for escaped Oms, this film really underlines that, despite being an "animated" feature, not all animation is appropriate for children—especially such a profound and deeply upsetting animated classic. **MK**

► The film began production in Czechoslovakia, but was forced to relocate to Paris after the Soviet invasion in 1968. The social unrest is echoed in the movies's images of racial prejudice and genocide.

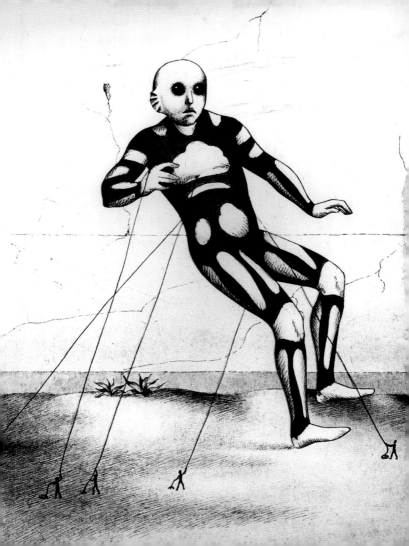

SLEEPER 1973 (U.S.)

Director Woody Allen **Producers** Jack Grossberg, Jack Rollins, Charles H. Joffe
Screenplay Woody Allen, Marshall Brickman **Cinematography** David M. Walsh
Music Woody Allen **Cast** Woody Allen, Diane Keaton, John Beck, Mary Gregory,
Don Keefer, John McLiam, Bartlett Robinson, Chris Forbes, Marya Small, Peter Hobbs

Woody Allen has never been ashamed of his influences. His early films, in particular, recall nearly every major comedian or comic style from the silent days of cinema onward. *Sleeper* is essentially Mack Sennett meets Bob Hope or Red Skelton in the future. Allen wisecracks like Hope, mugs like Skelton, and tangles with modern or, in this case, futuristic technology as if he were Buster Keaton or Charlie Chaplin.

Allen plays Miles Monroe, a health-food store owner cryogenically frozen in 1973, and now, 200 years later, awoken to a world where everyone lives in totalitarian bliss under a single leader. Miles is thawed in order to help a revolutionary Underground to overthrow the fascist regime. On the way, he meets a "poet" named Luna (Keaton), and the two are thrown together in a series of slapstick chases, brainwashes, and counterbrainwashes, ultimately teaming up to kidnap the only thing actually remaining of the leader—his nose.

With neither Allen nor Keaton playing it straight, the film sustains the hysterical pitch of a classic screwball comedy. Keaton matches Allen riff for riff in a performance that is more layered than his. Just as Woody Allen does, say, Bob Hope,

◄
Sleeper is one of Allen's very few experiments with science fiction, and he allegedly discussed his ideas with renowned master of science fiction, Isaac Asimov.

Diane Keaton proceeds to do Woody Allen *doing* Bob Hope. The scene where they are disguised as surgeons pretending to reattach the leader's nose is a fantastic dual performance in which, through their clumsy stalling and stammering, both actors try to out-Woody each other.

The production design is 1960s Pop and 1970s chic brought to absurd utilitarian levels. A silver orb that looks like a piece

"SCIENCE IS AN INTELLECTUAL DEAD END . . . IT'S A LOT OF LITTLE GUYS IN TWEED SUITS CUTTING UP FROGS." MILES

of minimalist sculpture is passed around at a party to provide a communal sci-fi high. The Orgasmatron, a sleek, closetlike cylinder, provides its occupants with automated orgasms, replete with mechanical moans. The costume designs, by a young Joel Schmacher, are fun and frivolous.

The futuristic setting allows Allen to poke fun not only at the sex and drug culture but at everything and everyone from the film's own era: Richard Nixon, Howard Cosell, Rod McKuen, high-brow artists, low-brow revolutionaries, science, politics, religion. Just as in a Marx Brothers movie, no person or institution is too sacred to be spared. Asked by Luna about what he *does* believe in, Miles states unequivocally, "Sex and death." But these words can't escape a classic Allen wisecrack: "Two things that come once in a lifetime, but at least after death you're not nauseous." **GC**

► The movie is very loosely based on the classic science-fiction novel *When The Sleeper Wakes*, by H. G. Wells.

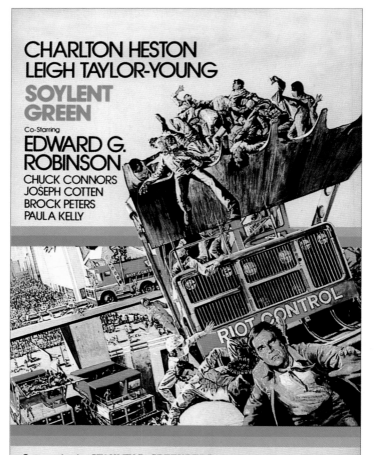

CHARLTON HESTON
LEIGH TAYLOR-YOUNG

SOYLENT GREEN

Co-Starring
EDWARD G. ROBINSON

CHUCK CONNORS
JOSEPH COTTEN
BROCK PETERS
PAULA KELLY

RIOT CONTROL

Screenplay by **STANLEY R. GREENBERG**
Based upon a novel by **HARRY HARRISON**
Original music by **FRED MYROW**
Produced by **WALTER SELTZER** and **RUSSELL THACHER**
Directed by **RICHARD FLEISCHER**

SOYLENT GREEN 1973 (U.S.)

Director Richard Fleischer **Producers** Walter Seltzer, Russell Thacher
Screenplay Stanley R. Greenberg (from the novel *Make Room, Make Room!* by Harry
Harrison) **Cinematography** Richard H. Kline **Music** Fred Myrow **Cast** Charlton
Heston, Edward G. Robinson, Leigh Taylor-Young, Chuck Connors, Joseph Cotten

Of the three apocalyptic sci-fi films in which Charlton Heston
appeared between 1968 and 1973, *Soylent Green* is—despite
hearty competition—the bleakest and most pessimistic. In
essence a police procedural crime thriller, its real purpose is as a
moral tract, warning against the threats of overpopulation and
environmental despoilment, while also taking subtle shots at
consumer culture, the decline of literacy, cultural standards,
and the encroaching State.

It is the year 2022, and in a massively overpopulated New
York the majority sleep rough, packed into any available space;
without any fresh food, they subsist on a hard, biscuitlike
substance called Soylent Green, for which they grovel on
weekly distribution days. Heston plays a cop investigating
the death of one of the minority still able to afford private
housing: a wealthy businessman (played by an under-used
Joseph Cotten) who lives in a swanky apartment that comes
complete with "furniture"—girls employed as live-in sex slaves.
What seems like a routine robbery is, in fact, a well-planned
assassination, and as Heston uncovers the motive he learns a
horrifying secret about Soylent Green.

◄

Despite a lack
of true hellishness,
Soylent Green
remains an
entertaining
thriller and a still-
powerful protest
against the twin
perils of hubris
and apathy.

The film is stolen by Edward G. Robinson as Heston's ornery old roommate, a "book" (a man who can read) who helps him with his investigations and regales him with stories of his youth, when fruit and vegetables were abundant and there were green open spaces. It was the actor's final film; he knew he was dying and would not make another, and his death scene—opting for voluntary euthanasia while watching film

"YOU'VE GOTTA TELL THEM! SOYLENT GREEN IS PEOPLE! WE'VE GOTTA STOP THEM SOMEHOW!" DETECTIVE THORN

images of running water, meadows, and animals—was the last scene he ever shot. He died less than two weeks later.

The film's principal fault is that its ideas are more imaginative than both the budgetary resources and what Richard Fleischer's direction can convey. In particular, the hellishness of everyday city life is never convincingly realized; there is little real sense of lawlessness or danger. Heston's cop lives in an apartment block unmolested by the seething hordes lining the corridors and stairwells, and the masses themselves are remarkably docile, unthreatening, and stiffly choreographed: they don't even try to get out of the slow-moving mechanical scoops that are used to facilitate crowd control on "Soylent Green day." But the film's ultimate revelation that—as Heston memorably screams—"Soylent Green is made out of people!" has entered genre lore. **MC**

► Apocalyptic cop Robert Thorn (Heston) maneuvers through a grim, overpopulated, and impoverished human landscape.

WESTWORLD 1973 (U.S.)

Director Michael Crichton **Producers** Paul Lazarus, Michael I. Rachmil
Screenplay Michael Crichton **Cinematography** Gene Polito **Music** Fred Karlin
Cast Richard Benjamin, Yul Brynner, James Brolin, Norman Bartold, Victoria Shaw,
Alan Oppenheimer, Dick Van Patten, Linda Scott, Steve Franken, Sharyn Wynters

One of the hallmarks of a good science-fiction film is evoking
in the viewer a strong desire to visit the world of the film and
experience the thrills of the fictional universe. *Westworld* not
only evokes that desire but, almost a decade before *Blade
Runner* (1982), presents a postmodern reflection on that desire.

The adult Disneyland-like amusement park, Delos, is divided
into three different "worlds": Medieval World, Roman World, and
Western World. For $1,000 a day, tourists immerse themselves
in the period play of these Delos resort sections, which are
populated by super-lifelike androids who are well programmed
in Asimov's Laws of Robotics (never hurt a human, or allow a
human to be hurt). But, as is typical of Crichton's work as both
a writer and director, perfect systems always go wrong (see
Jurassic Park for another example).

At Delos, and it is never explained why, the androids rebel
(or malfunction) from their centrally-computerized control, and
instead of always being slain by the tourists, turn the tables and
begin to kill the humans. Two city-slicker friends from Chicago,
enjoying the rough-and-tumble of the Western World,
challenge the "gunslinger" android (Brynner) who kills one of

◄

**Michael Crichton
supposedly got
inspired to write
this film after a
trip to Disneyland,
where he saw
the *Pirates of the
Caribbean* ride and
was impressed by
the animatronic
characters.**

them in the process. The film concludes with a relenting chase sequence as the gunslinger goes after the last remaining guest throughout all three worlds of the park, including the futuristic laboratory complex underneath it. Brynner's portrayal of the unrelenting and emotionless pursuer was the inspiration for John Carpenter's Michael Myers in *Halloween* (1978). *Westworld* plays with the central film-audience fantasy of creating a world

"WELL, AS WE'VE ALWAYS SAID: DELOS IS THE VACATION OF THE FUTURE, TODAY."

INTERVIEWER OF DELOS GUESTS

where we are able (for a hefty price) to enter into the cinematic fantasies we desire, to fight and kill, woo and sleep with all these projections of our cinematic fantasies. But what happens when those fantasies turn against us?

▶
Yul Brynner's automaton, "The Gunslinger," was a robotic recreation of his character from *The Magnificent Seven*, shown here burning with acid thrown by an increasingly desperate Richard Benjamin.

What is most significant about *Westworld* for a modern audience is just how ahead of its time it was. Delos presents not just any kind of historically accurate depiction of these worlds, but mass media constructions where grown-ups get to play out their sexual and violent fantasies, much like (and ever-so-slightly prefiguring) the blockbuster films of Steven Spielberg. The worlds of Delos are predicated upon the artifice of cinema, with then-contemporary average Joe movie stars like Brolin and Benjamin playing our surrogates on screen, while older Hollywood stars, like Brynner, are self-consciously evoking their own stardom. **MK**

The Spaced Out Odyssey.

DARK STAR

The Mission of the Strangelove Generation!

Bryanston Presents • A Jack H. Harris Production • DARK STAR • Starring Dan O'Bannon and Brian Narelle • Produced and Directed by John Carpenter
Written by Dan O'Bannon and John Carpenter • Executive Producer Jack H. Harris • A Bryanston Release • Color

G **GENERAL AUDIENCES**

DARK STAR 1974 (U.S.)

Director John Carpenter **Producer** John Carpenter **Screenplay** John Carpenter, Dan O'Bannon **Cinematography** Douglas Knapp **Music** John Carpenter **Cast** Brian Narelle, Andrew "Dre" Pahich, Dan O'Bannon, Cal Kuniholme, and the voices of Adam Beckenbaugh, Nick Castle, Cookie Knapp, Joe Saunders

Alien as beachball, bomb as Cartesian subject, astronaut as surfer: Welcome to the new frontier; you are entering uncharted territory. Starting out as an ultra-low-budget student project by film enthusiasts, *Dark Star* became one of the wittiest sci-fi movies in the history of the genre.

The comic element was twofold: On the one hand, John Carpenter used all kinds of production limitations in order to bring back a disarming naïveté to the genre, a naïveté that is actually (with Georges Méliès as founding father) something like ground zero of the science-fiction oeuvre. On the other hand, the director developed poignant parodic sentiments as a much-needed answer to recent tendencies in the genre whereby false grandeur and pretentiousness were just a mask to cover up an urgent lack of substance and insight. *Dark Star* was an infantile antidote: Sci-fi's metaphysical vision was here transformed into an ironic one . . . and suddenly the genre was philosophical again.

As a result of Carpenter's carefully calculated understatement, you can sense the existential anxiety of the crew members, on a mission to destroy all unstable planets in their way.

◄

It is Powell's cryogenically preserved mind, pictured on the poster, that tells Doolittle to try and talk the bomb out of detonating with a discussion about phenomenology.

The task is nonsensical, they are unstable too, and humor is present to mask despair, loneliness, and dissatisfaction. The idea of any absolute is transformed into the absurd with the constant technical deterioration of the spaceship. This meltdown is reflected in the progressive alienation between the crew members, who (without their ineffective, dead captain) can no longer cope with problems.

"DARK STAR *WAS TELLING SOME KIND OF TRUTH REGARDING OUR LIVES."*

JOHN CARPENTER

▶

John Carpenter and Dan O'Bannon started making *Dark Star* **while both were students at the University of Southern California, the influential film school that also listed Lucas, Spielberg, and Coppola among its former pupils.**

Where does all this lead? To the new, albeit tiny, Big Bang. Things were explosive anyway. Carpenter's main references are two Stanley Kubrick movies. The birth of the "Star-Child" in *2001* (1968), is matched by the destruction at the end of *Dark Star*, which also functions as a reversal of the whole atomic bomb logic of *Doctor Strangelove* (1964). When the bomb in *Dark Star* finally "comes to its senses" and says, "Let there be light," it is a proclamation of the new cosmology, emancipation from the previous deadlock. This polemical act of creation also serves as the realization of the astronauts' fantasies: Talby (Pahich) will join the asteroids, and Doolittle (Narelle) will catch the biggest of all waves, to surf through infinite space. The last we see of Talby is the shimmering of asteroids; the last we see of Doolittle is the glow from his encounter with a planet's atmosphere. Let there be light, indeed. **AB**

THE MAN WHO FELL TO EARTH

1976 (U.K.)

Director Nicholas Roeg **Producers** Michael Deeley, Barry Spikings **Screenplay** Paul Mayersberg (from the novel by Walter Tevis) **Cinematography** Anthony Richmond **Music** John Phillips **Cast** David Bowie, Rip Torn, Candy Clark, Buck Henry, Bernie Casey, Rick Riccardo, Tony Mascia, Jackson D. Kane, Linda Hutton, Adrienne Larussa

---

Based on Walter Tevis's 1963 novel, *The Man Who Fell to Earth* starred a wan, androgynous David Bowie emergent from his Ziggy Stardust phase, and was among the first science-fiction films to argue that "Aliens 'R US," registering an inward turn. Instead of boldly going, a lone extraterrestrial, Thomas Jerome Newton (Bowie), on a mission to save his drought-stricken planet, plummets into an idyllic turquoise lake in a remote area of the West. Pieter Brueghel's painting of the fall of Icarus is an allusion, and Newton "falls" in other ways. He creates a mega-corporation, World Enterprises, enters a codependent relationship with hotel maid Mary-Lou (Clark), finds consolation in alcohol, television, and sex and, losing touch with his family, forgets his purpose. So, in a meaningful sense, does the film.

Newton falls like Alice into Wonderland, and initially unrelated scenes and broken sequences recreate his sense of disorientation. We are plunged into the dazzling strangeness and poignancy of life on Earth as Newton succumbs to its spell, and we follow into the tailspin of his descent as his mission erodes. But the film was out of sync with its time, confounding

◄

The surreal and hallucinatory imagery throughout the film has won *The Man Who Fell to Earth* a strong cult following over the years.

audiences with its "channel surfing" narrative and lack of futuristic effects, while anticipating films like *Memento* (2000) and *Mulholland Drive* (2001). Time-lapses, abrupt crosscuts, visual and musical allusions, subplots and jostling genres—including drama, love story, western, satire, and philosophical meditation—thwart a linear trajectory. A western motif, for instance, includes disparate flashes of wagon trains

"TOMMY, YOU'RE A FREAK. I DON'T MEAN THAT UNKINDLY. I LIKE FREAKS. AND THAT'S WHY I LIKE YOU." *MARY-LOU*

and locomotives that suggest parallels, both hopeful and portentous, among American pioneer spirit, Manifest Destiny, and World Enterprises.

Ultimately Newton falls into excesses of global capitalism, dissolving into schizophrenia. In the film's most memorable scene, Newton, drinking gin before a bank of television screens, in a crisis of information overload, screams "Get out of my mind . . . All of you!" When he attempts to return to his planet, government agents arrest him, converting his quarters, which are dominated by a huge television screen, into a bizarre laboratory.

On another level, Newton is an angelic messenger whose message goes unheard. The film's fate was similar when its American theatrical release was cut by some 20 minutes, and as a result, found incomprehensible. **LB**

▶
Using X-rays to penetrate his disguise, government agents fuse Newton's (Bowie) contact lenses to his eyes, sealing him in medicated alienation.

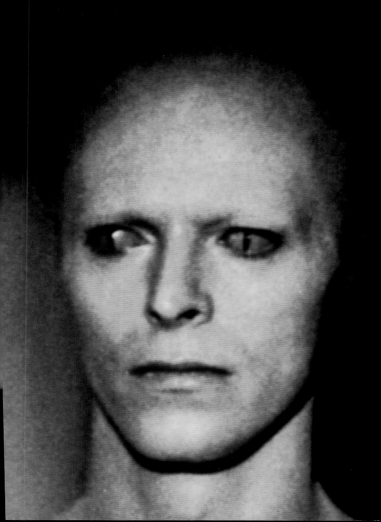

WELCOME TO THE 23RD CENTURY.
The perfect world of total pleasure.

...there's just one catch.

METRO-GOLDWYN-MAYER presents A SAUL DAVID PRODUCTION "LOGAN'S RUN" starring MICHAEL YORK · JENNY AGUTTER · RICHARD JORDAN · ROSCOE LEE BROWNE FARRAH FAWCETT-MAJORS & PETER USTINOV · Screenplay by DAVID ZELAG GOODMAN Based on the novel "LOGAN'S RUN" by WILLIAM F. NOLAN and GEORGE CLAYTON JOHNSON Music—JERRY GOLDSMITH · Produced by SAUL DAVID · Directed by MICHAEL ANDERSON

PG PARENTAL GUIDANCE SUGGESTED — Filmed in TODD-AO and METROCOLOR [NOW A BANTAM BOOK!]

MGM United Artists

LOGAN'S RUN 1976 (U.S.)

Director Michael Anderson **Producer** Saul David **Screenplay** David Zelag
Goodman (based on the book by William F. Nolan & George Clayton Johnson)
Cinematography Ernest Laszlo **Music** Jerry Goldsmith **Cast** Michael York, Jenny
Agutter, Richard Jordan, Peter Ustinov, Roscoe Lee Browne, Farrah Fawcett-Majors

The makers of 1970s sci-fi were largely agreed on just one
thing regarding the future: The outlook is bleak. Here, in the
23rd century, humans live in the mall-like serenity and sterility
of a great domed city. When their "life clock" reaches its end at
the age of 30, they are selected to appear on *Carousel*, a kind
of game show where the excited audience cheers, for their
favorites to be "renewed." Meanwhile, the Runners, those who
have instead choosen to run for their lives, are hunted down
and terminated by Sandmen like Logan (York), who never
questions his job (the word "kill" offends him) until he finds his
own time running out.

Seen now, *Logan's Run* is pure kitsch, its futurist iconography
dominated typically by elaborate glass and silver architecture,
model vehicles, and togas. But on the level of ideas, the film
has gained something with the passage of time: Where once
it seemed somewhat random in its satirical predictions, it can
now be seen to have hit a number of bullseyes.

The society in which all is geared to the pursuit of ephemeral
sensation seems strikingly prescient, and the film takes
effective aim at the emerging horrors of reality television, mall

◀
**The film is similar
to George Lucas's
THX 1138 (1971)
in its theme of
two lovers fleeing
a hedonistic,
hermetically-
sealed society.
It also bears
comparison
to 1977's
Damnation Alley.**

culture, vanity (as represented by the shop where citizens choose new faces to replace their boring old ones), and the commodification of sexual desire. Iconic in the latter capacity is Jenny Agutter as Jessica, conjured up by a remote control unit for the perfect night in.

The first *Carousel* game-show sequence—shown before we are exactly certain what is going on—is excellently staged,

"YOU DON'T HAVE TO DIE! NO ONE HAS TO DIE AT 30! YOU COULD LIVE! LIVE! . . . . I'VE SEEN IT!" LOGAN

as is the subsequent *Blade Runner*-like pursuit of the Runners. The architecture of the older, disused parts of the city, with the splendid gleaming chrome giving way to low-tech wheels and cogs, is also effective.

The main problem with the movie—and a common enough one it is—is that the first half is much more interesting than the second. The "run" sequence itself is a reasonably exciting affair of pursuing assassins, floods, and homicidal robots, but little is as interesting as the early sequences in the city. The section with Peter Ustinov as an old man who knew his parents is anti-climactic, and the ending itself is somewhat hokey.

Despite these problems, it remains a fondly thought of and frequently referenced work, with at least two elements that have stood the test of time since the 1970s: the design of escalators, and Farrah Fawcett's hairdo. **MC**

► Ironically, Michael York was already over 30 years old when he starred in *Logan's Run* with Jenny Agutter.

CLOSE ENCOUNTER
OF THE FIRST KIND
Sighting of a UFO

CLOSE ENCOUNTER
OF THE SECOND KIND
Physical Evidence

CLOSE ENCOUNTER
OF THE THIRD KIND
Contact

CLOSE ENCOUNTERS
OF THE THIRD KIND

A COLUMBIA/EMI Presentation
CLOSE ENCOUNTERS OF THE THIRD KIND A PHILLIPS Production A STEVEN SPIELBERG Film
Starring RICHARD DREYFUSS Also Starring TERI GARR, MELINDA DILLON with FRANCOIS TRUFFAUT as Lacombe
Music by JOHN WILLIAMS Visual Effects by DOUGLAS TRUMBULL Director of Photography VILMOS ZSIGMOND, A.S.C.
Produced by JULIA PHILLIPS and MICHAEL PHILLIPS Written and Directed by STEVEN SPIELBERG
Read the Dell Book   Panavision®   DOLBY SYSTEM

CLOSE ENCOUNTERS OF THE THIRD KIND 1977 (U.S. • U.K.)

Director Steven Spielberg **Producers** Julia Phillips, Michael Phillips, Clark L. Paylow
Screenplay Steven Spielberg **Cinematography** Vilmos Zsigmond **Music** John
Williams **Cast** Richard Dreyfuss, François Truffault, Teri Garr, Bob Balaban, Melinda
Dillon, Cary Guffey, J. Patrick McNamara, Warren Kemmerling, Roberts Blossom

The first scene in *Close Encounters of the Third Kind* establishes
the problem of translation. World War II fighter planes long-
reported missing suddenly reappear in perfect condition in
the middle of the Sonora Desert in Mexico. Spanish, French,
and English-speaking officials meet to discuss the strange
phenomenon but cannot understand each other: "Can you
translate English to French and French to English?" The officials
soon realize, however, that they face far greater problems
of translation, for the newly deposited fighters somehow
represent the intergalactic analogue of "Hello."

At the same time, the aliens extend similar greetings to
ordinary folk around the world in various forms. A delighted
five-year-old boy sees "toys" descend from the clouds.
Spacecraft circle ranches, leaving nighttime sunburns on the
faces of witnesses, and ideas in their minds that ultimately
become obsessions: An image of a mountain, the primary
colors, some simple math, and a memorable five-note melody.
At first, people like Roy Neary (Dreyfuss, teaming up again with

◄

**The movie was
sold on the
prospect of alien
contact. The poster
exemplifies the
iconic simplicity
of the successful
marketing campaign.**

Spielberg after the mammoth *Jaws*) are baffled. Looking down at the mountain he has sculpted in his house from his mashed potatoes, Neary doesn't know what to say: "I can't describe it . . . This means something. This is important."

But all soon becomes clear as these images and tones steadily draw the invited to Devils Tower National Monument in Wyoming, where an alien mothership descends to play a

> ## "I DON'T THINK WE COULD HAVE ASKED FOR A MORE BEAUTIFUL EVENING, DO YOU? O.K., WATCH THE SKIES." *PROJECT LEADER*

▶
The aliens seen in the movie's climax were played by children. Many ideas were considered for their appearance, including sped-up motion, and wires so they would appear to be flying. However, this more naturalistic approach was ultimately adopted.

simple musical game of mimicry that quickly ascends to the complexity of a symphonic dialogue between species. Scientists watch in awe: "It seems they're trying to teach us a basic tonal vocabulary." "It's the first day of school fellas." The aliens teach the humans the foundations of a perfect and universal cinematic language.

The film's true brilliance lies precisely here in its own self-consciousness. Like all great works, *Close Encounters* tells us something essential about its medium. Through a remarkable synthetic unity of mathematically organized and musically set images and tones and montage, *Close Encounters* transcends all racial and religious divisions of humanity in a language that translates itself. "They communicated through lights, colors, and music," Spielberg says of the aliens. The same could be said of Spielberg's supreme genre-defining film. **JA**

STAR WARS 1977 (U.S.)

Director George Lucas **Producer** Gary Kurtz **Screenplay** George Lucas
Cinematography Gilbert Taylor **Music** John Williams **Cast** Mark Hamill, Harrison
Ford, Carrie Fisher, Alec Guinness, Kenny Baker, Anthony Daniels, Peter Mayhew,
James Earl Jones (voice), David Prowse, Peter Cushing, Phil Brown, Shelagh Fraser

Once in a while a film comes along that so grabs the popular imagination that it will seemingly live forever, both as an iconic example of popular culture and as a cult hit loved by fans. *Star Wars*, the folktale of a young hero embarking on a quest to save a princess, do battle with the dark side, and rid the world of an evil ruler, is just such a film. More than that, though, it is a loving response to cinema by its creator and director, George Lucas.

In framing the journey of Luke Skywalker (Hamill), from farm boy to hero of the resistance, through the observations of two droids, Lucas draws on the device of a pair of peasant farmers caught up in a war from Akira Kurosawa's *The Hidden Fortress* (1958). This Japanese classic also features a general in disguise, a haughty princess, and an escape from behind enemy lines. *Star Wars* clearly has a pedigree, but Lucas's homage is also a roundabout reworking of the western (which Kurosawa was recreating in his Samurai films).

Further stylistic references are made to 1930s' matinee serials such as *Flash Gordon*. *Star Wars* opens with a scroll of "the story so far," and then throws viewers straight into an action sequence as the Rebel Alliance ship is boarded and Princess Leia (Fisher)

◄
Visually and stylistically quite unlike anything on screen before, *Star Wars* cleaned up at the 1978 Oscars, with Art Direction, Costumes, Visual Effects, Editing, Original Score, Sound and a Special Achievement for Ben Burtt, who created the creature voices.

taken prisoner—though not before hiding the plans in R2–D2, who escapes with C–3PO to Tatooine. This prologue could well be the resolution of a cliffhanger from the previous episode, and once this is resolved the film proceeds to introduce new characters and their adventures: Luke Skywalker, Obi-Wan Kenobi (Guinness), Han Solo (Ford), and Chewbacca (Mayhew), as they rescue Leia and destroy the Death Star.

"I WANTED VERY MUCH TO START IN THE MIDDLE—I DIDN'T WANT [A] BEGINNING; I DON'T LIKE BEGINNINGS." GEORGE LUCAS

This sense of ongoing, episodic excitement is certainly what Lucas intended. When the film was rereleased prior to *The Empire Strikes Back* (1980), Lucas even added the (now firmly established) *Episode IV: A New Hope* subtitle at the beginning of the scroll, though this was not present in the original release. (He has since tweaked the film on a further two occasions, principally to update the effects sequences, but also to add a scene with Jabba the Hutt, and to make Han less of a ruthless gunslinger by shooting Gredo in self-defense).

So in drawing on the western, the fairytale, the episodic serial, and samurai drama, Lucas crafts an engaging version of the archetypal hero's journey. No amount of clunky dialogue and special effects or continuity tinkering can detract from the sheer spectacle and wow moments of a film that forever changed the shape of science-fiction cinema. **BC**

► **The famous sound made by the TIE fighters was created by combining an elephant's scream with the noise of a car on wet tarmac.**

Сценарий А. Стругацкого, Б. Стругацкого
Постановка Андрея Тарковского
Главный оператор А. Княжинский
Главный художник А. Тарковский
Композитор Э. Артемьев
В ролях:
А. Фрейндлих,
А. Кайдановский,
А. Солоницын,
Н. Гринько

Художественный фильм
в двух сериях

СТАЛКЕР

Производство киностудии "Мосфильм"

STALKER 1979 (WEST GERMANY · U.S.S.R.)

Director Andrei Tarkovsky **Producer** Aleksandra Demidova
Screenplay Arkadi and Boris Strugatsky (based on their novel *Roadside Picnic*)
Cinematography Aleksandr Knyazhinsky **Music** Eduard Artemyev **Cast** Aleksandr Kaidanovsky, Alisa Freindlich, Anatoli Solonitsyn, Nikolai Grinko, Natasha Abramova

Something falls from the sky. Troops are sent into the area (the Zone) and never return. Physical laws do not apply there. The government promptly encloses it, forbidding entry. Allegedly, there is a room in the Zone that fulfills one's innermost wish. Only a select few are brave enough to sneak in. The guides that lead people through this singular space are called Stalkers.

If this were an American film, the Zone would be filled with monsters, elaborate visual effects, and stupendous twists. However, this being a Russian art film by a spiritual author like Andrei Tarkovsky (*Solaris* [1971]), such tropes are not necessary. Those looking for adventure, excitement, amazement, and thrills should look elsewhere. Tarkovsky is not after your adrenalin or your money—he wants to reach your soul. This is not to say that *Stalker* isn't an exciting meditation on human nature, filled with amazing visuals and thrilling in its (ambiguous) conclusions.

Set in a uniquely drab (perhaps post-apocalyptic) state, *Stalker* is filmed in startling sepia tones. Mud, mist, and decay hold domain over all, except for the Zone, which retains its natural colors. The three characters we follow are nameless,

◄

The setting for the movie, the Zone, was inspired by a nuclear accident that took place near Chelyabinsk in 1957, although naturally there was no official mention of it at the time.

called only by their professions: Stalker (Kaidanovsky), Scientist (Grinko), and Writer (Solonitsyn). The latter two stand for the key ways of approaching the mystery of existence: reason and imagination. Yet, confronted by the Zone and the darkness in their own hearts, they are ultimately powerless.

Some hope remains only for the Stalker, who seems to stand for love (and faith). For him the world is a prison. The Zone, with

"THE ZONE WANTS TO BE RESPECTED. OTHERWISE IT WILL PUNISH."

STALKER

its mysteries that defy analysis, is the original Nature, unspoiled by the horrendous machinery and smoke of civilization. Going to the Zone, over and over again, he attempts to retain the original purity of Man before The Fall. He is driven not by curiosity, greed, or any other selfish motive. Like a fallen Christ who wants to return to his Father's Kingdom, he realizes that what has hardened will never win. The Zone allows only the wretched, those who have lost all hope, but who remain humble and open-hearted, like children. That is why the film ends with his daughter (Abramova), a "mutant" affected by his Zone-altered genes. The Scientist, the Writer, and even Stalker himself, are forced to wander through the Zone, accomplishing little. The little girl sits morosely and moves glasses on the table only with her look. *Stalker* remains a hauntingly atmospheric and deeply affecting spiritual event. **DO**

► The Stalker's inexplicable love of the Zone is developed during the middle section of the film.

IMAGINE!
A SCIENTIFIC GENIUS NAMED H. G. WELLS
STALKS A CRIMINAL GENIUS NAMED JACK THE RIPPER
ACROSS TIME ITSELF
IN THE MOST INGENIOUS THRILLER
OF OUR TIME.

A HERB JAFFE Production
MALCOLM McDOWELL · DAVID WARNER · MARY STEENBURGEN
"TIME AFTER TIME"
Music by MIKLOS ROZSA   Screenplay by NICHOLAS MEYER
Story by KARL ALEXANDER & STEVE HAYES   Produced by HERB JAFFE
Directed by NICHOLAS MEYER   PANAVISION ®

ORIGINAL MOTION PICTURE SCORE ON ENTR'ACTE RECORDS.

DOLBY STEREO   PG PARENTAL GUIDANCE SUGGESTED
IN SELECTED THEATRES   SOME MATERIAL MAY NOT BE SUITABLE FOR CHILDREN

A WARNER BROS./ORION PICTURES RELEASE
thru WARNER BROS. ©
A WARNER COMMUNICATIONS COMPANY

TIME AFTER TIME 1979 (U.S.)

Director Nicholas Meyer **Producer** Herb Jaffe **Screenplay** Nicholas Meyer
Cinematography Paul Lohmann **Music** Miklós Rózsa **Cast** Malcolm McDowell,
David Warner, Mary Steenburgen, Patti D'Arbanville, Charles Cioffi, Kent Williams,
Andonia Katsaros, James Garrett, Leo Lewis, Keith McConnell, Byron Webster

Though he remains best known in science-fiction circles for
his involvement in three of the best-regarded and most literary
*Star Trek*s, director/writer Nicholas Meyer started his career in
a different vein with *The Seven-Per-Cent Solution*, a speculative
novel about therapy sessions for Sherlock Holmes at the hands
of Sigmund Freud. The idea of joining these pop culture figures
immediately caught fire, and while occasional cinematic one-
offs like *A Study in Terror* had paired Holmes with Jack the Ripper
(as did 1979's underrated *Murder by Decree*), it took a slight tweak
in the form of Meyer's *Time After Time* to produce the crowning
achievement of this narrative formula.

Along with its immense entertainment value, *Time After
Time* benefits by adhering fairly to the biographical facts
surrounding its main characters, science-fiction novelist H. G.
Wells and the infamous maniac Jack the Ripper. Although the
idea of these figures pursuing each other via time machine into
modern-day San Francisco isn't exactly "realistic," the film
lays down its own rules clearly at the beginning and never
cheats the viewer, even offering a surprising, emotionally
resonant finale that dovetails beautifully with real life. The

◄
**With a stirring,
nostalgic score by
Hollywood veteran
Miklós Rózsa,
and enchanting
visual effects
by future *TRON*
(1982) pioneer
Richard Taylor,
Time After Time
remains one of the
most endearing
and completely
satisfying
time-travel films
ever made.**

science-fiction aspects also remain wholly in keeping with Wells's own outlook as he responds with curiosity and dismay at humankind's evolution over a few decades. His understanding of man's capacity for barbarism had already found its root in the bloodlust lurking within his friend, a noted surgeon (Warner) revealed to be the Ripper, who claims he is the one at home in this future age, not Wells.

"HUMAN HISTORY BECOMES MORE AND MORE A RACE BETWEEN EDUCATION AND CATASTROPHE." *H. G. WELLS*

However, the film produces a powerful counterargument in the form of Amy Robbins (Steenburgen, whom McDowell married afterward), a bank teller with whom Wells forms an unlikely romantic partnership. Their bond is the true core of the picture and represents a subtle but optimistic viewpoint for humanity; if people this far apart can find a way to work everything out, why can't we all? In keeping with Wells's philosophy, people have the choice to veer toward barbarism and greed, but the inclination toward enlightenment and positive advancement always reaps greater rewards. Although countless movies have wrung suspense by having a hero race against time to rescue his beloved from a ruthless villain, this one makes the approach fresh by investing the viewer's emotions so deeply with the leads and demonstrating so clearly its villain's capacity for harm. **NT**

► **Mary Steenburgen and Malcolm McDowell, cast as lovers, met for the first time on this movie and were married soon afterward. The couple's romance gives the movie an authentic air.**

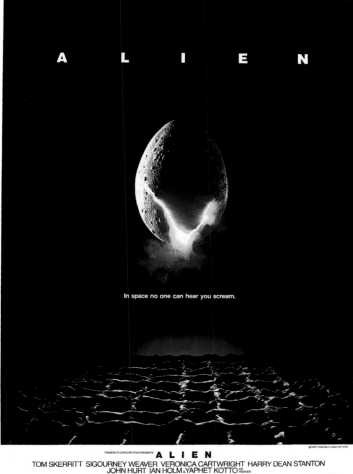

ALIEN 1979 (U.S. • U.K.)

Director Ridley Scott **Producers** Gordon Carroll, David Giler, Walter Hill
Screenplay Dan O'Bannon (story by Dan O'Bannon and Ronald Shusett)
Cinematography Derek Vanlint **Music** Jerry Goldsmith **Cast** Sigourney Weaver,
Tom Skerritt, Veronica Cartwright, Harry Dean Stanton, Ian Holm, John Hurt

Along with *Star Wars* (1977) and *2001: A Space Odyssey* (1968), *Alien* is a landmark science-fiction film. Its historical significance lies in the way it mixes Kubrick's slowness of space with the special effects and marketability of Lucas's franchise but keeps the film within the domain of gory adult entertainment.

The crew of the mining ship *Nostromo*, returning to Earth after a long voyage, is brought out of cryogenic sleep by the ship's computer, which has received an emergency beacon message asking for rescue. Arriving on a desolate planet, the crew discovers a room filled with strange egglike sacks. While investigating further, one of the eggs bursts open and a strange alien creature attaches itself to Kane's (Hurt) face. Kane is brought back to the ship and put into isolation. The creature detaches itself after a few days, and the crew member seems to be recovering. During one final meal before they returned to their frozen sleep, however, the "face-hugger" had apparently laid some kind of an egg in Kane's chest for incubation, for it is at the dinner table that the alien (named in the literature and in later films as a xenomorph) graphically bursts forth from Kane's chest in what is now an iconic moment of screen terror.

◄

Alien is another film that has an immediately recognizable, unique look. It picked up an Oscar for Best Visual Effects, and a nomination for Best Art Direction.

The creature scurries off and quickly grows to monstrous size, picking off each remaining crew member one at a time, until only Ripley (Weaver) is left. The two do battle before she blows the monster from the ship's airlock out into space.

Not since the classic 1950s films of intergalactic invasion has science fiction been so closely linked with horror as it is in *Alien*. While the monster and its gory rampage is clearly the generic

"IT'S EXOTIC BEYOND YOUR POSSIBLE EXPERIENCE, BUT IT'S ALSO VERY REAL."

RIDLEY SCOTT

property of horror, *Alien* is equally successful as a sci-fi movie, particularly in its depiction of a future society where human beings are secondary to corporate interests, and the gradual revelation that, while the *Nostromo*'s primary concern was its mining mission, it was equally important for the ever-present company that they bring back a xenomorph specimen for the company's bio-weapons interests. The crew is expendable.

The alien creature itself, based on a design by the Swiss artist H. R. Geiger, fuses the industrial, the sexual, and the human. From the film's very opening, tracking through the sleeping ship, the engine's thudding sounds like a heartbeat. As the crew awakens from their cryogenic sleep, the images evoke birth—but clean and antiseptic, particularly in juxtaposition with the bloody and visceral birth images of the alien baby at the dinner table. **MK**

▶
The impact of Dan O'Bannen's earlier experiences with the low budget *Dark Star* left him with a hunger for realism: The alien in *Alien* couldn't be further from *Dark Star*'s infamous "beachball" alien.

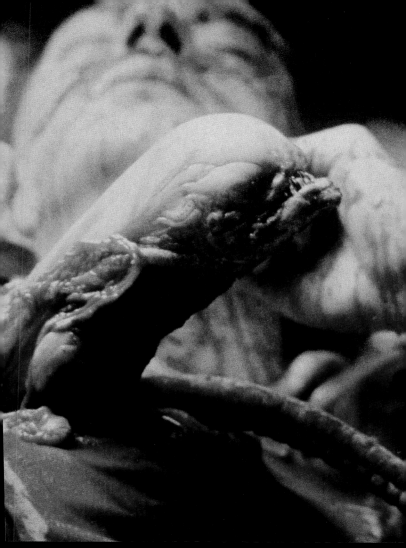

THE *STAR WARS* SAGA CONTINUES

Starring MARK HAMILL · HARRISON FORD · CARRIE FISHER
BILLY DEE WILLIAMS · ANTHONY DANIELS as See-Threepio
Co-starring DAVID PROWSE · KENNY BAKER · PETER MAYHEW · FRANK OZ
Directed by IRVIN KERSHNER   Produced by GARY KURTZ
Screenplay by LEIGH BRACKETT and LAWRENCE KASDAN   Story by GEORGE LUCAS
Executive Producer GEORGE LUCAS   Music by JOHN WILLIAMS
ORIGINAL SOUNDTRACK ON RSO RECORDS

STAR WARS: EPISODE V THE EMPIRE STRIKES BACK 1980 (U.S.)

Director Irvin Kershner **Producers** Gary Kurtz, George Lucas **Screenplay** Leigh Brackett, Lawrence Kasdan **Cinematography** Peter Suschitzky **Music** John Williams **Cast** Mark Hamill, Carrie Fisher, Harrison Ford, Billy Dee Williams, David Prowse, Peter Mayhew, Anthony Daniels, Kenny Baker, Alec Guinness

For most moviegoers *The Empire Strikes Back*, the second film made of George Lucas's *Star Wars* saga, is a favorite of the entire series. "Officially" the film is *Episode V*, and acts as the penultimate chapter in the saga. As *Star Wars: Episode VI—A New Hope* (1977) ends, the Death Star has been destroyed and the Rebel Alliance is enjoying its first real success in the battle against the Empire.

As *Empire* opens, Darth Vader (Prowse) has tracked the rebels to the ice planet Hoth, where they are defending their base. The base is destroyed, and our heroes scatter across the galaxy: Luke (Hamill) and R2-D2 are off to Dagobah so Luke can complete his training as a Jedi knight under the ancient Jedi master Yoda, while Han (Ford), Leia (Fisher), Chewbacca (Mayhew), and C-3PO look for a safe haven to repair their ship, the *Millennium Falcon*. They arrive at the Cloud City seeking sanctuary from an old smuggler buddy of Han's, Lando Calrissian (Williams), only to find that Lando has betrayed them all by selling them back to the Empire. Luke, through the powers of the Force,

◄
George Lucas was able to rerelease *Empire* in 1999, harnessing technological developments that allowed him to digitally tweak the special effects in ways unavailable to him in 1977, 1980, and 1983.

learns of his friends' predicaments, and leaves his training to go to their rescue. Once there, Luke falls into the Empire's trap and must battle Darth Vader face-to-face.

Despite the huge amount of story that *Empire* tells, and its position within the structure of the overall *Star Wars* narrative (being the middle part of the original trilogy), the film manages to bring the human characters to life much more than in

"THE FORCE IS WITH YOU, YOUNG SKYWALKER, BUT YOU ARE NOT A JEDI YET." DARTH VADER

any of the other *Star Wars* movies. Although some of this credit belongs to screenwriters Leigh Brackett and Lawrence Kasdan in enabling the emerging love between Han and Leia, developing Luke's fear of being a Jedi and the draws of the Dark Side, Vader's relentless searching for Luke and, to a lesser extent, Lando being torn between betraying his friends or establishing a higher place in the Empire, director Irvin Kershner is able to bring out performances that center the human dimension more than George Lucas ever could as a director, making this the strongest entry in the series.

► **The Imperial AT-AT Walkers were intoduced in the battle of Hoth at the start of *The Empire Strikes Back*.**

In preparation for the 1999 release of *The Phantom Menace*, Lucas rereleased the original three films in the saga, but even with the improved effects their impact is in the background, as the character arcs in *The Empire Strikes Back* are still the core of the film. **MK**

FLASH GORDON 1980 (U.S. • U.K.)

Director Mike Hodges **Producer** Dino De Laurentiis **Screenplay** Lorenzo Semple **Cinematography** Gil Taylor **Music** Queen, Howard Blake **Cast** Sam J. Jones, Melody Anderson, Topol, Max Von Sydow, Brian Blessed, Timothy Dalton, Ornella Muti, Peter Wyngarde, John Osborne, Richard O'Brien, Suzanne Danielle

When *Flash Gordon* first came out, many 12-year-olds (at whom it was aimed) just didn't know what to make of it. In the wake of other science-fiction blockbusters, such as *Star Wars* and *The Empire Strikes Back*, and television programs like *Battlestar Galactica* and *Buck Rogers*, they expected a big-budget, Dino De Laurentiis–produced space opera. Twelve-year-olds are not necessarily the best audiences for "retro camp."

Football star Flash Gordon (Jones) is caught up with reporter Dale Arden (Anderson) and former NASA scientist Dr. Hans Zarkov (Topol) in fighting the intergalactic villain Ming the Merciless (von Sydow), who is trying to destroy the earth. While on Ming's planet, Mongo, the trio find themselves at odds, and eventually allies with, various other alien races trying to survive under Ming's merciless rule.

Based on the 1930s comic strip by Alex Raymond, and a series of 1930s and 1940s movie serials, director Mike Hodges sought to create a film aesthetic that directly reflected this origin, much like Robert Altman tried to do in his 1980 film, *Popeye*. The opening credits of *Flash* use illustrations from those early comic strips, along with Queen's now famous theme song.

◄

Flash Gordon **picked up a handful of BAFTA nominations for Film Music, Production Design, and Costume Design.**

But throughout the movie, Hodges chooses film angles, framings, and colors to evoke the reading of a comic strip.

Despite Jones winning a "Razzie" for the worst performance by an actor in the film, the blandness of the heroic leads was designed to likewise reflect the story's comic-strip origins. Having Ming played by an actor most known for his collaborations with Ingmar Bergman was a genius move in

"[FLASH IS] A BIT THICK . . . A BIT DUMB. KIND OF LIKE AMERICAN FOREIGN POLICY, IT SEEMS TO ME . . . " MIKE HODGES

casting against type. Ratcheting up the film's campiness, Hodges casts veteran stage actors Timothy Dalton (in his pre-Bond days) as Prince Barin of the Ardentians and Brian Blessed as Prince Vultan of the Hawkmen, as well as *The Rocky Horror Picture Show*'s creator and star, Richard O'Brien.

Of course the cleverness of the casting and its kitchiness was lost on adolescent audiences, as were Hodges's allusions to American foreign policy, particularly the 1979 capturing of the American embassy in Tehran, during the Iranian revolution. Flash, Dale, and Zarkov's stumbling into the complexities of the politics on Mongo, particularly under a despotic dictator like Ming, has echoes in post-war American foreign policies. Apparently, much of the film's merits were also lost on executive producer Dino De Laurentiis, who was under the impression that he was making a great space epic to rival *Star Wars*. **MK**

► **Director Hodges has compared his version of *Flash* to the making of a soufflé, recognizing that both would need a very light touch.**

SCANNERS 1981 (CANADA)

Director David Cronenberg **Producer** Claude Heroux **Screenplay** David Cronenberg **Cinematography** Mark Irwin **Music** Howard Shore **Cast** Jennifer O'Neill, Stephen Lack, Patrick McGoohan, Lawrence Dane, Michael Ironside, Fred Doederlein, Robert A. Silverman, Lee Broker, Mavor Moore, Adam Ludwig

Scanners is first and foremost the exploding-head movie, film history's most impressive moment of brain splatter. Ten minutes into the story a battle of minds between two adversaries ends with the head of one of them blasting off its torso. The 47 frames of gushing gore contained in that one masterful shot, composed by leading special-effects wizards Dick Smith, Gary Zeller, and Chris Walas, became an invitation for audiences to experiment with a new gadget: the VCR remote. As one critic wrote: "It's the kind of scene where you go 'yuck!' and then play it over, in slow motion, about six times."

The exploding-head shot in itself should make *Scanners* memorable. But there is more to the film than just a radical cure for headaches. Coming at the pinnacle of a series of conspiracy thrillers such as *Coma* (1978), *Capricorn One* (1978), and *Telefon* (1977), *Scanners* exemplifies science fiction's era of ultimate suspicion: No government agency, no drug, no one can be trusted, and maybe it's all in your head. In the case of *Scanners*, this is to be taken literally. The story revolves around 237 "scanners," people who can scan (or read) minds, and whose mind powers can kill. Upon the orders of their "creator,"

◀

Scanners was David Cronenberg's most commercially successful movie until *The Fly* six years later; not coincidentally, it was also the closest thing to a conventional sci-fi thriller he had made up until then.

Dr. Paul Ruth (McGoohan), one of them, derelict Cameron Vale (Lack), infiltrates the network of a shady operation run by scanner Daryll Revok (Ironside), who is out to turn the world population into a super-race of scanners. Cameron confronts Revok in a battle of wills that literally sparks fireworks. Besides its spectacular stuntwork and special effects, most of *Scanners'* power lies in the overall atmosphere of paranoia

"KABOOM! UNDOUBTEDLY, THE FINEST EXPLODING HEAD OF ALL TIME."

JASON ARNOPP

and desolation. Much of this is achieved through a mature treatment of the story, with explicit horror, violence, abuse, and a constant blurring of the boundaries between good and bad. In the end the viewer is left in confusion over who has won, Cameron or Revok, but also in a grounding in realism. It gave *Scanners* an edgy and militant look, one that stood in stark contrast to the more outworldly science fiction of *Star Wars* and *Star Trek*.

Whether it was because of this militancy, or the exploding head, or because of a shooting at one of the early New York screenings of the film, *Scanners* became a surprise box-office success, director David Cronenberg's biggest at the time. Its subsequent video release was equally profitable. It led to several sequels and reworkings, and a cult reputation—all evidence of its enduring appeal. **EM**

► **William S. Burroughs's novel *Naked Lunch* (loosely adapted by Cronenberg in 1991) contains a chapter concerning "Senders," a hostile organization of telepaths bent on world domination, a clear influence on the movie.**

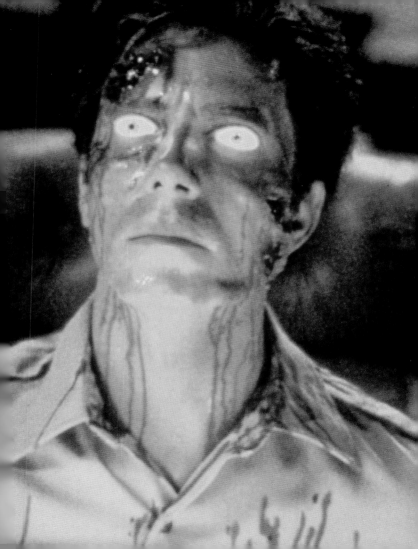

ESCAPE FROM NEW YORK 1981 (U.S. • U.K.)

Director John Carpenter **Producer** Shinya Tsukamoto **Screenplay** John Carpenter, Nick Castle **Cinematography** Dean Cundy **Music** John Carpenter
Cast Kurt Russell, Lee Van Cleef, Isaac Hayes, Donald Pleasence, Ernest Borgnine, Harry Dean Stanton, Adrienne Barbeau, Season Hubley, Tom Atkins, Charles Cyphers

In conjunction with films like George Miller's *Mad Max 2* (or *The Road Warrior*, 1981), John Carpenter's *Escape from New York* helped establish a more pessimistic vision of the future in the early 1980s. Originally written during the tail end of the Nixon administration, the screenplay offers a forecast of the decade's rising crime rate and a strong attitude toward the duplicity and secrecy of government.

It's the future (the setting is 1997, only 16 years after the film was made) and embittered former Special Forces Lieutenant S. D. "Snake" Plissken (Russell), captured recently during a robbery, is on his way to a life sentence at the Manhattan Island maximum security prison when his unique services come into need. Rebels have hijacked Air Force One and slammed it into a skyscraper in the Manhattan skyline. However, the president (Pleasence) survived in an escape pod and is somewhere inside this walled-off prison. Plissken is offered a deal by Bob Hauk (Van Cleef)—get in, bring the president out alive, and receive a full pardon. After finding out he is injected with mini-explosives to ensure his loyalty, Plissken makes it to Manhattan Island with a time limit to locate the president.

◄
The only scene actually filmed in New York was the opening dolly shot, which follows a character who passes the Statue of Liberty.

Once there, Plissken enlists the aid of several prisoners, including Cabbie (Borgnine), Brain (Stanton), and Maggie (Barbeau). Together, they find out that the president is being held hostage by The Duke (Hayes), the local crime boss who intends on using his high-value hostage as a ticket to freedom. Carpenter and cowriter Nick Castle's bleak vision of 1997 is a dystopia of zero tolerance (escapees are blown up in the first

> ## "IT'S THE SURVIVAL OF THE HUMAN RACE, PLISSKEN. SOMETHING YOU DON'T GIVE A S**T ABOUT." HAUK

few minutes) where any undesirables shipped off to the prison have an option for self-termination if requested. The penal system has been abandoned in favor of an anarchistic free-market structure that sees the rise of everyone from crime lords to oil producers to cannibals.

Like Carpenter's previous *Rio Bravo* redo *Assault on Precinct 13* (1976), *Escape* is essentially a western in a modern setting, with Russell doing his admittedly best Clint Eastwood impersonation. And whereas a big-budget action movie starring a former Walt Disney child star would be questionable today, the duo of Carpenter and Russell make it work. The inventive screenplay also leads to some unforgettable action scenes (a gladiator challenge with spiked baseball bats; a car chase across a mined bridge), with Carpenter's memorable score speeding the anarchy at a rhythmic rate. **WW**

► **Resisting the urge to use older, studio-suggested stars like Steve McQueen and Charles Bronson, Carpenter insisted on casting Russell, with whom he had worked on the television miniseries *Elvis* (1979).**

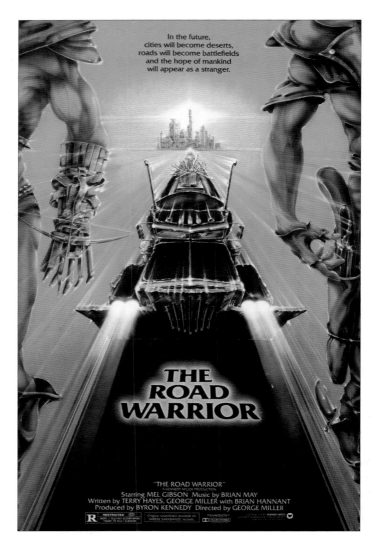

THE ROAD WARRIOR (MAD MAX 2)
1981 (AUSTRALIA)

Director George Miller **Producer** Bryon Kennedy **Screenplay** Terry Hayes, George Miller, Brian Hannant **Cinematography** Dean Semler **Music** Brian May
Cast Mel Gibson, Bruce Spence, Mike Preston, Max Phipps, Vernon Wells, Kjell Nilsson, Emil Minty, Virginia Hey, William Zappa, Arkie Whiteley, Steve J. Spears

There exists only a very loose connection to the first *Mad Max* movie directed by George Miller in 1979 and this sequel (also released in other parts of the world as *Mad Max 2*). You don't have to have seen *Mad Max* in order to understand *The Road Warrior*. For director amd co-writer Miller, past and future are nothing. The present is everything. Max lives in a post-apocalyptic world, located in another time, another place. He wanders through a wasteland, a deserted land (in fact fittingly the Australian outback). It is an extinct countryside where a nuclear holocaust has made it tough to eke out a life let alone a living, and only the fittest, the fastest, and the fiercest survive. Mad Max (Gibson, still a relative unknown to U.S. audiences) is a man who doesn't go looking for Australia, as he knows he can't find it any more. The only thing that still counts in the wilderness is the ruthless search for fuel.

While Australia was recovering from the global oil crisis of the late 1970s, *The Road Warrior* takes up the idea of a post-Industrial future ruled by gas-siphoning warloads. Toying with the fear of running out of natural resources, it levels criticism

◄
The original *Mad Max* (1979) had a limited U.S. release, so calling this movie *Mad Max 2* would have been difficult to market there. It was renamed *The Road Warrior* for North American distribution.

at excessive car culture on the one hand while glorifying car fetishism through spectacular action sequences on the other.

Miller's direction is never really serious as he aims for a campy, over-the-top approach. But his car, truck, and bike stunts are stunningly choreographed, while Gibson comes on all Eastwood, spaghetti-western style machismo. The movie boasts a strong cartoonish feel, stripping down all characters

"WE TOLD THESE POST-APOCALYPTIC ALLEGORIES TO . . . EXPLORE THE DARKER SIDE OF OURSELVES." GEORGE MILLER

and situations to archetypes, then blowing them all up again in an immensely flamboyant comic-book style.

The storyline, for what it's worth, has a gang of barbaric Hell's Angels terrorizing a commune of settlers just like the savage Indians of Hollywood's classical westerns. In one battle after another Max fights them off, culminating in a masterfully staged showdown chase sequence that lasts almost one-third of the movie: an orgy of gas, guns, and guts. When Max has done his job he returns to the wilderness knowing that there can be no place for him in civilized life.

► **Although Max (Gibson) is featured in almost every frame of the film, he speaks only about a dozen lines.**

Max is a post-modern remodeling of Ethan Edwards (John Wayne) just as *The Road Warrior* is a post-modern pastiche of John Ford's *The Searchers* (1956). The film's style—a combination of comic book violence, post-apocalyptic angst, and punk rock attitude—quickly led to its becoming a cult classic. **IR**

A STEVEN SPIELBERG FILM

E.T.

THE EXTRA-TERRESTRIAL

A STEVEN SPIELBERG FILM
E.T. THE EXTRA-TERRESTRIAL
DEE WALLACE   PETER COYOTE   DREW BARRYMORE
HENRY THOMAS AS ELLIOTT
MUSIC BY JOHN WILLIAMS   WRITTEN BY MELISSA MATHISON
PRODUCTION DESIGNER JAMES D. BISSELL
DIRECTOR OF PHOTOGRAPHY ALLEN DAVIAU   EDITED BY CAROL LITTLETON
PRODUCED BY STEVEN SPIELBERG & KATHLEEN KENNEDY

E.T.: THE EXTRA-TERRESTRIAL 1982 (U.S.)

Director Steven Spielberg **Producers** Steven Spielberg, Kathleen Kennedy
Screenplay Melissa Mathison **Cinematography** Allen Daviau **Music** John Williams
Cast Henry Thomas, Dee Wallace, Robert MacNaughton, Drew Barrymore, Peter
Coyote, K. C. Martel, Sean Frye, C. Thomas Howell, David M. O'Dell, Frank Toth

The image of young Elliott (Thomas) and his newfound space
alien friend, silhouetted as tiny hooded figures against a
luminous full moon, has become iconic, a symbol of inspiration,
the importance of friendship and home, and the magic of
cinema itself. (It is also the logo of Amblin Entertainment,
Spielberg's production company.) Spielberg has called this
his most personal film and it quickly became for a while the
highest-grossing motion picture of all time. The American Film
Institute has listed the movie among its top 25 greatest movies
ever made, and its also ranks among the AFI's ten most inspiring
films in history. The phrase "E.T. phone home," expressing the
movie's primary theme of an abandoned space creature who
must rely on his human friends to help him return to his origins,
has become one of the most memorable quotes in Hollywood
history. Spielberg's 20th-anniversary reissue of the film includes
never-before-seen footage, enhanced effects, and a digitally
remastered sound track.

The film expresses a heartwarming and humbling message
that has spoken to young and old viewers alike, a message
that is as ancient as the Mesopotamian epic of Gilgamesh,

◀
E.T. scooped the
Oscars for Best
Visual Effects,
Best Sound Effects
Editing, Best
Original Score, and
Best Sound. It was
also nominated for
Best Director, Best
Cinematography,
Best Film Editing,
Best Picture, and
Best Screenplay
Written Directly
for the Screen.

teaching that love is an emotional condition that transcends humanity itself and that there are indeed universal patterns connecting all living things.

And even though *E.T.* may be targeted chiefly toward children, it does not shy away from bigger real-life issues such as governmental surveillance, divorce, and the fear of death. In fact, Elliott's moments spent with his very sick alien friend are

"HE'S CALLING HIS PEOPLE, AND I DON'T KNOW WHERE THEY ARE, AND HE NEEDS TO GO HOME." *ELLIOT*

as serious and heartbreaking as, say, scenes of a mother dealing with a grown daughter's terminal illness in *Terms of Endearment* (1983). It is intriguing that Spielberg chose to include snippets of a romantic scene from John Ford's *The Quiet Man* (1952) when showing us a television-entranced *E.T.* We know from interviews that Spielberg, like many other contemporary American directors, was highly influenced by Ford. But what makes this clip choice especially interesting is that Ford's film, like *E.T.*, has also become a highly popular motion picture, one that masterfully balances unabashed sentimentality with an awareness of the pains and trials that the adult world can cause. Even more so, both films revolve around the basic theme of love—a love that can reveal the occasional poetry of life while also uniting individuals from different cultures (as in *The Quiet Man*) as well as different planets (as in *E.T.*). **KS**

► Although Henry Thomas gives a remarkable performance as the child Elliott, it is the wide-eyed and neck-craning title character that truly steals the viewers' hearts.

STAR TREK II: THE WRATH OF KHAN
1982 (U.S.)

Director Nicholas Meyer **Producer** Robert Sallin **Screenplay** Jack B. Sowards, Harve Bennett **Cinematography** Gayne Rescher **Music** James Horner
Cast William Shatner, Leonard Nimoy, DeForest Kelley, Ricardo Montalban, Kirstie Alley, Bibi Besch, James Doohan, Walter Koenig, George Takei, Nichelle Nichols

After the lumbering *Star Trek: The Motion Picture* (1979), at the time among Hollywood's costliest films ever, Paramount handed the reins of its potentially profitable *Star Trek* franchise to executive producer Harve Bennett, who had run several very successful television shows. Bennett, along with screenwriter Jack B. Sowards and director Nicholas Meyer (*Time After Time* [1979]), brought fresh thinking to the project, unsaddled with preconceived notions of how *Star Trek* was "supposed to be."

Perhaps their brightest decision was upping the comic-strip action content; *Star Trek II* is the fastest-paced and most violent of the series, and Ricardo Montalban a suitably nasty adversary for Admiral Kirk (Shatner). The self depreciating humor helps too. Another smart move occurred when Leonard Nimoy was hesitant to return as Spock, perhaps the series' most popular character. Bennett coaxed Nimoy back into the fold by promising to kill Spock off, believing no actor could resist performing a dramatic death scene. When word of Spock's death leaked to the fans, it spawned a heap of publicity that, whether or not the fans approved, could not help but benefit the film's release.

◄

Thanks in part to Meyer's snappy direction, outstanding Industrial Light and Magic visual effects, and James Horner's rousing score, *Star Trek II: The Wrath of Khan* is arguably the best of the ten Trek films (to date).

Set more than a decade after the TV show's original five-year mission, *Star Trek II* finds the U.S.S. *Enterprise* suddenly ordered to investigate murder on a scientific outpost run by Dr. Carol Marcus (Besch). Marcus and her team have been developing the top-secret Genesis Device, amazing technology able to create life from scratch, and everything needed to sustain human existence. In the wrong hands, however, Genesis

"GALLOPING AROUND THE COSMOS IS A GAME FOR THE YOUNG, DOCTOR."

ADMIRAL JAMES T. KIRK

could be a devastating weapon. Those hands belong to Khan Noonian Singh (Montalban, reprising his role from the *Star Trek* episode *Space Seed*), whose ultimate goal is vengeance against his old foe, Admiral James T. Kirk (Shatner).

Star Trek II is a rare breed in modern moviemaking—a summer blockbuster that simultaneously thrills, enlightens, and touches its audience. Clothing his actors in thick Napoleonic uniforms and bathing the sets in red mood lighting, Meyer created a tense action picture anchored by its two charismatic stars: Shatner, whose middle age imbues his swaggering hero with surprising depth and vulnerability, and Montalban, whose magnetic vigor makes Khan a worthy adversary. Adding piquancy to Shatner's performance is his superlative work in the final reel, in which he and Nimoy perform one of science-fiction cinema's most powerful goodbyes. **MM**

► **Captain Spock (Nimoy) gives Dr. McCoy (Kelley) a Vulcan inspection.**

BLADE RUNNER 1982 (U.S. • SINGAPORE)

Director Ridley Scott **Producer** Michael Deeley **Screenplay** Hampton Fancher, David Webb Peoples (based on *Do Androids Dream of Electric Sheep?* by Philip K. Dick) **Cinematography** Jordan Cronenweth **Music** Vangelis **Cast** Harrison Ford, Rutger Hauer, Sean Young, Edward James Olmos, M. Emmet Walsh, Daryl Hannah

The big theme of confronting the facts of life is presented with more than adequate ambition and grandeur in Ridley Scott's superior adaptation of Philip K. Dick's potent but awkward novel *Do Androids Dream of Electric Sheep?* The potential of science fiction to bypass realistic concerns and go beyond minutiae of everyday life to the essence beyond is magnificently realized in this masterpiece of the genre. Its pulp origins are present—but only in a transmuted, transcendent manner, as in the fiction of Raymond Chandler and William S. Burroughs (who coined the term "Blade Runner").

Trench-coated detective Rick Deckard (Ford) is hired to "retire" a group of renegade replicants (androids with limited life spans). He has qualms about his job, but the encounter with the replicants' leader will make him question his own identity and humanity. Roy Batty (Hauer, in his most iconic performance) is the group's mastermind, bent on meeting his maker and asking for an upgrade. Future-noir is present in terms of iconography (the gloomy, rain-swept streets of the 2019 Los Angeles metropolis), but also in the mood of noirish fatalism; the replicants are, basically, DOA.

◄

Despite its stunning set designs and visual effects, *Blade Runner*'s Oscar nominations for Best Art Decoration–Set Decoration and Best Effects, Visual Effects remained mere nominations—it was, after all, the year of *E.T.* as well.

Haunted by "accelerated decrepitude" their mission is futile from the very start. Still, Batty wants to find out if the maker can repair what he makes. "All he'd wanted were the same answers the rest of us want," muses Deckard. "Where did I come from? Where am I going? How long have I got?"

Like a Byronic rebel, Batty is a Lucifer figure who destroys his maker in a poignant scene whose tragic overtones are

"I STILL THINK IT'S ONE OF THE BEST FILMS I EVER MADE."

RIDLEY SCOTT

peerless not only in the sci-fi genre, but cinema in general. In a strangely poetic ending, Lucifer evolves into a Christ figure, saving the life of his would-be killer. Technically a machine, he poignantly strives for a soul: "I've seen things you people wouldn't believe. Attack ships on fire off the shoulder of Orion. I watched C-beams glitter in the dark near the Tannhauser Gate. All those moments will be lost in time, like tears in rain. Time to die."

The stunning art direction by David Snyder, production design by Lawrence G. Paull, and state-of-the-art visual effects result in one of the most unforgettable settings of any film, ever. The atmosphere is enhanced by the superb soundscape by Vangelis and Jordan Cronenweth's moody lensing, and the performances are excellent throughout, including Sean Young's memorable turn as a replicant femme fatale. **DO**

▶
Harrison Ford gives a vulnerably cool performance as Deckard against David Snyder's gothic-to-goth art direction.

THE THING 1982 (U.S.)

Director John Carpenter **Producers** Stuart Cohen, David Foster, Larry J. Franco, Wilbur Stark, Lawrence Turman **Screenplay** Bill Lancaster (based on the story by John W. Campbell Jr.) **Cinematography** Dean Cundey **Music** Ennio Morricone **Cast** Kurt Russell, Keith David, Wilford Brimley, T. K. Carter, David Clennon, Joel Polis

The Thing is a generic hybrid and, much like Ridley Scott's *Alien* (1979), arguments have long raged as to whether or not it is a science-fiction or a horror film. But whatever it is, one thing is for sure: This *Thing* is going to make you afraid…very afraid. Defying the maxim that remakes are always inferior copies of the original, John Carpenter's *The Thing* takes Howard Hawks's *The Thing from Another World* (1951) to a chillingly new level in the horror stakes. An American Antarctic research station is infiltrated by an alien creature with the ability to perfectly imitate any life-form that it comes into contact with. Paranoia takes over and, one by one, the crew are either taken over by the creature or murdered, until the station's pilot, R. J. MacReady (Russell), takes matters into his own hands, leading a virtual witch hunt in order to discern who is human and who is from another world.

Partly an out-and-out experiment in fear, partly a meditation on American cultural isolationism, there are strong echoes of McCarthyism in MacReady's single-minded pursuit of rooting out the aliens within the group. As the crew begin to realize the terror that is befalling them, they are forced to destroy the

◄

John Carpenter and Kurt Russell have both admitted that after all of these years they still do not know, at the end of the movie, who has been replaced by the creature and when.

station in order to kill the creature and prevent it from taking over the world, even though it will likely as not signal their own demise. By the end of the film there are only two survivors, neither of whom can be sure the other is still human.

The sense of isolation, of being "outside nature" is reinforced by the all-male cast (there is not a single female character present) and by Dean Cundey's washed-out blue and faded

"WHY DON'T WE JUST WAIT HERE FOR A LITTLE WHILE . . . SEE WHAT HAPPENS?" R. J. MACREADY

white visuals, which lend the film a feeling of impenetrable bleak desolation. *The Thing* was the fourth pairing of Carpenter and Cundey, who previously worked together on *Halloween* (1978), *The Fog* (1980), and *Escape from New York* (1981, which also starred Kurt Russell), but it was the director's collaboration with special-effects guru Rob Bottin that transformed this picture from thriller to high-class chiller.

In the days before CGI-ubiquity, *The Thing*'s special effects are a real tour de force, showing a technician at the top of his craft and marking a real "landmark in gore." Gruesome, bloody, and frighteningly real, they lent the film an edgily visceral quality. Indeed, such was Bottin's dedication, working seven days a week for an entire year, that he was admitted to a hospital by the director for exhaustion when shooting the movie finally wrapped. **RH**

► Special effects pioneer Rob Bottin was only 22 when he started work on *The Thing*.

A world inside
the computer
where man
has never been.

Never before now.

Enter its world this summer.

TRON   A LISBERGER-KUSHNER PRODUCTION
Starring JEFF BRIDGES BRUCE BOXLEITNER DAVID WARNER CINDY MORGAN and BARNARD HUGHES
Executive producer RON MILLER Music by WENDY CARLOS Story by STEVEN LISBERGER and BONNIE MACBIRD
Screenplay by STEVEN LISBERGER Produced by DONALD KUSHNER Directed by STEVEN LISBERGER
Songs by JOURNEY from WALT DISNEY PRODUCTIONS

TRON 1982 (U.S. • TAIWAN)

Director Steven Lisberger **Producer** Donald Kushner **Screenplay** Steven
Lisberger, Bonnie MacBird **Cinematography** Bruce Logan **Music** Wendy Carlos
Cast Jeff Bridges, Bruce Boxleitner, David Warner, Cindy Morgan, Barnard Hughes,
Dan Shor, Peter Jurasik, Tony Stephano, Craig Chudy, Vince Deadrick, Sam Schatz

In spite of its groundbreaking use of computer-generated
effects, this costly, somewhat embarrassing box-office failure
soon developed a growing fan base of nostalgically minded
computer "geeks" who ended up bestowing a reputation upon
it that it barely deserves. Already a quaint, outdated narrative
at the time of its release, the fairly tacky costume design—
bringing to mind nothing more futuristic than the sci-fi serials
of the 1930s—and the minimal amount of detail in the synthetic
computer-animated elements, kept it from making its mark on
the pop culture of the time the way *Star Wars* (1977) had done
so effortlessly before. Nor did the movie end up doing very
much for computer animation either, as it was perceived by
most to be too expensive and unappealing.

Indeed, the extent to which computer animation was even
employed in *TRON* is drastically lower than the film's promotional
campaign or popular image would have us believe. Instead of
costly CGI, traditional cell-drawn animation and old-fashioned
compositing were the techniques used for most special-effects
sequences in the film. Several Disney animators actually refused
to work on the film out of fear that they might lose their jobs

◄
Rumor has it that
the Motion Picture
Academy refused
to nominate
TRON for a Best
Special Effects
Oscar because
they felt the use
of computer-
generated graphics
was a cheat.

to computers. This "mini-strike" ultimately turned out to be eerily prescient, as two decades later, Disney closed down its traditional animation division in favor of computer work.

What the film did give us, however, was the first major feature that visualizes formerly abstract terms like *cyberspace* at a time when the home computer market was still in its infancy. Its depiction of a computer's insides as a neon-on-black

"ON THE OTHER SIDE OF THE SCREEN, IT ALL LOOKS SO EASY."

KEVIN FLYNN

realm remains a dominant paradigm: a three-dimensional landscape inhabited by anthropomorphized avatars engaged in gladiatorial gaming rituals. The way it brought to life this exciting new frontier, even if it did so in strangely childlike dimensions, was of great delight to many young males for whom computer science formed a then unusual hobby.

TRON may actually be a more interesting film today than it was 25 years ago, at least from a design perspective. Its curiously over-the-top costume design gives it a camp value that has made it popular among aficionados of 1980s nostalgia, and the film's narrative content and pioneering technology have endeared it to computer programmers everywhere. But in the end, *TRON*'s most enduring legacy may be its popular, addictive, and financially more successful spin-off arcade game. **DH**

► After being filmed in black-and-white, all the live action that took place within the computer was subsequently colorized using photographic and rotoscopic techniques.

First it controls your mind
Then it destroys your body

A VISION OF ENORMOUS PHYSICAL IMPACT !

FROM DAVID CRONENBERG

VIDEODROME
A TERRIFYING NEW WEAPON

starring

JAMES WOODS · DEBORAH HARRY

Released by **filmways**

VIDEODROME 1983 (CANADA)

Director David Cronenberg **Producer** Claude Héroux **Screenplay** David Cronenberg **Cinematography** Mark Irwin **Music** Howard Shore **Cast** James Woods, Sonja Smits, Deborah Harry, Peter Dvorsky, Leslie Carlson, Jack Creley, Lynne Gorman, Julie Khaner, Reiner Schwartz, David Bolt, Lally Cadeau, Henry Gomez

Videodrome is a prophetic film, a unique look into a future that has since become reality. The reason lies with its subject, the media: the fastest-developing branch of technology in the last few decades. We still largely fly the same planes and drive the same cars, but our relation to media technology has changed dramatically.

The basis of the story can almost be seen as a blueprint for contemporary fears over the effects of media violence. Small television station owner Max Renn (Woods) is in search of tough material for his niche broadcasts. He stumbles upon the illegal torture show *Videodrome*, which is so powerful it sends him into hallucination. Soon, he believes he is part of an ultra-paranoid plot, pushed around by shady figures and media prophets competing for control over the viewer's mind. Max becomes violent, and eventually his body mutates (a slit in his stomach appears, for video cassette insertion; and a gun grinds itself into his arm). He assassinates several people, retreats into isolation, and commits suicide.

Videodrome is a messy film. As the plot becomes gradually more muddled, and Max gets more messed up, more

◄

Videodrome **predicted many media intrusions, including virtual reality, first-person shooter games, 24-hour surveillance, media piracy, and pay-per-view porn.**

clutter appears. In this rubble lies the film's true meaning: *Videodrome*'s network media do not so much send a directive to their viewers as they bury them under mindless garbage. It is not the violence in the media that makes Max mad, but the fact that he cannot tear himself away from *any* broadcast. It becomes his drug. It doesn't help either that the basis of *Videodrome* is Pittsburgh, the hometown of zombie director

"VIDEODROME *IS THE* CLOCKWORK ORANGE *OF THE 1980S.*"

ANDY WARHOL

George Romero and pop icon Andy Warhol (who foresaw that everyone would have their "fifteen minutes of fame"). There is only one location that is "clean" (though not spotlessly shiny), and that is the renaissance room of Videodrome's main opponents the O'Blivions, a sanctuary from a media-infested real world where they defiantly try to preserve art treasures from contamination.

Videodrome had an unfortunate initial reception; not even the presence of rock idol Debbie Harry in a kinky role could save it at the box office. In the long run, however, it became so accurate in its predictions of how the media would creep up on our daily lives—first-person shooter games and pay-per-view porn, for instance—that it is uncanny. Most films with which reality has caught up look the worse for it, but in the case of *Videodrome* it was a vindication of its quality.   **EM**

► The character of Brian O'Blivion (Creley) is based on Marshall McLuhan. Cronenberg was a college student of McLuhan's.

PRIX SPECIAL DU JURY AVORIAZ 83

PRIX DE LA CRITIQUE AVORIAZ 83

LE DERNIER COMBAT

un film de **LUC BESSON**

PIERRE JOLIVET

JEAN BOUISE

FRITZ WEPPER

JEAN RENO

CINÉMASCOPE

DOLBY STEREO

Directeur de la photographie CARLO VARINI   Montage SOPHIE SCHMIT   Musique ERIC SERRA   Scénario LUC BESSON et PIERRE JOLIVET

THE FINAL COMBAT 1983 (FRANCE)

Director Luc Besson **Producers** Luc Besson, Pierre Jolivet **Screenplay** Luc Besson, Pierre Jolivet **Cinematography** Carlo Varini **Music** Eric Serra **Cast** Pierre Jolivet, Jean Bouise, Jean Reno, Fritz Wepper, Christiane Krüger, Maurice Lamy, Pierre Carrive, Jean-Michel Castanié, Michel Doset, Bernard Havet, Marcel Berthomier, Petra Müller

Post-apocalyptic films were still big in 1983 when Luc Besson made his feature debut, based on his 1981 short *L'Avant Derniere*. But *Mad Max* (1979) and its sequel *Road Warrior* (1981)—not to mention a number of their cheap imitations—are of minor relevance for understanding Besson's film. *The Final Combat* (a.k.a. *Le Dernier Combat*) is a completely different beast from the typical post-apocalyptic movie. It has more in common with John Boorman's underrated *Zardoz* (1974), or even Chris Marker's short *La Jetée* (1962).

The first and most obvious curiosity is actually more than that and becomes an important plot point—the absence of any dialogue during the film, barring the two whispered words that come on one important occasion. The "explanation" for this lack of speech is that the atmosphere has become so polluted that speaking is no longer possible. Without communication there is also no need for names. Each nameless character is described in one or few words, as simply The Man, or The Brute, The Doctor, The Captain, and so on. The wasted landscape is gorgeously shot in black–and-white, and the resounding silence is counterbalanced by Eric Serra's atmospheric score.

◄

The Final Combat's post-apocalyptic vision asks what you should do with your remaining time when you're not even sure how you should be feeling.

In the beginning of the film, The Man (Jolivet) is building an aircraft and just wants to escape. Then he finds some unexpected company in a desolate city and everything changes. Besson's world is a wasteland haunted by memories of past times, but his bleak depiction of the future doesn't automatically invoke the sense of nihilism already familiar from George Miller's post-apocalyptic films. On the contrary,

"ONE OF THE MOST UNUSUAL 'ENTRY INTO MANHOOD' MOVIES OF RECENT TIMES." *OVERLOOK FILM ENCYCLOPEDIA*

Besson is reaching toward an almost childlike innocence in the way his characters perceive their "brave new world." Even their conflicts are reminiscent of some sort of carefully choreographed game. At first they're just struggling to survive, but buried beneath their primal instincts are still some leftovers of distorted humanity that could be triggered with some simple, forgotten craft: like trying to read a book, to play Ping-Pong, even to speak. Those moments are both touching and funny . . . and sometimes downright weird. One of the most bizarre scenes is when it suddenly rains fish. In almost any other film, in a different context, that would surely seem pretty random—but here it comes naturally.

► **While *Le Dernier Combat* was begun in color, it is Besson's stunning use of black-and-white Cinemascope that lends the film its polished, big-budget look.**

If *Mad Max* is about physically surviving the apocalypse, *The Final Combat* asks, How are you supposed to feel and think and, basically, become a human being again? **MCv**

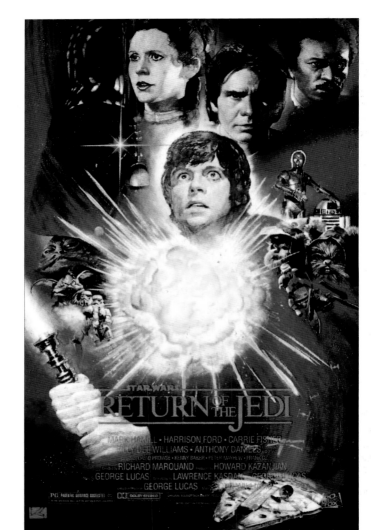

STAR WARS: EPISODE VI RETURN OF THE JEDI 1983 (U.S.)

Director Richard Marquand **Producer** Howard Kazanjian **Screenplay** George Lucas, Lawrence Kasdan **Cinematography** Alan Hume **Music** John Williams
Cast Mark Hamill, Harrison Ford, Carrie Fisher, Ian McDiarmid, Billy Dee Williams, David Prowse, Jeremy Bulloch, Anthony Daniels, Peter Mayhew, Sebastian Shaw

By the release of the third installment in the "original" *Star Wars* trilogy, the mythology was well established and the franchise hugely successful. In keeping with the notion of a serial, *Return of the Jedi* is itself formed of an episodic plot, with each segment escalating the action en route to a spectacular climax and a fairy tale happy ending.

So the story opens with a sequence depicting the release of Han Solo (Ford) from Carbonite, followed by the death of Boba Fett (Bulloch) and the triumphant escape from the Sarlaac Pit. This is then followed by sequences in which Luke Skywalker (Hamill) returns to Dagobah to complete his training, Han and Princess Leia (Fisher) destroy the shield generator that is protecting the incomplete replacement Death Star, Luke resists The Emperor's (McDiarmid) attempt to turn him to the Dark Side, and Darth Vader (Prowse) gains redemption, before Lando Calrissian (Williams) destroys the second Death Star.

This works well as a thoroughly enjoyable, fun-packed romp, although it does have an uneven feel (particularly when

◄

At the time, the climactic battle in outer space featured more optical effects in one scene than had ever been previously committed to film.

it comes to the cavorting Ewoks). *Return of the Jedi* certainly lacks the gravitas and the darker edge of *The Empire Strikes Back* (1980). It is a more emotionally manipulative film than its predecessor, but even though it can lapse into the cute at times, it is still charged with tension during key sequences, resolves the family drama, and sees Luke reach the end of his rite of passage. The dénouement between Luke and The

"IT'S NOT ABOUT THE WORDS ON THE PAGE, IT'S ABOUT YOUR EMOTIONAL IMPRESSION OF BEING THERE." *GEORGE LUCAS*

Emperor with Vader torn between his master and his son is still powerful, and Anakin Skywalker's death moving (despite the lack of quite such a gruesome visage under Vader's mask than was suggested in *Empire*). It must be kept in mind that this is primarily a children's movie, so credit must go to a production that can still hold such deep and enduring meaning for adults.

Return of the Jedi remains visually stunning and the cultural legacy of the trilogy is also indisputable. The merchandising is massive and has kept on growing, but more significant are the cultural references, including most famously the discussion in Kevin Smith's *Clerks* (1994) about the fate of the Death Star workers. And of course, *Jedi* finally portrays the fall of a dictatorship, providing the movie with lasting impact. As the initial Star Wars trilogy must be seen as a whole, so *Jedi* leaves the fan sad that it is all over yet still desperate for more. **BC**

▶
Jabba the Hutt's death was partly inspired by a scene in *The Godfather* (1972), in which Luca Brasi (Lenny Montana) is choked to death with a garrote.

REPO MAN 1984 (U.S.)

Director Alex Cox **Producers** Peter McCarthy, Michael Nesmith, Gerald Olson, Jonathan Wacks **Screenplay** Alex Cox **Cinematography** Robby Müller **Music** Steven Hufsteter, Humberto Larriva **Cast** Emilio Estevez, Harry Dean Stanton, Tracey Walter, Olivia Barash, Sy Richardson, Susan Barnes, Fox Harris, Tom Finnegan

Alex Cox's *Repo Man* was produced entirely outside of Hollywood—when the independents were still independent—and then ultimately bought by Universal for worldwide distribution. Exactly the same thing happened 15 years earlier to Dennis Hopper's *Easy Rider* (1969), which was ultimately snapped up by Columbia. From New Hollywood to post-classical Hollywood, from modernism to post-modernism: from *Easy Rider* to *Repo Man*. Two road movies. Two utterly different films.

There is nothing left of Dennis Hopper's great pathos in Alex Cox. All the hippies are dead. Gone for good. And the world has become a play. The staging of a quote of a quote of a quote. To live a life is no longer a question of politics but a question of aesthetics. Caustic irony and a camp sensibility dominate *Repo Man*, a picture that mocks every genre in sight: the youth movie, the thriller, the science-fiction film—hardly shying away from even the foolish and fatuous.

Not a sci-fi movie but a film about sci-fi movies. A cinematic discourse. A motion of running to and fro, of comings and goings, of steps and complexities. Everything is put into

◀
Sci-fi meets punk, ranking number seven in *Entertainment Weekly*'s "Top 50 Cult Films of All-Time."

quotation marks by Cox. It's as if *Repo Man* is about an insane nuclear physicist. It's as if *Repo Man* is about a secret agent conspiracy. It's as if *Repo Man* is about a weird alien landing. It's as if *Repo Man* tells a story. It's as if *Repo Man* is a movie.

They own the night. They go to bed at 3:00 P.M. They get up again at 4:00 P.M. They are professionals: professional thieves. They are repossessors: repo men. Cox weaves a loose network of

"GODDAMN-DIPS**T-RODRIGUEZ-GYPSY-DILDO-PUNKS. I'LL GET YOUR ASS." BUD

stories around these car snatchers, assembling a kaleidoscope of a Los Angeles far away from neon glamor. A world where logic is nothing and speed is everything. Where nothing is lasting and everything is intense.

Few if any films come as close to capturing the feeling of early 1980s punk culture as vividly as *Repo Man*. Composed of fluid camera work by Robby Müller and featuring an epochal sound track by Iggy Pop and the Circle Jerks, Fear, and the Juicy Bananas, the movie gives us not only images of the time, but a time-image: the direct presentation of time, the very passion of thought. A space opens up between the images, appealing to our body and mind simultaneously, setting free sentiment(s). That is the point where *Repo Man* becomes an authentic work of art again: in its desire to go for anything *but* authenticity. **IR**

► **Except for white punk Otto Maddox (Estevez), all the repo men in the movie are named after beers.**

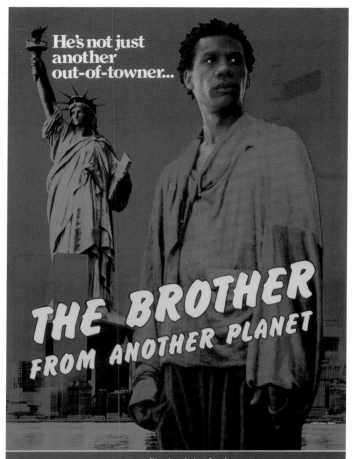

He's not just
another
out-of-towner...

THE BROTHER
FROM ANOTHER PLANET

a new film by John Sayles

Written, Directed and Edited by JOHN SAYLES
Produced by PEGGY RAJSKI and MAGGIE RENZI
Starring JOE MORTON Director of Photography ERNEST R. DICKERSON
Production Designer NORA CHAVOOSHIAN Music MASON DARING
Original Soundtrack Album Available on Daring/Rounder Records Cinecom
INTERNATIONAL FILMS

THE BROTHER FROM ANOTHER PLANET 1984 (U.S.)

Director John Sayles **Producers** Peggy Rajski, Maggie Renzi **Screenplay** John Sayles **Cinematography** Ernest Dickerson **Music** Martin Brody, Mason Daring **Cast** Joe Morton, Daryl Edwards, Steve James, Leonard Jackson, Bill Cobbs, Maggie Renzi, Olga Merediz, Tom Wright, Minnie Gentry, Ren Woods, Peter Richardson

Shakespearean actor and Tony Award nominee Joe Morton plays the nameless character of Brother in John Sayles's *The Brother From Another Planet*, and has the power to heal and fix things, as well as the power to perceive present thoughts and voices of the dead.

After his spaceship crashes just off of Ellis Island in New York City, Brother seeks refuge inside a small neighborhood bar in Harlem. Brother is an alien whose demeanor as a mute, dark-skinned deadpan makes him confusing to others, but they still take pity on him. As Brother experiences life in Harlem, he is particularly puzzled by the interaction between blacks and whites. He also sees the effects of drug addiction on its inhabitants, and a subplot deals with his own encounter with heroin. The film follows Brother as he tries to run from two extraterrestrial bounty hunters who are trying to recapture him and bring him back to his home planet.

It is safe to say that writer-director John Sayles has mastered the art of the American independent film. He shot *The Brother*

◄

Although they are not named in the film or end credits, the "Men In Black" are named Uno (John Sayles) and Dos (David Strathairn), according to subsequent interviews with Sayles.

From Another Planet on a budget of $400,000 total, using a star-filled sky that was made with construction paper and a pin; and Brother's glowing, healing hand was effected with a concealed lightbulb. Stylistic and technical innovations also came into play: The entrance and exit scenes of the bounty hunters' first appearance in a bar, for example, were filmed entirely in reverse with the camera upsidedown.

"FUNNY-LOOKIN' MOTHERF***ER, BUT HE CAN SHOOT, CAN'T HE?"

BASKETBALL PLAYER

Because Brother is mute and has literally dropped out of the sky, he lacks an opinion about anything, which enables Sayles to subtly incorporate a degree of satire and social commentary into the story. There is no hint of stereotyping as Brother mixes with the bros and barflies. When Brother first walks the streets, he sees a crucifix in a store window and, across the street, a similar spread-'em pose of another brother who is being rousted by the police. He can't seem to understand why people would go out of their way to be cruel to one another. His surprise comes off as sweet and uncomplicated rather than ignorant and thus stands as one of the most effective elements of the whole movie.

The movie remains a weird mix of science fiction, amusing farce, and some biting satire that is hard to pigeonhole and stands out as an auteur's work. **CK**

► **Joe Morton gives a deft and expressively understated performance as an alien in Harlem.**

GEORGE ORWELL'S TERRIFYING VISION COMES TO THE SCREEN.

JOHN HURT RICHARD BURTON
in Michael Radford's film of George Orwell's "NINETEEN EIGHTY-FOUR"
with SUZANNA HAMILTON   CYRIL CUSACK
A Virgin Films/Umbrella-Rosenblum Films Production   Director of Photography ROGER DEAKINS
Editor TOM PRIESTLEY   Production Designer ALLAN CAMERON   Music by EURYTHMICS & DOMINIC MULDOWNEY
Executive Producer MARVIN J. ROSENBLUM   Co-Producers AL CLARK & ROBERT DEVEREUX   Produced by SIMON PERRY
Written and Directed by MICHAEL RADFORD   FROM ᴀᴙ ATLANTIC RELEASING CORP ©1984

Title Theme "Sexcrime — 1984" performed by Eurythmics | Original Soundtrack on RCA Records and Cassettes

NINETEEN EIGHTY-FOUR 1984 (U.K.)

Director Michael Radford **Producer** Simon Perry **Screenplay** Michael Radford (from the novel by George Orwell) **Cinematography** Roger Deakins **Music** Dominic Muldowney **Cast** John Hurt, Suzanna Hamilton, Richard Burton, Cyril Cusack, Gregor Fisher, James Walker, Andrew Wilde, David Trevena, David Cann

Few novels written in the 20th century have proved as influential as Orwell's dystopian masterpiece *1984*. Far from losing relevance as time passes, Orwell's vision of a totalitarian society seems to become more ubiquitous with each passing year. Its influence has been strongest in the sci-fi genre, where Orwell's work has been cited as the main source of inspiration for all kinds of works, ranging from *Logan's Run* (1976) to *The Matrix* (1999). It wasn't intended to be a description of a remote and distant future, however. Orwell's tale was originally titled *1948* after the year in which it was written: It was meant to depict an allegorical exaggeration of Britain post 1939–45, combined with cautionary elements drawn from the Soviet Union's Stalinist era.

　1984 saw its first film adaptation in 1956, with a strong emphasis on the futuristic trappings that so aggravated the book's author, and a watered-down version of the novel's political message. After that, filmmakers were unsuccessful in securing the rights to the book from Orwell's widow, who remained reluctant to see another Hollywood version of the novel reach cinema screens.

◄
John Hurt later appeared in James McTeigue's 2006 film *V for Vendetta*, playing the High Chancellor Adam Sutler, who appears Big-Brother-like on a massive television screen in several scenes.

It was on the condition that his production contain no science-fiction trappings that British director Michael Radford finally succeeded in obtaining those film rights. His pitch was to do a completely faithful adaptation that would be released in the actual year 1984, with several scenes to be shot on the exact dates on which they were originally set in the novel. As laudable as this over-determined fidelity seems, it is a ploy

"IF YOU WANT A VISION OF THE FUTURE . . . IMAGINE A BOOT STAMPING ON A HUMAN FACE FOREVER." O'BRIEN

that ultimately seems to have more value as a promotional tool than anything else, for protagonist Winston Smith (Hurt) soon comes to the realization that he has no way of knowing what day or even what year it is; the government has such complete control over every aspect of everyone's life that all dates have become unreliable, even irrelevant, as history is continuously rewritten.

But even though its setting in the year 1984 is ultimately not the point, Radford's adaptation is in all other aspects not only a faithful version of Orwell's book, but also an excellent film in its own right. Visually, it seems more like a period picture than a science-fiction piece; rather than a depiction of a future society, Radford therefore succeeded in reversing the digits once more by creating a frighteningly believable world that seems like an alternate version of 1948. **DH**

►
Richard Burton and John Hurt, engaged in playful dentistry.

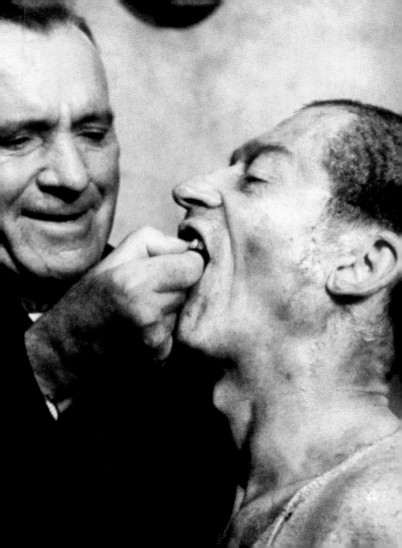

THE TERMINATOR 1984 (U.K. • U.S.)

Director James Cameron **Producer** Gale Anne Hurd **Screenplay** James Cameron, Gale Anne Hurd **Cinematography** Adam Greenberg **Music** Brad Fiedel **Cast** Arnold Schwarzenegger, Michael Biehn, Linda Hamilton, Paul Winfield, Lance Henriksen, Bess Motta, Earl Boen, Rick Rossovich, Dick Miller, Shawn Schepps

When a man claims that he's traveled across time to protect you and your unborn son who will become a future leader of human resistance against the "machines," you may find his story a bit hard to swallow. But when the television reports that several women bearing the same name as you have already been "terminated" in L.A., execution-style, you may begin to wonder. And then, when you're confronted with a humanoid, bulletproof hulk bent on killing you for no apparent reason, you may finally start believing.

"That terminator is out there," says Kyle Reese (Biehn), the man from the future. "It can't be bargained with. It can't be reasoned with. It doesn't feel pity, or remorse, or fear. And it absolutely will not stop, ever, until you are dead." And it's as simple as that.

The terminator is a cyborg from the year 2029 A.D., when computers and robots have caused a nuclear war in order to exterminate the redundant human race. The metal shall inherit the devastated earth. The sole obstacle: human freedom fighters, whose leader can be eradicated only by killing his mother 45 years in the past.

◄

The blockbuster announced in no uncertain terms the arrival of James Cameron and his revolutionary amalgam of action and sci-fi—to be further explored and enriched in *Aliens* (1986), *The Abyss* (1989), *Terminator 2* (1991), and *Avatar* (2009).

As played by Arnold Schwarzenegger in a career-defining performance, the terminator is an unstoppable, merciless killing machine, a Jason Vorhees with large-caliber firearms. Like an angel of death, he kills everyone in his path, and his relentless dedication to the mission makes him a terrifying figure. This brings *The Terminator* very close to a horror movie, especially in its prolonged slasherlike culmination in which, even when

"A BLAZING, CINEMATIC COMIC BOOK . . . VIRTUOSO MOVIEMAKING, TERRIFIC MOMENTUM . . . COMPELLING." *VARIETY*

reduced to a bare metallic endoskeleton, the damned thing keeps coming back, running and crawling after Sarah Connor (Hamilton: an excellent blend of frailty and perseverance).

The script (inspired by Harlan Ellison's *Outer Limits* teleplay) is witty, full of memorable catchphrases and action set pieces. Cameron's direction is bursting with energy and innovation (fighting against the low-budget and less-than-stellar special effects), driven with a manic, almost terminatorlike devotion that would become his trademark. After his inauspicious gun-for-hire debut, *Piranha II* (1981), *The Terminator* is the first real Cameron movie, a blast of action, horror, and science fiction that will mark all of his best films. Although essentially humanistic and warm, it also remains his bleakest film to date. It ends with the words: "There's a storm coming in." This refers to the storm of impending apocalypse. **DO**

▶
The Terminator (Schwarzenegger) undertakes some messy self-repairs.

A WORLD BEYOND YOUR EXPERIENCE,
BEYOND YOUR IMAGINATION.

DUNE

DINO DE LAURENTIIS PRESENTS
A DAVID LYNCH FILM "DUNE"
SCREENPLAY BY DAVID LYNCH BASED ON THE NOVEL BY FRANK HERBERT EDITED BY ANTHONY GIBBS MECHANICAL SPECIAL EFFECTS BY KIT WEST
SPECIAL PHOTOGRAPHIC EFFECTS BY BARRY NOLAN ADDITIONAL VISUAL SPECIAL EFFECTS BY ALBERT WHITLOCK CREATURES CREATED BY CARLO RAMBALDI MUSIC BY TOTO
PROPHECY THEME BY BRIAN ENO COSTUME DESIGN BY BOB RINGWOOD PRODUCTION DESIGNED BY ANTHONY MASTERS DIRECTOR OF PHOTOGRAPHY FREDDIE FRANCIS
ASSOCIATE PRODUCER JOSE LOPEZ RODERO PRODUCED BY RAFFAELLA DE LAURENTIIS DIRECTED BY DAVID LYNCH DOLBY STEREO READ THE BOOK
SOUNDTRACK AVAILABLE ON RECORDS AND TAPES A UNIVERSAL RELEASE

DUNE 1984 (U.S.)

Director David Lynch **Producer** Raffaella de Laurentiis **Screenplay** David Lynch (from the novel by Frank Herbert) **Cinematography** Freddy Francis **Music** Toto **Cast** Kyle MacLachlan, Francesca Annis, Brad Dourif, Siân Phillips, José Ferrer, Jurgan Prochnow, Sean Young, Max von Sydow, Leonardo Cimino, Linda Hunt, Freddie Jones

Dune is an epic, telling a complex and still very relevant story about warring factions thousands of years in the future when humanity has spread throughout the galaxy. It is also a deeply intimate story concerning the coming of age and rise to power of Paul Atreides (MacLachlan) as he takes on his predestined messianic role as the Kwisatz Haderach. And above all else, *Dune* tells the story of a planet. Arrakis is a desert world populated by the Sufi-like Freman (who fight against the outsiders who exploit their world) and giant all-devouring worms that are the only source of "spice"—a drug that is for all intents and purposes what drives the transportation system, and thus the economy, on a galactic scale. In other words, it is the equivalent of our oil, found in the deserts of the Middle East. As all this suggests, in its themes, in its scope, and in its cast of characters, the "world" of *Dune* seems always about to overwhelm the story.

And if any film project could be predicted to fail, it was *Dune*. A tortuous ten-year period in development hell, passing through the hands of David Lean, Alejandro Jodorowsky, and Ridley Scott before David Lynch took the helm, merely

◄
During the film's original release, "cheat-sheets" explaining much of the story's setting and its more obscure vocabulary were handed out to moviegoers at some theaters.

hinted at the potential difficulties of such a project. Herbert's immensely popular novel depicts complex groupings; Mentats, Bene Gesserit, Spacing Guild, the Landsraad, and the Sardaukar, together with the fiefdoms of Corrino, Atreides, and Harkonnen. Moreover, Herbert's prose looks forward and back at the same time as it relates events in the present. It is to Lynch's great credit that he manages to retain a flavor of all

"I PROBABLY SHOULDN'T HAVE DONE THAT PICTURE, BUT I SAW TONS OF POSSIBILITIES FOR THINGS I LOVED." LYNCH

this in full. But in doing so, he has to encapsulate the written memoirs of Princess Irulan (a character who takes no part of the action), the inner thoughts of the major characters (particularly Atreides), and a range of dreams and visions. Lynch's recreation of these narrative devices and internal monologues does not entirely work in that they can seem awkward or distracting. In addition, the sometimes impenetrable dialogue renders the fullness of the film inaccessible to all except those with an intimate knowledge of the source novel. Nevertheless, the film is visually impressive, with large-scale operatic sequences that require only music and image.

The movie was poorly received by all but a few critics on first release and failed at the box office, but in the way of many, another flawed masterpiece is now a beloved cult film with its own "lost" versions. **BC**

► **Paul Atreides (MacLachlan, right),** *Dune*'s **visionary Messiah-to-be.**

STARMAN 1984 (U.S.)

Director John Carpenter **Producers** Larry J. Franco, Michael Douglas
Screenplay Bruce A. Evans, Raynold Gideon **Cinematography** Donald M. Morgan
Music Jack Nitzsche **Cast** Jeff Bridges, Karen Allen, Charles Martin Smith, Richard
Jaeckel, Robert Phalen, Tony Edwards, John Walter Davis, Ted White, Dirk Blocker

Following horror and sci-fi scare flicks like *Halloween* (1978) and *The Thing* (1982), director John Carpenter switched thematic gears with *Starman*, an examination of the human condition that was both other-worldly and emotional.

It's 1977 and NASA launches the Voyager 2 probe containing a "Greetings from Planet Earth." Journeying through outer space, the probe enters an unknown planet where the inhabitants discover the message and take up the invitation. A reconnaissance ship dispatches to Earth, but is shot down by the U.S. military, crashing in upper Wisconsin. A ghostly orb exits the scene of the crash and enters the home of recently widowed Jenny Hayden (Allen). Using DNA from hair found in a scrapbook, the alien entity takes the form of Hayden's deceased husband, Scott (Bridges). Kidnapped at gunpoint, Jenny is forced by this simulacrum of her husband to drive him to his preordained destination in Arizona. Hot on this ultimate illegal alien's trail are merciless military man George Fox (Jaeckel) and empathetic S.E.T.I. (Search for Extraterrestrial Intelligence) researcher Mark Shermin (Smith). Much like Steven Spielberg's *Close Encounters of the Third Kind* (1977) and

◄
The film inspired a short-lived TV series of the same name in 1986, starring Robert Hays and Christopher Daniel Barnes.

E.T. : The Extra-Terrestrial (1982), *Starman* presents a scenario where the middle class of America is touched by a celestial being. Over the three-day journey, the alien visitor is privy to the American way of life through truck stops, gas stations, and motels where ordinary Americans are more than willing to lend a helping hand. Highlights include Starman learning local vernacular ("Take it easy" and "Up yours!") and how to

" . . . TELL THE PRESIDENT AN ALIEN HAS ASSUMED THE IDENTITY OF A DEAD HOUSEPAINTER?" GEORGE FOX

drive ("Red light, stop. Green light, go. Yellow light, go very, very fast."); studying how to kiss from a TV viewing of *From Here to Eternity* (1953); a run-in and subsequent brawl with a group of deer hunters after Starman resurrects their kill; and an accidental Las Vegas detour where he manipulates the slot machines to accommodate their penniless plight.

> It is the building relationship between Bridges and the equally strong Allen that ultimately carries the narrative, resulting in the most well rounded movie in Carpenter's filmography.

All of this Americana works thanks to the incredible performance of Jeff Bridges. Playing on a childlike innocence and inquisitiveness, Bridges allows audiences to experience his learning process over the course of the film. It is an entirely natural portrayal that asks the audience to trust the protagonist and grow alongside the personality, much like Karen Allen's character is forced to do. The performance earned Bridges an Academy Award nomination for Best Actor, a rarity for a science-fiction feature. **WW**

JONATHAN **PRYCE**   BOB **HOSKINS**   ROBERT **DE NIRO**

Brazil

A FILM BY TERRY GILLIAM

BRAZIL 1985 (U.K.)

Director Terry Gilliam **Producer** Arnon Milchan **Screenplay** Terry Gilliam, Tom Stoppard, Charles McKeown **Cinematography** Roger Pratt **Music** Michael Kamen **Cast** Jonathan Pryce, Robert De Niro, Katherine Helmond, Ian Holm, Michael Palin, Peter Vaughan, Kim Greist, Jim Broadbent, Ian Richardson, Charles McKeown

Terry Gilliam's fiercely imaginative and blackly comic adaptation of George Orwell's dystopia, alternatively titled *1984½*, converts the novel's chilling indictment of fascism and Stalinism into a satire on modern bureaucracy, consumerism, and the Thatcher-Regan era, making it the director's most outspokenly conceptual film. *Brazil* opens at "8:49…, somewhere in the [totalitarian] 20th century" when a (literal) bug in the system replaces the last name of a suspected terrorist (Tuttle) with that of an innocent shoe repairman (Buttle), who is interrogated and killed.

Meanwhile, minor functionary and latter-day Winston Smith Sam Lowry (Pryce) escapes in his dreams where, accompanied by the kitschy samba strains of *Aquarela do Brasil* (1939), he soars above the clouds, an Icarus-winged knight who rescues a gauze-shrouded blonde damsel (Greist). Promoted to the Ministry of Information, he tracks down the error and meets the Buttles' outraged neighbor and his "dream girl," who actually chain-smokes and drives a monster truck. Breaking protocol left and right and getting in far over his head, Sam is inevitably interrogated as a terrorist himself.

◀

Gilliam spent months in a battle to get the film distributed in America. He refused Universal's demands (20 minutes of cuts and an upbeat ending) and eventually a modified version was released as compromise. The Director's Cut is available on DVD.

Brazil is the darkest of Gilliam's trilogy (including *Time Bandits* [1981] and *The Adventures of Baron Munchausen* [1988] about the (supposedly) triumphant imagination. True, Sam's nightmares are often revelations—the cyclopean Samurai Warrior (composed out of microchips) whose face is revealed to be his own, or the dreams of flying broken by skyscrapers erupting out of the ground. But his daydreams are escapist and

"A TERRIFIC MOVIE HAS ESCAPED THE ASYLUM WITHOUT A LOBOTOMY."

RICHARD CORLISS

utterly conventional in a Walter Mittyish way, and the film's true revolutionary, Tuttle (De Niro), a guerilla heating-duct repairman who zooms down from the tops of skyscrapers to short-circuit Central Services, is literally smothered in swirling paper and vanishes, the last figment of Sam's extinguished mind.

Gilliam goes the Kafka rather than the Orwell route, conveying his ideas through art design, visual style, and a wildly comic sensibility. Swarming with sight gags and visual delights—a pastiche of Keatonesque balletic slapstick from *Metropolis* (1927), and monolithic *Blade Runner* (1982) architecture, among its resonances—the film obsessively repeats an "iron cage" motif of blocklike building units, cubicles, and boxes. A black comedy of brilliant excess about surveillance, terrorism, and office culture, *Brazil* remains topical, and is recognized as Gilliam's masterpiece and one of the most visionary films of the 1980s. **LB**

► Dr. Jaffe (Broadbent) shows Mrs. Lowry (Helmond) how much room there is for improvement in the tautness of her skin.

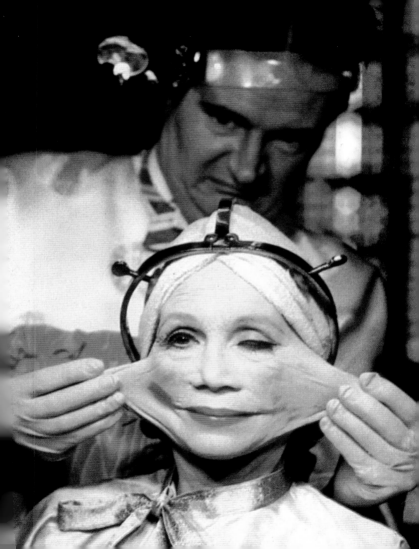

STEVEN SPIELBERG Presents

BACK TO THE FUTURE

A ROBERT ZEMECKIS Film

He was never in time
for his classes...

He wasn't in time
for his dinner...

Then one day...
he wasn't in his
time at all.

"BACK TO THE FUTURE"   MICHAEL J. FOX
CHRISTOPHER LLOYD · LEA THOMPSON · CRISPIN GLOVER
ROBERT ZEMECKIS & BOB GALE   ALAN SILVESTRI   BOB GALE   NEIL CANTON
STEVEN SPIELBERG KATHLEEN KENNEDY   FRANK MARSHALL
ROBERT ZEMECKIS   A UNIVERSAL Picture

BACK TO THE FUTURE 1985 (U.S.)

Director Robert Zemeckis **Producers** Neil Canton, Bob Gale **Screenplay** Robert Zemeckis, Bob Gale **Cinematography** Dean Cundey **Music** Alan Silvestri
Cast Michael J. Fox, Christopher Lloyd, Lea Thompson, Crispin Glover, Thomas F. Wilson, Claudia Wells, Marc McClure, Wendie Jo Sperber, James Tolkan, Billy Zane

No science-fiction film is more typical of the 1980s than *Back to the Future*, even though (and maybe because) it is partly set in the 1950s. After all, the 1980s were the first decade in which looking at the past became more sexy than imagining the future, especially after the election of Ronald Reagan, a movie star of past glory campaigning for a return to old values. Of the many time-travel movies that this sentiment spawned, *Back to the Future* is by far the most entertaining—a comedy with an optimistic, never-say-die spirit and the pace of a theme-park ride that stood in sharp contrast to the dystopian futures usually painted in contemporary sci fi.

The story is deviously simple. Marty McFly (Fox) ends up in 1955, where, with the help of loony professor Doc (Lloyd, in his best performance ever), he must ensure that his future father and his mother-to-be fall in love or else he will never be born. But that story is layered thickly with witty asides and topical overtones that make each scene burst with weighty themes (even the word *heavy* is singled out for a discussion); it's also laced with off-the-cuff anachronistic observations, and even silly product placement. In fact *Back to the Future* is so chockablock

◄

Back to the Future won an Oscar for Best Effects, and Sound Effects Editing. *The Power of Love* **by Huey Lewis and The News, that played over the movie's skateboard opening, was nominated for Best Original Song.**

with overt references to commercial and materialist culture, that the film stands as both an expression and a critique of 1980s consumer excesses. Marty introduces sneakers, rock 'n' roll attitude, and skateboards to the 1950s, and constantly sings the praise of prestigious automobiles (the titanium-coated DeLorean—a prime example of 1980s excess—key among them). On top of it all came marvelous production design and

"I GUESS YOU GUYS AREN'T READY FOR THAT YET. BUT YOUR KIDS ARE GONNA LOVE IT." *MARTY*

Oscar-winning special effects matching the expectations one would have for a collaboration of Robert Zemeckis (director) and Steven Spielberg (executive producer).

At the time of its release, *Back to the Future* was frequently compared to another time-travel movie instigated by nostalgia for the 1950s, Francis Ford Coppola's *Peggy Sue Got Married* (1986). The comparison often depicted *Back to the Future* as the more reactionary and materialistic of the two, with less interest in ideals than in fun and excess—cars in *Peggy Sue Got Married* are laughed away. The sustained box-office success of *Back to the Future* muted such critical denouncements, however, and ever since, the film has garnered a cult following for whom the expression "1.21 Gigawatts" is not just a reference to a physical requirement for time travel, but to a type of sparkling cinematic excitement of which the 1980s saw too little. **EM**

▶

John Lithgow and Jeff Goldblum were both considered for the role of Doc Brown before it went to Christopher Lloyd.

THE QUIET EARTH 1985 (NEW ZEALAND)

Director Geoff Murphy **Producers** Sam Pillsbury, Don Reynolds **Screenplay** Bill Baer, Bruno Lawrence, Sam Pillsbury (based on the novel written by Craig Harrison) **Cinematography** James Bartle **Music** John Charles **Cast** Bruno Lawrence, Alison Routledge, Pete Smith, Anzac Wallace, Norman Fletcher, Tom Hyde

Apocalyptic science fiction doesn't need the overblown hyperbole of an *Armageddon* (Michael Bay, 1997) or a *Deep Impact* (Mimi Leder, 1997). This New Zealand–made end-of-the-world thriller features very little big-budget sfx and no reliance at all on the now ubiquitous over-use of CGI to convey its sense of the end. Made for approximately $1,000,000 back in 1985, *The Quiet Earth* is a textbook example of how to make an effective science-fiction film without a Hollywood-sized budget.

It's 6:12 A.M., and Zac Hobson (Lawrence) awakes that morning to discover he is the last man on earth. Something has happened, referred to as "the effect"; everyone in Auckland appears to have vanished, leaving no trace of their departure —no bodies, no residue, nothing. Meals are left half eaten on tables, airplanes have fallen out of the sky, and kettles are boiling over. The phones still work, but there is no one around to answer them. Zac goes off to the laboratory, where he has been working on something called "Project Flashlight," which may be responsible for "the effect." (This international project is being led by the Americans to somehow create a defensive shield around the entire planet.) At first, Zac enjoys being the only

◀

The film won a huge number of New Zealand Film and TV Awards: Best Film, Best Director, Best Actor (Lawrence), Best Supporting Actor (Smith), Best Editing, Best Cinematography, Best Production Design, and Best Adapted Screenplay.

person on the planet—living it up with whatever he can find—but gradually that decadence and loneliness starts moving toward madness. Just in time comes Joanne (Routledge) and then Api (Smith), demonstrating that not everyone vanished in "the effect." The three also have something else in common—all three seem to have died at the moment of the cataclysm, and their deaths at that moment seem to have saved them: Zac

"THE MORAL [OF THE FILM IS]: 'DON'T F**K WITH THE INFINITE!'"

DEREK ADAMS

had just overdosed on sleeping pills because of the realization of what Project Flashlight entailed, Api was engaged in a fight with his former best friend over a woman, and so on. Gradually the three come across others who survived, but unlike themselves, could not cope with being on their own so have ended their new lives. Zac, as the film's central scientist, observes that another "effect" is imminent, and the three plot to try to stop it from happening, by blowing up one of Project Flashlight's grid relays. The second "effect" occurs at the moment Zac drives his dynamite-laden truck into the relay station, and our hero awakens on the shores of a distant planet in an ambiguous ending that echoes Kubrick's *2001*. Sadly, the more plot-oriented activities dominate the second half of the film (once Joanne and Api enter the scene), distracting from the film's overall power. **MK**

► The first half of the film is very chilling, as Zac (Lawrence) roams around the empty city, surrounded by the detritus left behind by the capitalist West.

ALIENS 1986 (U.K. • U.S.)

Director James Cameron **Producer** Gale Ann Hurd **Screenplay** James Cameron
Cinematography Adrian Biddle **Music** James Horner **Cast** Sigourney Weaver,
Lance Henrikson, Paul Reiser, Bill Paxton, Carrie Henn, Michael Biehn, Jenette
Goldstein, William Hope, Al Matthews, Mark Rolston, Ricco Ross, Colette Hiller

Common wisdom has it that, at the root of each cinematic
franchise, there must always be a strong and unique original.
More frequently, however, the second film, the sequel, turns
out to be the one that proves the staying power of a particular
cinematic vision, cements its world or characters in the popular
imagination, and truly initiates the series.

Nobody knows this better than James Cameron. During the
course of his career, he has stepped up from his moderately
profitable *Terminator* (1984) to its wildly successful sequel
Terminator 2: Judgment Day (1991). More important, Cameron
managed, with his sequel to Ridley Scott's science-fiction/horror
hybrid *Alien* (1979), both to initiate a phenomenally successful
franchise with a total of six (four, if you are a purist) films so far,
and to help shape the science-fiction/action adventure genre
that, since the mid-1980s, has dominated both the American
and global box office, until the post-millennial shift toward
fantasy, that is.

Despite its formulaic progeny, *Aliens* proves that one director's
idiosyncratic vision can mesh serendipitously with the spirit
of the original and the changing times. Cameron sustains the

◄
**The movie won
Oscars for Best
Visual Effects
and Best Sound
Effects Editing,
and received
a multitude
of nominations:
Aliens can do
no wrong.**

look of Scott's quietly creepy original, inspired by H. R. Giger's biomechanical gothic, which, in a startling paradigm shift, had broken with the symmetrical white interiors of Kubrick's *2001: A Space Odyssey* (1968).

True to Scott's original, and similar to the *Terminator* films, *Aliens'* sympathies lie with the working-class characters. But *Aliens* is a loud and fast film with skillfully orchestrated action

> ## "MOMMY ALWAYS SAID THERE WERE NO MONSTERS—NO REAL ONES— BUT THERE ARE." NEWT

sequences; whereas Scott transplants the horror film into outer space, Cameron borrows from the combat movie. When Ellen Ripley (Weaver), freshly awoken after 57 years of hypersleep, revisits and overcomes the first film's traumatic experiences— this time with a group of overconfident marines and a repulsive yuppie representing Big Business (Reiser)—Cameron has transformed Scott's gothic heroine into the proverbial 1980s action babe. Fully armored, her pumped-up physique decked out with guns and ammo, Ripley is that ambiguously gendered creature that, like Sarah Connor in *Terminator 2*, issues the post-feminist challenge to all men: Can you measure up? (Ripley remains nonetheless all woman.) Despite their initial swagger, the marines' mission reenacts the catastrophically humiliating Vietnam War experience the Reagan administration was so eager to erase. **SH**

► **Ripley's iconic line "Get away from her, you bitch!," opens the film's climactic battle: a fight to the death between two mean mothers.**

THE VOYAGE HOME
STAR TREK IV
THEY TRAVELLED BACK
WHERE 23RD CENTURY MAN
HAD NEVER GONE BEFORE.
TO A MAD, CRAZY,
OUTRAGEOUS TIME.
1987
MAXI HOTEL
DO NOT ENTER
NO RIGHT TURN
MOVIES
NCISCO BANK
PARAMOUNT PICTURES PRESENTS · A HARVE BENNETT PRODUCTION · A LEONARD NIMOY FILM · STAR TREK™ IV: THE VOYAGE HOME · WILLIAM SHATNER · LEONARD NIMOY · DeFOREST KELLEY
CO-STARRING JAMES DOOHAN · GEORGE TAKEI · WALTER KOENIG · NICHELLE NICHOLS · EXECUTIVE CONSULTANT GENE RODDENBERRY · MUSIC BY LEONARD ROSENMAN
DIRECTOR OF PHOTOGRAPHY DON PETERMAN, A.S.C. · EXECUTIVE PRODUCER RALPH WINTER · BASED UPON STAR TREK CREATED BY GENE RODDENBERRY
SCREENPLAY BY STEVE MEERSON & PETER KRIKES AND HARVE BENNETT & NICHOLAS MEYER · STORY BY LEONARD NIMOY & HARVE BENNETT · PRODUCED BY HARVE BENNETT
DIRECTED BY LEONARD NIMOY · A PARAMOUNT PICTURE · ORIGINAL SOUNDTRACK ALBUM AVAILABLE ON MCA RECORDS AND TAPES
READ THE BOOK · PANAVISION®

STAR TREK IV: THE VOYAGE HOME
1986 (U.S.)

Director Leonard Nimoy **Producer** Harve Bennett **Screenplay** Steve Meerson,
Peter Krikes, Harve Bennett, Nicholas Meyer **Cinematography** Donald Peterman
Music Leonard Rosenman **Cast** William Shatner, Leonard Nimoy, DeForest Kelley,
James Doohan, George Takei, Walter Koenig, Nichelle Nichols, Catherine Hicks

---

Star Trek IV: The Voyage Home is the most lighthearted film of
the entire *Star Trek* movie franchise, which began with *Star Trek:
The Motion Picture* (1979). *The Voyage Home* sends 23rd-century
Admiral Kirk (Shatner) and his crew to San Francisco in 1986.
This narrative device both allows the film to discuss a relevant
late-20th-century issue—species extinction—and provides a
setting in which Kirk and his comrades can be humorously out
of touch.

The crux of the film's plot proceeds from the necessity for
Kirk and his crew to locate humpback whales, whose song is
the only thing that will keep an alien probe from destroying
23rd-century Earth. The catch: humpback whales have long
since been hunted to extinction, and our heroes must literally
travel back in time to find, catch, and transport two live
whales back to their own era. Successfully sling-shotting their
ship around the sun, the crew do indeed find themselves in
a time and place where the humpback whale still exists: late-
20th-century San Francisco. After parking their cloaked ship in
Golden Gate Park, the crew divides up into three teams: Kirk

◄

**This, the fourth
Star Trek film,
was Oscar-
nominated for Best
Cinematography,
Best Visual Effects,
Sound Effects
Editing, Best
Original Score,
and Best Sound.**

and Spock (Nimoy) venture off to find the whales, Scotty (Doohan), McCoy (Kelley), and Sulu (Takei) work to arrange for the safe transportation of the whales, and Chekov (Koenig) and Uhura (Nichols) embark upon a quest to find the necessary resources to repair their ship, which was damaged as a result of the time travel. Much of the humor of the picture results from the difficulties faced in meeting these objectives: Cold

"[SPOCK]'S HARMLESS. PART OF THE FREE SPEECH MOVEMENT. I THINK HE DID A LITTLE TOO MUCH LDS." KIRK

War–wary citizens look askance on Chekov's aim to find the location of a "nuclear wessel"; a clueless Scotty futilely shouts commands at a desktop computer; Spock tries to fit in by awkwardly peppering his already formal speech—"to hunt a species to extinction is not logical"—with profanity. Most of the film's serious moments, however, are appropriately related to Kirk and Spock's attempt to obtain whales for safe transport back to the future. They discover two whales at the Cetacean Institute that are about to be released back into the open sea, where they will become targets for prowling whaling ships.

► As part of the deal that enabled Spock to get reincarnated, Leonard Nimoy took the director's chair for both Star Trek III and IV.

Fun, funny, and socially conscious, The Voyage Home was a change of pace for the franchise, and it was embraced by many fans and newcomers alike. J. J. Abram's "prequel" film, titled simply Star Trek, aims to explore the early life of James T. Kirk, and hopes to become as popular. **AK**

SCHWARZENEGGER
Nothing like it has ever been on Earth before.
It came for the thrill of the hunt.
It picked the wrong man to hunt.
PREDATOR
SOON THE HUNT WILL BEGIN
TWENTIETH CENTURY FOX A GORDON-SILVER-DAVIS ARNOLD SCHWARZENEGGER PREDATOR CARL WEATHERS
ALAN SILVESTRI DONALD McALPINE JOHN VALLONE R/GREENBERG ASSOCIATES, INC. STAN WINSTON
JIM THOMAS JOHN THOMAS LAWRENCE GORDON, JOEL SILVER JOHN DAVIS JOHN McTIERNAN
R

PREDATOR 1987 (U.S.)

Director John McTiernan **Producers** John Davis, Lawrence Gordon, Joel Silver **Screenplay** Jim Thomas, John Thomas **Cinematography** Donald McAlpine **Music** Alan Silvestri **Cast** Arnold Schwarzenegger, Carl Weathers, Bill Duke, Elpidia Carrillo, Jesse Ventura, Sonny Landham, Richard Chaves, R. G. Armstrong, Shane Black

Effortlessly combining the rugged commandos-in-war plot with science fiction, the Arnold Schwarzenegger–starring *Predator* helped further establish the 1980s trend of adrenaline-pumping, ultra-violent sci-fi alongside such films as *The Terminator* (1984), *Aliens* (1986), and *RoboCop* (1987).

Giving the audience a heads-up over the characters, the film opens with a shot of an alien spacecraft heading toward Earth. In the jungles of Central America, a Special Forces unit led by Major Alan "Dutch" Schaefer (Schwarzenegger) heads into the fictional country of Val Verde to rescue a kidnapped presidential cabinet member. Assisted by CIA agent Major George Dillon (Weathers), Dutch and his team glimpse the skinned bodies of another Special Forces unit near a rebel encampment. Quickly disposing of the camp, Dutch discovers he has been lied to by Dillon in an effort to kill the rebels. What no one in the group knows, however, is that they are being followed by a chameleonic alien that has journeyed to Earth in an effort to hunt the greatest, most exotic sport of all—man.

As with most action vehicles from this decade, the film is essentially overwhelmed by Schwarzenegger's muscular

◄

The original title of *Predator* was *Hunter*, but that title was scrapped to avoid confusion with the Fred Dreyer cop series of the same name.

physique, and the slim script offers little in terms of innovation (unless one counts the otherworldly addition to this *Ten Little Indians/Most Dangerous Game* variation). However, like the previous year's *Aliens* from James Cameron, director John (*Die Hard*) McTiernan builds efficient tension and slam-bang action so effectively that one can sit back and enjoy the chase. Familiar traumas ensue as soldiers are beheaded and blown

"COME ON . . . ! DO IT! DO IT! COME ON! KILL ME! I'M HERE! KILL ME! I'M HERE! COME ON! DO IT NOW! KILL ME!" DUTCH

apart until only Schwarzenegger stands to face the alien where, reverting to a more primal state, he is able to defeat the hunter using rudimentary, handcrafted weapons.

Predator further cemented Schwarzenegger's public recognition with science fiction, a genre that has consistently delivered his highest box-office returns beginning with *The Terminator* (1984) and continuing with *Total Recall* (1990) and two *Terminator* sequels (1991, 2003). In the wake of the film's box-office success, *Predator* turned into a highly profitable franchise for the studio. The sequel, *Predator 2*, set in the urban jungle of Los Angeles, premiered in 1990. In 1989, a comic-book series pitting the Predator monster against the Aliens from the *Alien* franchise debuted. The studio finally released the long-gestating *AVP: Alien vs. Predator* (2004) and the continuation *AVPR: Aliens vs. Predator – Requiem* (2007). **WW**

► Schwarzenegger does his best to blend in to his surroundings in *Predator*. He shed pounds to get into shape for his action role.

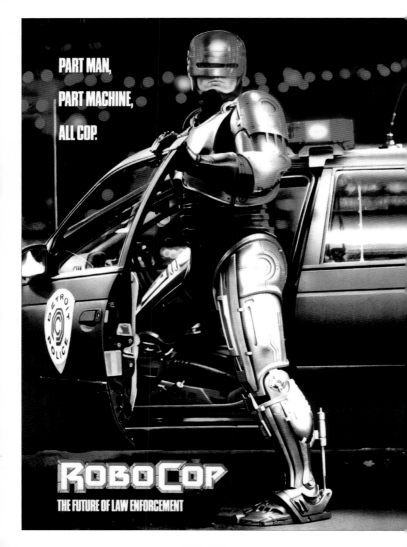

ROBOCOP 1987 (U.S.)

Director Paul Verhoeven **Producer** Arne Schmidt **Screenplay** Edward Neumeier, Michael Miner **Cinematography** Jost Vacano **Music** Basil Poledouris **Cast** Peter Weller, Nancy Allen, Dan O'Herlihy, Ronny Cox, Kurtwood Smith, Miguel Ferrer, Robert DoQui, Ray Wise, Felton Perry, Paul McCrane, Jesse Goins, Del Zamora

Where pulp and art meet, where the boundaries between genre and "auteur" cinema are muddled and rendered pointless—Paul Verhoeven stands, and makes his best films. With *RoboCop*, his bleak view of humanity and his penchant for vivid, memorable imagery are perfectly blended in a delightfully cynical, yet frighteningly accurate satire of America.

The plotline has the country governed by soulless corporations; big business runs hand in hand with the military and the police who serve and protect the big money interests; an overflowing population is zombified by consumerism and imbecilic daily TV shows; larger-than-life criminals have a field day. The future of law enforcement is embodied in a half-dead policeman augmented by robot parts, programmed to uphold the law—as long as small fry are concerned. What makes him perfect is not that he is armored in metal. He is ideal for the Corporation that bought the Detroit Police because "He doesn't have a name. He has a program. He's a product." The big fish are protected by a secret code in his program that forbids him to take action against any employee of the Corporation. After all, "We can't have our products turn against us." But that old fear

◀

The character of *RoboCop* was inspired by Judge Dredd along with the Marvel Comics superhero Iron Man.

of renegade machinery (also seen in *The Terminator*, [1984]) is given a fresh twist: Here the humans are corrupt and only a "product" can redeem them.

The sci-fi themes of human identity and what makes us human are here brought back with a vengeance through memories and dreams that remind officer Alex Murphy (a perfectly cast Weller) of his human past. *RoboCop* follows

"ROBOCOP *IS AS TIGHTLY WORKED AS A FILM CAN BE, NOT A MOMENT OR LINE WASTED.*" *VARIETY*

Murphy's gradual humanization, from a thing that "doesn't have a name" to the last lines in the film, which provide a simple human touch to the kill-the-villains action that preceded it. "Nice shooting, son", comments the corporate head, "What's your name?" RoboCop replies: "Murphy." And that is that: You can stick all the metal parts and questionable software you want inside him, but as long as there are memories and dreams, there is hope for humanity. If *The Terminator* peeled away Schwarzenegger's fake flesh to expose a murderous metallic thing, *RoboCop* removes the metal casing to reveal Weller's human heart.

Verhoeven here directs with a priceless economy and a unique sense for perfectly framed composition, his action scenes bursting with impact that doesn't shy away from the splatter effects that stress the frailty of the human body. **DO**

▶
Always provocative and always entertaining, in *RoboCop* Verhoeven adds a necessary touch of European seriousness to the comic-book material, creating one of the genre's timeless classics.

AKIRA 1988 (JAPAN)

Director Katsuhiro Ôtomo **Producers** Haruyo Kanesaku, Shunzo Kato, Ryohei Suzuki, Hiroe Tsukamoto **Screenplay** Izô Hashimoto, Katsuhiro Ôtomo (from the graphic novel) **Cinematography** Katsuji Misawa **Music** Shoji Yamashiro **Cast** Mitsuo Iwata, Nozomu Sasaki, Mami Koyama, Tesshô Genda, Hiroshi Ôtake

Based on his epic manga of the same name, Katsuhiro Ôtomo's 1988 masterpiece, *Akira*, has become a cyberpunk classic. Arguably the most influential work of Japanese anime ever created, *Akira* introduced many European and North American fans of science fiction and fantasy to a long-standing Japanese aesthetic tradition made up of highly imaginative works packed with frenetic action, spectacular battles, and plots that engaged in compelling scientific speculation.

Backed by a then-record budget of around $10 million U.S., *Akira* was the most expensive feature-length anime ever created. Its cutting-edge artwork rivaled anything yet produced by Disney studios and other major Western creators of popular animation, and its sophisticated storyline, replete with multidimensional characters and scenes of graphic violence, appealed to both adult and teenage audiences worldwide. Upon its release in Tokyo, *Akira* shattered box-office records for an animated feature, and its subsequent success in North America inevitably sparked plans for a big-budget live action remake. (The astronomical amount of funding necessary for a live-action version, however,

◄

One of the first Japanese anime films to have the characters' voices recorded before they were animated. Though standard practice in U.S. animation, in Japan the animation tends to be created first.

inevitably led Hollywood producers to shelve their plans.) Set in the sprawling 21st-century metropolis of Neo-Tokyo several years after the end of World War III, *Akira* follows the exploits of Shôtarô Kaneda (Iwata) and Tetsuo Shima (Sasaki), two members of a teenage biker gang engaged in a brutal turf war with a rival group of thugs called the Clowns. While running for his life with two Clowns in close pursuit, Tetsuo

"THE FUTURE IS NOT A STRAIGHT LINE. THERE ARE MANY DIFFERENT PATHWAYS." *KIYOKO*

Shima encounters the mysterious Takashi (Nakamura), a young boy recently rescued from a government research facility by a terrorist group known as the Resistance. Almost immediately, government soldiers arrive in helicopters, taking Takashi, as well as Tetsuo, Shôtarô Kaneda, and the rest of the biker gang into custody. Thus begins *Akira*'s sprawling, action-packed narrative.

► *Akira*'s impact was profound, influencing a generation of writers and graphic artists and permeating popular culture across multiple media, from comic books and collectibles to videogames.

A fast-paced adventure that encompasses several planes of action, *Akira* features explosive skirmishes between Neo-Tokyo's military leadership and Resistance fighters determined to disrupt inhuman biological experiments, a battle of wills between Shôtarô Kaneda and Tetsuo Shima, two friends whose relationship is stretched to the breaking point by petty jealousies, and, lastly, the arrival of eponymous posthuman entity Akira, a being whose rage sends the film's narrative rocketing toward its unforgettable apocalyptic finale. **JM**

THE NAVIGATOR 1988 (AUSTRALIA · NEW ZEALAND)

Director Vincent Ward **Producer** John Maynard **Screenplay** Geoff Chapple, Kely Lyons, Vincent Ward **Cinematography** Geoffrey Simpson **Music** Davood A. Tabrizi **Cast** Hamish McFarlane, Bruce Lyons, Marshall Napier, Chris Haywood, Noel Appleby, Paul Livingston, Sarah Peirse, Mark Wheatley, Tony Herbert

The different subtitles given to *The Navigator* in different territories and on different formats suggests the problem in classifying this film as belonging to any particular genre, or indeed any genre at all. Its original subtitle—*A Medieval Odyssey*—has been supplemented by *An Odyssey Across Time* for the U.S. release and *A Time-Travel Adventure* for the later U.S. DVD release. The original title holds no suggestion of science fiction, and it is clear that for the American market the generic undertones in the form of time travel needed to be played up.

Clearly, *The Navigator* is a time-travel adventure of sorts. With its focus on the visions of the young boy Griffin (McFarlane), the film depicts the journey of a group of men from 14th-century Cumbria to 20th-century New Zealand. They achieve this astonishing feat with no more technology than an "engine for digging rock" that allows them to tunnel through to the other side of the world. This is not depicted in any realistic way, for believing the world to be flat, they merely have to dig through a crust of rock and soil. They carry a cross with them, an offering they must deliver to the great cathedral in order to save their village from the Black Death.

◀

Vincent Ward's talent for creating haunting visual poetry is on full display in this film about the healing power of dreamers.

Ward suggests the journey from the "evil" of a land beset by the plague to the "goodness" of the future with a change from monochrome to color film stock. Yet the modern city they reach is a terrifying and awe-inspiring vision seen through the eyes of these time travelers, and they are driven to the point of madness by all they see. A key scene that draws parallels between the Black Death of the Middle Ages and the AIDS

"IT'S A DIALOGUE BETWEEN PAST AND PRESENT, BETWEEN FAITH, LOGIC OR SKEPTICISM." VINCENT WARD (DIRECTOR)

epidemic anchors the meaning of the picture, just as the travelers are anchored by the cross that they carry. The fact that this cross perfectly fits the church they find waiting in the city does suggest, however, that it is perhaps a little too perfect a vision.

Indeed, the revelation that it is only a dream, a story that Griffin relates as they wait out the night in a mine, lends a touch of frustration to the ending. Whether these events occur in actuality or within the realms of imagination should, though, be irrelevant. The focus is on characters who are drawn with economy and grace, and the film is shot with a sparse beauty against the night sky and the great city. In the end, it hardly matters that the time travel is merely a parable. Ward himself went on to write the story for *Alien³* but has never bettered the fantasy time travel offered here with such originality. **BC**

►
Griffin (McFarlane) in a distinctly "un-medieval" part of the odyssey.

TETSUO 1989 (JAPAN)

Director Shinya Tsukamoto **Producer** Shinya Tsukamoto **Screenplay** Shinya Tsukamoto **Cinematography** Shinya Tsukamoto, Kei Fujiwara (with art direction also by Shinya Tsukamoto) **Music** Chu Ishikawa **Cast** Tomorowo Taguchi, Shinya Tsukamoto, Kei Fujiwara, Nobu Kanaoka, Renji Ishibashi, Naomasa Musaka

Featuring rapid editing, an aggressive industrial sound track, and grainy black-and-white cinematography, Shinya Tsukamoto's *Tetsuo* is a wholly individual plunge into the underground world of Japanese sci-fi cyberpunk that explodes onto the screen.

Tetsuo opens with a Metal Fetishist (Tsukamoto) inserting a metal pipe into his leg. When he sees maggots squirming over the open wound, the man runs into the street, only to be hit by a car. The film then focuses on a character known simply as Man (Taguchi), who, while shaving, discovers a metal shard growing out of his face. As Man goes about his day, he encounters a woman on the subway who becomes possessed and mutates after touching a piece of metal. Returning home, Man finds that a frankly sexual breakfast with his girlfriend (known simply as Woman) results in the emergence of his robotic penis. Initially scared, the girlfriend feels she can handle this newfound growth, only to have it result in her death via fornication. It is then that the Metal Fetishist appears outside of his confines in order to confront the Man. From here on out, the pair wage war in the streets, an epic battle that results in the duo melding together with the promise to rust the entire world.

◄

One of the most extraordinary pieces of micro-budgeted, underground filmmaking in the history of Japanese (and arguably world) cinema.

Playing like a Japanese manga bursting to life, *Tetsuo* was produced in conjunction with regular collaborators found in Tsukamoto's Kaijyu Theater. With a background in painting and advertising, Tsukamoto is a one-man silver screen army as he directed, scripted, designed, co-photographed, and edited the film. Tsukamoto's cinematic influences are varied. Stylistically, the surreal imagery echoes works like avant-garde

"TOGETHER, WE CAN TURN THIS F*****G WORLD TO RUST!"

METAL FETISHIST

filmmakers Maya Deren's *Meshes of the Afternoon* (1943) and Luis Buñuel's *Un Chien Andalou* (1929). The stark black-and-white cinematography and the "man residing in the metal" recall David Lynch's cult classic *Eraserhead* (1976). Thematically, *Tetsuo* is similar to the early works of David Cronenberg, particularly *The Brood* (1979) and *Videodrome* (1983), where the concept of anger being a physically altering force is displayed.

▶ The underlying theme of *Tetsuo* is similar to that of many David Cronenberg films—flesh and technology have become warring forces on a mutable battleground.

That is not to say the film has no original ideas of its own. Tsukamoto comments on the growth of industrial cityscapes into the countryside and the resulting growing alienation. In addition, there is a prescient quality to the film in regards to the idea of man being consumed by technology. And although the narrative is initially confounding, further inspection unveils a revenge story where Man and Woman are being punished for their hit-and-run of the Metal Fetishist. **WW**

THERE'S EVERYTHING YOU'VE EVER KNOWN ABOUT ADVENTURE...

AND THEN THERE'S

THE
ABYSS

TWENTIETH CENTURY FOX PRESENTS A GALE ANNE HURD PRODUCTION A JAMES CAMERON FILM THE ABYSS   ED HARRIS · MARY ELIZABETH MASTRANTONIO · MICHAEL BIEHN MUSIC BY ALAN SILVESTRI
PRODUCTION DESIGNER LESLIE DILLEY DIRECTOR OF PHOTOGRAPHY MIKAEL SALOMON PRODUCED BY GALE ANNE HURD WRITTEN AND DIRECTED BY JAMES CAMERON

THE ABYSS 1989 (U.S.)

Director James Cameron **Producer** Gale Ann Hurd **Screenplay** James Cameron
Cinematography Mikael Salomon **Music** Alan Silvestri **Cast** Ed Harris, Mary
Elizabeth Mastrantonio, Michael Biehn, Leo Burmester, Todd Graff, John Bedford
Lloyd, Adam Nelson, J. C. Quinn, Kimberly Scott, Capt. Kidd Brewer Jr., George R. Klek

At the time of its first release, *The Abyss* was widely seen as a
stumble in the career of writer-director James Cameron, whose
previous two films—*The Terminator* (1984) and *Aliens* (1986)—
had established him as the world's leading director of action.
The Abyss's pronounced elements of melodrama and sentiment
seemed to separate it out from the more hard-edged approach
evident in Cameron's earlier work, and these elements did not
always sit easily with the film's own action scenes. Matters were
not helped by the fact that Cameron's version of the movie
was initially deemed too long and shorn of a large part of its
conclusion. In retrospect, and especially since the 1992 release
of Cameron's cut, *The Abyss* has come to appear a far more
significant achievement.

As one might expect from Cameron, *The Abyss*'s numerous
action set pieces—most notably a protracted chase and fight
scene between two mini-subs—are, without exception, state-
of-the-art masterworks, and all the more remarkable for being
filmed in extremely demanding underwater conditions. By
contrast, the film's narrative, which deals with an encounter with
aliens during an attempt to salvage a downed submarine, has

◄
**Beauty and
terror commingle
beneath the seas
in this film that
won an Oscar for
Best Visual Effects.**

proved more contentious. Some have compared *The Abyss* to Kubrick's *2001: A Space Odyssey* (1968), but a more apt comparison would be with Robert Wise's 1951 film *The Day the Earth Stood Still*, which also features aliens who are essentially peaceful but who are prepared to issue some pretty serious threats in order to curtail the human species' warlike tendencies. In the case of *The Abyss*, this involves the aliens apparently resolving Cold

"HE SEES HATE AND FEAR. YOU HAVE TO LOOK WITH BETTER EYES THAN THAT." LINDSEY BRIGMAN

War tensions through engineering a series of immense tidal waves that threaten major cities around the world (in a scene that was missing from the original release version, an omission that arguably rendered the aliens pointless).

The view this entails of humans as childlike and desperately in·need of some alien authority might not be politically astute, but it is presented with conviction and great cinematic skill. In particular, the structuring of the film's lengthy conclusion through a descent—Ed Harris's epic but suicidal journey into the abyss where the aliens reside—followed by an ascent, when the aliens' massive craft rises to the surface, succeeds in eliciting an emotional response, mixing apprehension with wonder. And it is in this invoking of intense emotions, negative and positive, that *The Abyss*, for all its awkward moments, retains the power to fascinate and move us. **PH**

► **Much of the underwater filming for *The Abyss* took place in the world's largest underwater set (seven million gallons) within a half-completed nuclear reactor facility in South Carolina.**

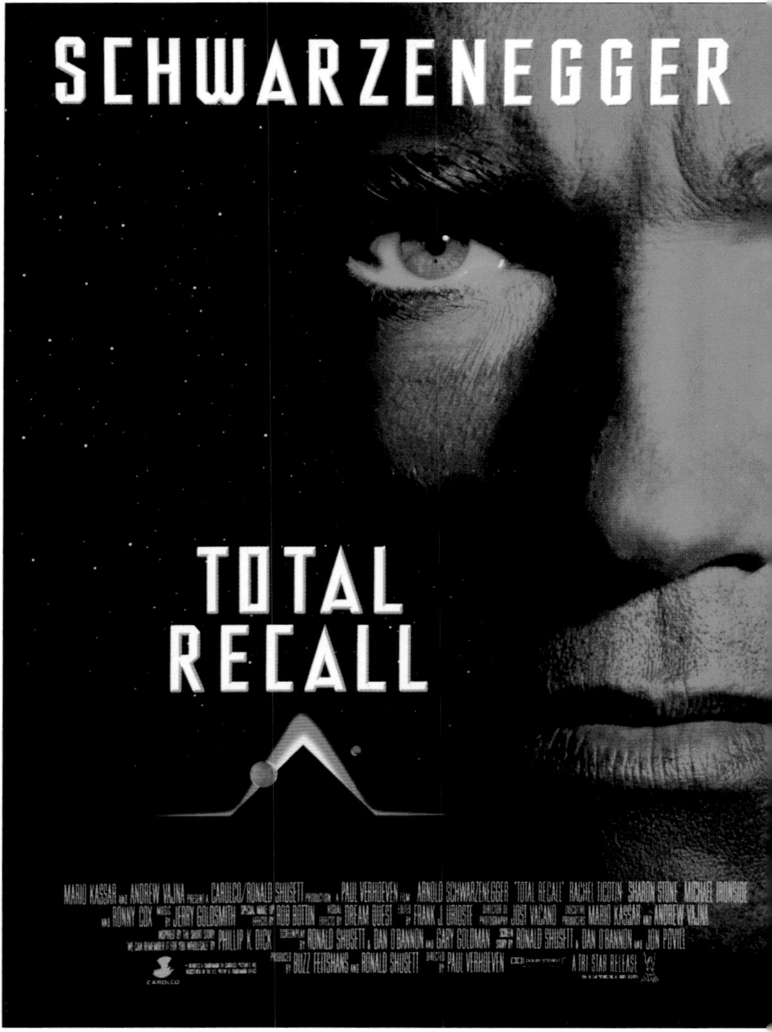
SCHWARZENEGGER
TOTAL RECALL
MARIO KASSAR AND ANDREW VAJNA PRESENT A CAROLCO/RONALD SHUSETT PRODUCTION A PAUL VERHOEVEN FILM ARNOLD SCHWARZENEGGER "TOTAL RECALL" RACHEL TICOTIN SHARON STONE MICHAEL IRONSIDE
AND RONNY COX MUSIC BY JERRY GOLDSMITH SPECIAL MAKE-UP EFFECTS BY ROB BOTTIN VISUAL EFFECTS BY DREAM QUEST EDITED BY FRANK J. URIOSTE DIRECTOR OF PHOTOGRAPHY JOST VACANO EXECUTIVE PRODUCERS MARIO KASSAR AND ANDREW VAJNA
PHILLIP K. DICK SCREENPLAY BY RONALD SHUSETT & DAN O'BANNON AND GARY GOLDMAN SCREEN STORY BY RONALD SHUSETT & DAN O'BANNON AND JON POVILL
PRODUCED BY BUZZ FEITSHANS AND RONALD SHUSETT DIRECTED BY PAUL VERHOEVEN
A TRI-STAR RELEASE
CAROLCO

TOTAL RECALL 1990 (U.S.)

Director Paul Verhoeven **Producers** Ronald Shusett, Mario Kassar, Andrew G. Vajna **Screenplay** Dan O'Bannon, Ronald Shusett, Gary Goldman, John Povill **Cinematography** Jost Vacano **Music** Jerry Goldsmith **Cast** Rachel Ticotin, Sharon Stone, Ronny Cox, Michael Ironside, Marshall Bell, Ray Baker, Arnold Schwarzenegger

In 2084, everyman Douglas Quaid (Schwarzenegger) has an ideal life with a steady construction job and a loving wife, Lori (Stone). But constant dreams of another life on the now-colonized Mars lead Quaid to Rekall, a retail outlet that implants fantastic virtual-reality memories into your brain. Opting to enjoy a spy fantasy, Quaid's procedure fails when Rekall workers uncover previously embedded memories in his mind. Following his Rekall visit, Quaid has no memory, but is suddenly attacked by coworkers and even his wife, who explains that she is really an agent pretending to be his spouse. On the run, Quaid receives a suitcase from Hauser, his former self, which includes a video explaining that he must get to Mars. Once on the red planet, Quaid meets up with Melina (Ticotin), the girl seen in his dreams, in a small mining colony tightly restricted by Cohaagen (Cox), a ruthless politician who controls the price and flow of air. In addition, Cohaagen's shoddy buildings have created mutants from Mars's atmosphere and an insurgency, which Quaid soon discovers he was a part of.

Walking a fine line between reality and imagination, Paul Verhoeven's *Total Recall* plays like a sci-fi version of *North*

◄

The film, that won a Special Achievement Award at the Oscar for its effects, features a wide array of mutants, including resistance leader Kuato (overleaf).

by *Northwest* (1959). Although hardly the embodiment of the average man, Schwarzenegger is commendable as the paranoid Quaid, never quite sure if he is living or dreaming. Verhoeven actually shot the film to support either the reality or hallucination theory, as Quaid's adventure does not truly begin until he is in the Rekall chair. In the end, it is up to audiences to decide.

"WHAT ABOUT THE GUY YOU LOBOTOMIZED? DID HE GET A REFUND?"

DOUGLAS QUAID

As with his previous movie, *RoboCop* (1987), Verhoeven piles on the ultra-violence (enough to originally receive an X-rating from the MPAA), but leaves out much of the black comedy that made his sci-fi debut unique. And despite being a blockbuster action flick filled with trademark Schwarzenegger one-liners, the screenplay retains elements of its inspiration, Philip K. Dick's short story *We Can Remember It For You Wholesale*, notably wariness about government agencies and corporations.

Total Recall displays a dazzling collection of practical special effects courtesy of Rob Bottin's crew, such as Schwarzenegger pulling a tracking device out of his head through his nose, and a disguise head that comes apart in sections. Ironically, this was overtaken the next year by the even-bigger Schwarzenegger vehicle *Terminator 2*, which officially ushered in the era of computer-generated effects. **WW**

► **Marshall Bell had full-body makeup for the Kuato scenes. The head of Kuato was completely animatronic.**

TERMINATOR 2: JUDGMENT DAY
1990 (U.S. • FRANCE)

Director James Cameron **Producers** James Cameron, Gale Anne Hurd, Mario Kassar **Screenplay** James Cameron, William Wisher Jr. **Cinematography** Adam Greenberg **Music** Brad Fiedel **Cast** Arnold Schwarzenegger, Linda Hamilton, Edward Furlong, Robert Patrick, Joe Morton, Earl Boen, S. Epatha Merkerson

Having displayed a knack for action-oriented, sci-fi sequels with *Aliens* (1986), director James Cameron advances the popular *The Terminator* (1984) with *Terminator 2: Judgment Day*—an adrenaline-fueled special-effects showcase that is one of the most significant science-fiction pictures of the 1990s.

Picking up roughly 13 years after the original, *Terminator 2* follows the basic architecture as a cyborg is sent back from the year 2029 to assassinate future leader John Connor (Furlong), now a techno-savvy juvenile living in a foster home. Led to believe his mother is delusional with her stories of Terminator killing machines and a time-traveling father, John has no contact with the institutionalized Sarah Connor (Hamilton). This changes when John is confronted by a T-800 (Schwarzenegger), the machine that tried to kill his mother. But this Terminator is different—it has been reprogrammed and sent back by John himself in order to protect him from the T-1000 (Patrick), a shape-shifting Terminator currently in Los Angeles disguised as a police officer. Realizing his mother isn't crazy and fearing for her safety, John orders the T-800 to break Sarah out of the

◀

The *Terminator* franchise expanded with the Cameron-less sequel *Terminator 3: Rise of the Machines* (2003), a television series, and a fourth theatrical entry (2009).

mental institution. Together, the trio take off with the T-1000 in hot pursuit, but things go awry when Sarah disappears with the goal of assassinating researcher Miles Dyson (Morton), head of Cyberdyne, the company that eventually generates Terminator-creating Skynet.

Famously the first film to command a $100 million budget, nearly all of the money is on-screen in over-the-top stunt set

"CHILL OUT, DICKWAD." TERMINATOR
"GREAT! SEE, YOU'RE GETTING IT!" O'CONNOR
"NO PROBLEMO." TERMINATOR

pieces involving cars, motorcycles, semitrucks, and helicopters and Oscar-winning special effects. Cameron also utilizes the CGI (Computer Generated Images) developed for his earlier *The Abyss* (1989) to display the various replications of the liquid metal T-1000 with astonishing effect. Amid all this Cameron still finds the time to elaborate on the series' theme of self-reliance in regard to one's future ("There is no fate but what we make"). *Terminator 2* is a rare sequel in that it successfully inverts the roles from the original. Perceptive of Schwarzenegger's popularity, the filmmakers effortlessly recast the iconic (and heretofore villainous) Terminator figure as this entry's hero without sacrificing the character's appetite for brutality. In addition, series heroine Sarah Connor morphs from innocent victim to tough warrior, an astonishing physical and mental transformation by Hamilton. **WW**

► **Sarah Connor (Hamilton) changes from victim in *Terminator* to hardened, if paranoid, survivor in *Terminator 2*.**

A STEVEN SPIELBERG FILM

An Adventure
65 Million Years In The Making.

UNIVERSAL PICTURES PRESENTS AN AMBLIN ENTERTAINMENT PRODUCTION SAM NEILL LAURA DERN JEFF GOLDBLUM
AND RICHARD ATTENBOROUGH "JURASSIC PARK" BOB PECK MARTIN FERRERO B.D. WONG SAMUEL L. JACKSON WAYNE KNIGHT
JOSEPH MAZZELLO ARIANA RICHARDS LIVE ACTION DINOSAURS STAN WINSTON FULL MOTION DINOSAURS DENNIS MUREN, A.S.C. DINOSAUR SUPERVISOR PHIL TIPPETT SPECIAL DINOSAUR EFFECTS MICHAEL LANTIERI
MUSIC BY JOHN WILLIAMS FILM EDITOR MICHAEL KAHN, A.C.E. PRODUCTION DESIGNER RICK CARTER DIRECTOR OF PHOTOGRAPHY DEAN CUNDEY, A.S.C. BASED ON THE NOVEL BY MICHAEL CRICHTON
SCREENPLAY BY MICHAEL CRICHTON AND DAVID KOEPP PRODUCED BY KATHLEEN KENNEDY AND GERALD R. MOLEN DIRECTED BY STEVEN SPIELBERG SPECIAL VISUAL EFFECTS BY INDUSTRIAL LIGHT & MAGIC
A UNIVERSAL PICTURE

JURASSIC PARK 1993 (U.S.)

Director Steven Spielberg **Producer** Kathleen Kennedy, Gerald R. Molen
Screenplay Michael Crichton, David Koepp (from the novel written by Michael
Crichton) **Cinematography** Dean Cundey **Music** John Williams **Cast** Sam Neill,
Laura Dern, Jeff Goldblum, Richard Attenborough, Joseph Mazzello, Ariana Richards

By 1993, while Steven Spielberg had established his position
as the preeminent Hollywood director, his films over the
previous decade had largely decayed into cloying cuteness
and overblown sentimentality. So the buzz that Spielberg
had secured the rights to Michael Crichton's cracking novel
Jurassic Park did not augur well (cuddly dinosaurs learning how
to speak in childlike voices?). But anyone emerging from the
auditorium after the two-hour screening must have felt that
dinosaurs were truly walking the earth. Spielberg was back on
form: *Jurassic Park* wasn't just good, it was *Jaws* good.

The high-concept novel by Crichton tells of a scientific
research laboratory that has developed the process of
extracting dinosaur DNA from mosquitoes caught in amber
and using amphibious DNA to complete the genome. With a
full genetic code, these scientists are able to effectively clone
animals that had been extinct for millions of years. With this
ability to clone dinosaurs, the next logical step is, of course, to
open a theme park/zoo on an isolated island where tourists
can see living dinosaurs in a reconstructed natural habitat. And,
as the park is about to open, the dinosaurs break free.

◄

**Visible in the shots
of the gift shop is a
book entitled *The
Making of Jurassic
Park* by Don Shay
and Jody Duncan.
This book was
actually published,
and tells the
behind-the-scenes
story of how the
movie was made.**

Jurassic Park is totally self-reflexive; it recognizes that, like the characters in the story, we would love to see real dinosaurs running around. And rather than give us Ray Harryhausen stop-motion effects, like in *Valley of the Gwangi* or *King Kong*, Spielberg and his team of special-effects artists needed to create these monsters so believably that we fall into a kind of sublime awe at their presence (as the characters in the

"THE LACK OF HUMILITY BEFORE NATURE BEING DISPLAYED HERE, UH . . . STAGGERS ME." *DR. IAN MALCOLM*

movie do). But *Jurassic Park* is smarter still; Spielberg includes a sequence, not in the novel, where we get a simple panning shot of the park's gift shop, full of *Jurassic Park* merchandise. All the stuff on display in this shot utilizes the graphic design of the film itself, and the excess—everything from pencil cases to lunchboxes and T-shirts—is also self-reflexive of the kinds of movie merchandise that Spielberg's own corpus has been instrumental in establishing.

What does this shot tell us? It tells us that Spielberg was aware of how overly commodified his films had become, and within the context of the movie, after the dinosaurs have broken loose and the park is clearly never going to open, this merchandising bubble must ultimately burst. Spielberg's films since *Jurassic Park* have been much less merchandised than they were in the 1980s. **MK**

► Dr. Alan Grant (Neill) stays still for the T-Rex, with a terrified Lex (Richards) under his arm.

GHOST IN THE SHELL 1995 (JAPAN • U.K.)

Director Mamoru Oshii **Producers** Mitsuhisa Ishikawa, Ken Iyadomi, Ken Matsumoto, Yoshimasa Mizuo, Shigeru Watanabe **Screenplay** Kazunori Itô (based on anime by Masamune Shirow) **Cinematography** Hisao Shirai **Music** Kenji Kawai **Cast** Atsuko Tanaka, Akio Ôtsuka, Tamio Ôki, Iemasa Kayumi, Kôichi Yamader

Japanese sci-fi anime movie *Ghost in the Shell* (a.k.a. *Kôkaku Kidôtai*) takes place in 2029, a time when nations have been replaced by city-states and mega-corporations, and the world has been tied inextricably together through a vast computer network. In this brave new world, Section 9 is a covert division of the Japanese police that investigates cyber-crime and crimes committed by runaway robots.

The story follows Major Motoko Kusanagi (Tanaka) of Section 9 and her partner Batô (Ôtsuka) in their investigation of what at first appears to be a hacker known as the Puppet Master, who specializes in implanting unsuspecting people with false memories and manipulating them to do his dirty work. As it turns out, the mysterious character that has been operating behind the scenes is in fact an Artificial Intelligence program, code-named Project 2501, that has become sentient and is now seeking asylum with Section 9. But the government agency that created the AI program isn't about to let it get away, and it still remains a mystery why the Puppet Master sought out Major Kusanagi in the first place—or indeed what it intends to do with her.

◀

Director Mamoru Oshii utilizes Cyberpunk tropes with enormous dexterity: cyber-brains being hacked, thermoptic suits, and the image of a typist with high-speed mechanical fingers.

Ghost in the Shell is one of the most influential anime films of all time, and is frequently referred to as the first truly adult animated motion picture. It was also the first anime film to be released simultaneously in Japan, Britain, and the United States. Mamoru Oshii was able to create a cinematic masterpiece with his dynamic, unforgettable images, each of which is choreographed for maximum impact, never lingering

"I MEAN, HAVE YOU EVER ACTUALLY SEEN YOUR BRAIN?"

ATSUKO TANAKA

too long at the expense of storytelling. For example, a fight scene between two cyber-enhanced characters takes place in a brief few shots, instead of dragging out for five minutes. This film opened the doors for events like Disney's pursuit of Hayao Miyazaki (*Princess Mononoke*, *Spirited Away*, *Howl's Moving Castle*, and the like), and eventually, the truly incredibly pace of anime that exists today.

The awsome success of *Ghost in the Shell* spawned an even more visually sensational (some would argue) sequel, *Ghost in the Shell 2: Innocence* (2004). Again, the anime characters speculate on what it means to be human and whether machines can feel anything (in this movie they are created for sexual pleasure). But ultimately, as with the original, it's best to dwell on the mesmerizing, futuristic cityscapes and forgo the metaphysical and poorly dubbed doodlings. **CK**

▶
In addition to the brilliant 2004 sequel, the *Ghost in the Shell* saga was continued in a 52-episode anime TV series entitled *Ghost in the Shell: Stand Alone Complex* (2002).

BRUCE WILLIS
MADELEINE STOWE
BRAD PITT
THE FUTURE IS HISTORY
A TERRY GILLIAM FILM
12 MONKEYS
BRUCE WILLIS MADELEINE STOWE BRAD PITT "12 MONKEYS" CHRISTOPHER PLUMMER
JULIE WEISS LLOYD PHILLIPS MICK AUDSLEY JEFFREY BEECROFT ROGER PRATT
CAVALLO GARY LEVINSOHN ROBERT KOSBERG CHRIS MARKER DAVID PEOPLES & JANET PEOPLES
PRODUCED BY CHARLES ROVEN DIRECTED BY TERRY GILLIAM A UNIVERSAL RELEASE

TWELVE MONKEYS 1995 (U.S.)

Director Terry Gilliam **Producer** Charles Roven **Screenplay** David Peoples, Janet Peoples, Chris Marker (from his film *La Jetée*) **Cinematography** Roger Pratt **Music** Robin Clarke **Cast** Bruce Willis, Madeleine Stowe, Brad Pitt, Christopher Plummer, Joseph Melito, Jon Seda, Michael Chance, Vernon Campbell, Bob Adrian

Terry Gilliam's *Twelve Monkeys* features Bruce Willis and an almost unrecognizable Brad Pitt working "for cheap" and playing against type in astonishing intense and eruptive performances. It is 2035, and the earth's surface is an uninhabitable winter wonderland in which wild animals roam among deserted skyscrapers. Some 40 years earlier, a virus killed off five billion people, but in a lab underneath Philadelphia scientists prepare to send a naked James Cole (Willis) back to 1996 to find its cause and reclaim the earth. Scientists have assumed the functions of the state and, like the fumbling bureaucracy of *Brazil* (1985), are prone to error. Arriving in 1990 instead of the designated destination, Cole is mistaken for a derelict, incarcerated and treated by Dr. Kathryn Railly (Stowe) and befriended by another patient, Jeffrey Goines (Pitt). Bounced back to a World War I battlefield, he at last finds himself in 1996, where he again meets Railly and Goines, now the leader of an animal rights terrorist organization called the Army of the 12 Monkeys.

Exhausted from unending temporal dislocation, Cole longs simply to be insane and in 1996, with its "clean" air, music (Louis Armstrong's "What a Wonderful World"), and his beautiful

◄ Caught in a deliriously strange loop, *Twelve Monkeys* leaves us haunted with its mood of lyrical nostalgia, yearning, melancholy, and endless déjà vu.

psychiatrist. His delirium is infectious, spreading to Kathryn and the audience during its final minutes, when images we have seen before or imagined are poised to come together in a series of *Vertigo* (1958) moments: Kathryn in a blonde wig, a herd of giraffes parading across a bridge, the fleeting sparks of life in Cole's dying gaze renewed in the mournful, ageless eyes of the child he now is, was, and will be again.

"YOU HAD A BULLET FROM WORLD WAR I IN YOUR LEG, JAMES! HOW DID IT GET THERE?" *KATHRYN RILEY*

▶
The movie is the converse of *The Terminator* (1984) and *Back to the Future* (1985): Cole (Willis) cannot change history, and his actions are destined to repeat themselves.

Like Gilliam's signature films, *Twelve Monkeys* is a can of worms, with the difference that no moment is gratuitous. Inspired by Chris Marker's 27-minute masterpiece *La Jetée* (1962), and with a debt to George Roy Hill's *Slaughterhouse-Five* (1972), the movie is dense with other cinematic and topical touchstones. Gilliam's vision of the world as an asylum/prison/interrogation run by frigid bureaucrats melds seamlessly with the script's multiple concerns: ecological disaster, pandemics, biological weapons, animal rights, terrorism, surveillance culture, Stockholm Syndrome, and "mental divergence." The asylum sequences channel *Marat Sade* (1967) and *One Flew Over the Cuckoo's Nest* (1975) with a wildly gesticulating Goines spitting out prophetic epigrams. Indeed, to classify *Twelve Monkeys* as a time-travel thriller understates the film's philosophical and psychological complexity. **LB**

The question of
whether or not
we are alone
in the universe
has been answered.

INDEPENDENCE DAY

Don't make plans for August.

JULY 3 EVERYWHERE
www.id4.com

INDEPENDENCE DAY 1996 (U.S.)

Director Roland Emmerich **Producer** Dean Devlin **Screenplay** Roland Emmerich, Dean Devlin **Cinematography** Karl Walter Lindenlaub **Music** David Arnold **Cast** Will Smith, Jeff Goldblum, Bill Pullman, Judd Hirsch, Robert Loggia, Randy Quaid, Vivica Fox, Mary McDonnell, Harvey Fierstein, Adam Baldwin, Margaret Colin

Roland Emmerich's *Independence Day* has been heavily criticized for its overly American patriotic rabble-rousing finale, but as far as big-budget Hollywood summer popcorn movies go, it really is the template for how to make a blockbuster. And closer textual analysis reveals some textbook ideas more Hollywood screenwriters should pay attention to.

The film takes place over three days, beginning two days before the annual Fourth of July celebrations. Alien aircraft appear over each of the major cities around the world, giving undeniable proof that there is intelligent life in the universe. But whether or not they are peaceful is unknown until, in a coordinated attack, each craft unleashes a deadly ray destroying everything in its path. Human military means are unable to stop the mass carnage. As a small, ragtag group of survivors make their way to Area 51 in the Nevada desert, two heroes, Captain Steve Hiller (Smith) and David Levinson (Goldblum), find a gap in the alien's technology and the two fly one of the alien craft back to the mothership and save humanity. Although *Independence Day* is clearly modeled on H. G. Wells's 1898 science-fiction novel *The War of the Worlds*, replacing the

◄

At first, 20th Century Fox wanted to change the name of the movie to *Doomsday* and release it on Memorial Day in order to avoid the traditionally fierce box-office competition on July 4th.

common cold that defeats the aliens with a computer virus, the film also has many echoes and homage to the history of science-fiction cinema: There are references to *The Day the Earth Stood Still* (1951), *Alien* (1979), *Star Wars* (1977), and even *2001: A Space Odyssey* (1968).

But equally referenced is the whole history and mythology surrounding UFOs in contemporary folklore: Area 51, Roswell,

"SPECIAL EFFECTS ARE MEANINGLESS IF YOU DON'T CARE ABOUT THE PEOPLE IN THOSE SPECIAL EFFECTS." DEAN DEVLIN

alien autopsy footage, alien abductions. The film could almost be said to work purely as a two-and-a-half-hour compendium of sci-fi cinema and UFO-ology. But in addition, Emmerich and co-writer Dean Devlin structure the story so that it has a kind of disaster movie logic to it: Reminiscent of the disaster films of the 1970s, *Independence Day* has multiple character plotlines that ultimately come together. Although Hiller and Levinson ultimately emerge as the film's heroes, named characters die, often surprisingly, leaving the audience wondering who will survive and who won't.

But for all the big-budget hoopla this blockbuster threw around, including Oscar-winning special effects, Emmerich and Devlin never lose sight of the human stories amidst the mayhem. *Independence Day* is the ultimate B-movie with a strong focus on the humanity of the characters. **MK**

► Audiences are lured into rooting for their heroes (Will Smith and Jeff Goldblum among others) as they are introduced in their private and human contexts, rather than by the status of their characters.

GAUMONT présente

BRUCE WILLIS

LE CINQUIÈME ELEMENT

GAUMONT présente un film de LUC BESSON - BRUCE WILLIS "LE CINQUIEME ELEMENT" GARY OLDMAN - IAN HOLM - CHRIS TUCKER et MILLA JOVOVICH musique ERIC SERRA costumes JEAN-PAUL GAULTIER superviseur des effets spéciaux visuels MARK STETSON producteur associé IAIN SMITH chef monteuse SYLVIE LANDRA chef décorateur DAN WEIL directeur de la photographie THIERRY ARBOGAST scénario original LUC BESSON adaptation et dialogues LUC BESSON et ROBERT KAMEN produit par PATRICE LEDOUX réalisé par LUC BESSON

http://www.gaumont.fr

THE FIFTH ELEMENT 1997 (FRANCE)

Director Luc Besson **Producers** Patrice Ledoux, John A. Amicarella, Iain Smith
Screenplay Luc Besson, Robert Mark Kamen **Cinematography** Thierry Arbogast
Music Eric Serra **Cast** Bruce Willis, Gary Oldman, Ian Holm, Milla Jovovich, Chris
Tucker, Luke Perry, Brion James, Tommy "Tiny" Lister Jr., Lee Evans, Charlie Creed Miles

In the year 2263, the world is in danger of being destroyed by a
molten ball of lava heading straight for Earth. In a colorful and
flamboyant future, with cosmic guns and weird-looking aliens,
it should come as no surprise that the salvation of mankind
rests upon the shoulders of a motley group of characters. These
include recently unemployed cabdriver Korben Dallas (Willis),
new-age priest Vito Cornelius (Holm), outspoken radio host
Ruby Rhod (Tucker), and a sexy female who is fond of saying
"Multi-pass" named Leeloo (Jovovich).

A story originally thought of by director Luc Besson when
he was only a teenager, *The Fifth Element* focuses on the eternal
struggle between Good and Evil. Set within the context of a
prophesy that the "Great Evil" will arrive every five millennia,
evil presents itself in the form of a large fireball that will
destroy the earth. Cornelius maintains that the only weapon
that can overcome evil is the Fifth Element. Unlike the other
four elements (earth, air, water, and fire), the Fifth Element is a
"'perfect being" named Leeloo, who is brought to Earth by the
Mondoshawans, a friendly alien race who aim to help humanity.
Afraid in this strange new world, Leeloo runs away from the

◄
**At the time of
its release, the
French-produced
The Fifth Element
was the costliest
movie ever
made outside
of Hollywood.
This is the original
French poster.**

scientists wishing to evaluate her, and runs into the arms of the cabbie, Dallas. Dallas, memorable for his no-nonsense attitude and his bright orange tank top, falls in love with Leeloo. As they are chased by Jean-Baptiste Emanuel Zorg (Oldman), an arms-dealer tycoon and supporter of the Great Evil, Dallas takes Leeloo on an adventure through the galaxy, helping her to save humanity.

"[BY] CREATING A LITTLE DESTRUCTION, I'M ACTUALLY ENCOURAGING LIFE. YOU AND I ARE IN THE SAME BUSINESS." ZORG

Though the film is perhaps best known for its costume design and cinematography, one should not let these appearances overshadow the film's presentation of the picture of good and evil in the human condition. This picture is personified through the human characters, and their endeavors toward creation and destruction. Cornelius represents that which is good, as his goal is to create a world of peace, whereas Zorg epitomizes evil in his quest to destroy life. While these two characters show the apparent extremes of good and evil, Leeloo wonders why she should even bother saving the human race, as she begins to believe that, collectively, human beings may be more evil than good, and could end up destroying each other. However, through Dallas's love, she is convinced that one should be optimistic and have hope that the human race can overcome the evil in themselves and become better beings. **SB & WD**

► **Korben Dallas (Willis) sees the light and delivers a customary tongue-in-cheek performance as an amiable spacefighter turned cabbie.**

PROTECTING THE EARTH FROM THE SCUM OF THE UNIVERSE

MR. JONES   MR. SMITH

MEN IN BLACK

COLUMBIA PICTURES PRESENTS AN AMBLIN ENTERTAINMENT PRODUCTION

IN ASSOCIATION WITH MacDONALD/PARKES PRODUCTIONS A BARRY SONNENFELD FILM STARRING TOMMY LEE JONES WILL SMITH "MEN IN BLACK" LINDA FIORENTINO VINCENT D'ONOFRIO RIP TORN MUSIC BY DANNY ELFMAN PRODUCTION DESIGNER BO WELCH SPECIAL VISUAL EFFECTS BY INDUSTRIAL LIGHT & MAGIC EDITED BY JIM MILLER DIRECTOR OF PHOTOGRAPHY DON PETERMAN ASSOCIATE PRODUCER STEVE R. MOLEN MAKE-UP DESIGNER RICK BAKER CO-PRODUCER GRAHAM PLACE EXECUTIVE PRODUCERS STEVEN SPIELBERG BASED ON THE COMIC BOOK BY LOWELL CUNNINGHAM SCREEN STORY BY ED SOLOMON SCREENPLAY BY ED SOLOMON AND EXECUTIVE PRODUCER WALTER F. PARKES AND LAURIE MacDONALD DIRECTED BY BARRY SONNENFELD

JULY 2   www.sony.com   COLUMBIA PICTURES

MEN IN BLACK 1997 (U.S.)

Director Barry Sonnenfeld **Producers** Laurie MacDonald, Walter F. Parkes
Screenplay Ed Solomon (from *The Men In Black* comic by Lowell Cunningham)
Cinematography Don Peterman **Music** Danny Elfman **Cast** Will Smith, Tommy Lee
Jones, Rip Torn, Linda Fiorentino, Vincent D'Onofrio, Tony Shalhoub, Siobhan Fallon

Based on the cult comic-book series of the same name, *Men in Black* was a movie project that had more than its fair share of problems before it finally saw the light of day as the surprise summer blockbuster of 1997. After Clint Eastwood turned it down, Tommy Lee Jones agreed to participate only after executive producer Steven Spielberg promised him the script would be rewritten to reflect the comic book's deadpan sense of humor more accurately. His costar Will Smith, then famous for the hit TV show *The Fresh Prince of Bel Air*, was not approached until Chris O'Donnell and David Schwimmer had passed on it. Even director Barry Sonnenfeld didn't come on board until several others (including Quentin Tarantino) had turned it down.

With all three principal contributors last-minute replacements and the production itself famously troubled by rewrites, on-set quarrels, and extensive reshoots, it came across as something of a miracle that the final product was so well received. Indeed, two subsequent attempts to make lightning strike in the same place twice (the abysmal *Wild Wild West* [1999] and the equally terrible *MIB* sequel [2002]) merely proved how

◄
In UFO conspiracy theories, the term "Men in Black" or "MIB" is used to describe men dressed in black suits claiming to be government agents who attempt to threaten or harrass UFO witnesses into silence.

unique this movie's genial brand of comedy really was. But its vast commercial appeal may be attributed to factors outside the film's mix of broad physical comedy, exciting action sequences, and understated banter. More than anything else, the producers managed to capitalize on Smith's popularity not only as a TV personality, but especially as a mainstream hip-hop star. For not only did the film quickly become an international

"THERE'S ONLY ONE WAY OFF THIS PLANET, BABY, AND THAT'S THROUGH ME." AGENT JAY

box-office behemoth, but it immediately catapulted Will Smith into the category of Hollywood superstar.

The movie's main marketing tool was in this case not the eye-catching poster, but its music video: a high-gloss mini-narrative that featured characters, sets, and props side by side with spectacular scenes from the actual film. Resampling Patrice Rushen's 1982 hit "Forget Me Nots" the track's catchy repetition of the movie's title guaranteed enormous international exposure for the film and its young star. But although Smith was the one who ended up reaping the main rewards, Tommy Lee Jones remains the true star of the picture, outshining even Rick Baker's award-winning creature effects. Effortlessly convincing as the seen-it-all, done-it-all, grizzled old veteran, he was able to bring both humor and unexpected conviction to lines like "Put up your arms and all of your flippers." **DH**

► **Will Smith originally turned down the part of Agent "J" but was coaxed into accepting it by his wife Jada Pinkett Smith.**

ETHAN HAWKE

G A T T A C A

UMA THURMAN

THERE IS NO GENE FOR THE HUMAN SPIRIT

COLUMBIA PICTURES PRESENTS

A JERSEY FILMS PRODUCTION   A FILM BY ANDREW NICCOL

STARRING ETHAN HAWKE UMA THURMAN "GATTACA"
ALAN ARKIN   JUDE LAW   LOREN DEAN   ERNEST BORGNINE
MUSIC COMPOSED BY MICHAEL NYMAN COSTUME DESIGNER COLLEEN ATWOOD
EDITOR LISA ZENO CHURGIN PRODUCTION DESIGNER JAN ROELFS DIRECTOR OF PHOTOGRAPHY SLAWOMIR IDZIAK
PRODUCED BY DANNY DeVITO MICHAEL SHAMBERG STACEY SHER
WRITTEN AND DIRECTED BY ANDREW NICCOL

GATTACA 1997 (U.S.)

Director Andrew Niccol **Producers** Danny DeVito, Michael Shamberg, Stacey Sher **Screenplay** Andrew Niccol **Cinematography** Slawomir Idzia **Music** Michael Nyman **Cast** Ethan Hawke, Jude Law, Uma Thurman, Gore Vidal, Xander Berkeley, Jayne Brook, Elias Koteas, Maya Rudolph, Elizabeth Dennehy, William Lee Scott

In the tradition of Jean-Luc Godard's *Alphaville* (1965) and Ridley Scott's *Blade Runner* (1982), Andrew Niccol's *Gattaca* (1997) blends traditional science-fiction themes with the visual feel of film noir. Far more than merely the movie that introduced Jude Law to American audiences, *Gattaca* presents a dystopian future where most humans are genetically engineered in vitro. The preference for creating children using eugenics has produced a caste system where favor and success are bestowed on those with whom the "local geneticist" has been most successful. Those born without the benefit of scientific intervention are immediately regulated to the society's bottom strata.

Gattaca's main character, Vincent Freeman (Hawke), is one such individual. Naturally born, Vincent is assessed at birth as having a short life expectancy because of his potential of developing a heart condition. Vincent spends his early life watching his genetically engineered younger brother receive the academic accolades, physical achievements, and paternal love withheld from him because of societal and biological prejudice. Vincent finds himself barred from school because of administrators' anxieties regarding his potential health issues,

◀

Gattaca's title is deliberately and appropriately made up only of letters used to label human DNA's nucleotide bases.

and as an adult, although self-taught and highly intelligent, Vincent can find only the most basic jobs. Alienated from his family and oppressed by social barriers, Vincent becomes restless. His continued dreams of space travel lead him to embrace an illegal option becoming a "borrowed ladder," a person who assumes the identity of a genetically superior individual who is somehow unable to perform as expected.

"I GOT THE BETTER END OF THE DEAL. I ONLY LENT YOU MY BODY—YOU LENT ME YOUR DREAM." JEROME

Vincent is then introduced to Jerome Eugene Morrow (Law), a genetic giant and former Olympic medalist whose glory is cut short when an accident abroad results in the loss of use of his legs. Now in a wheelchair, Jerome agrees to let Vincent take over his identity in exchange for financial compensation and, eventually, being able to live vicariously through Vincent's achievements. Posing as Jerome, Vincent's rise at Gattaca, the institution behind numerous space exploration missions, is indeed meteoric. All is set for Vincent's yearlong space expedition to Saturn's moon, Titan, until a murder at Gattaca renders all of its employees suspect and threatens to expose Vincent as an impostor.

Gattaca is a commentary on the dangers of scientific advancement that results in harming, rather than aiding, human society and development. **AK**

► **Identity theft in a chilly and stylized future: Ethan Hawke adds gravitas to the superb cast.**

STARSHIP TROOPERS 1997 (U.S.)

Director Paul Verhoeven **Producers** Jon Davison, Alan Marshall **Screenplay** Ed Neumeier (from the novel written by Robert A. Heinlein) **Cinematography** Jost Vacano **Music** Basil Poledouris **Cast** Casper Van Dien, Dina Meyer, Neil Patrick Harris, Denise Richards, Michael Ironside, Jake Busey, Clancy Brown, Patrick Muldoon

Paul Verhoeven's adaptation of Robert Heinlein's 1959 novel *Starship Troopers* is perhaps one of the most underrated and misinterpreted science-fiction movies of all times. Far from being a glorification of war, the film is highly critical and satirical of the media trappings that seduce us.

In the future, four teenagers graduate from high school and immediately join up for military service (the only way one can become a citizen in this dystopia future). While on basic training, the "bugs" of Klendathu, insectoid creatures, attack Earth and wipe out several million people. War is declared and the four friends find themselves in different arenas of the conflict.

Although it is easy to get sucked into viewing the film as a gung-ho Christmastime blockbuster, with all the $100 million budget on-screen with big explosions and thousands of Kendathu bug invasions, *Starship Troopers* is much more satirical in its evocation of World War II propaganda, particularly the kinds of propaganda films of the Third Reich that director Verhoeven grew up watching in occupied Holland. For Verhoeven, the kind of military hysteria the story was evoking was as much a reflection on the Third Reich as it was a warning

◀

Robert Heinlein's novel *Starship Troopers* won the Hugo Award in 1960, and from the very beginning attracted controversy for its political and social themes. Verhoeven's film is thus a faithful adaptation in this sense above all others.

about contemporary American politics and our media-saturated, 24-hour news broadcasting culture in fin-de-siècle America. When Carl (Harris), (co-opted by military intelligence) emerges wearing a black SS-like uniform, Verhoeven's satire of putting TV's *Doogie Howser* into a Nazi outfit was lost on most of the audience, who approached the film only on its most superficial level.

"THE CONTRARY OPINION THAT VIOLENCE DOESN'T SOLVE ANYTHING IS MERELY WISHFUL THINKING." MR. RASCZAK

The rest of the cast were also heavily criticized for being bland and wooden: Casper Van Dien as Johnny Rico, the film's central hero, Denise Richards as Carmen Ibanez, Johnny's high-school love interest who breaks his heart for a flyboy, and Dina Meyer as Dizzy Flores, Johnny's female best friend who has carried a torch for the hero since they were at school together, are absolutely comic-book-deep caricatures. But for Verhoeven, that's partially the point: these characters are cartoonlike, not real human beings. The picture has a sensibility of playing with Ken and Barbie dolls being attacked by giant bugs. To have humanized these characters would have been to detract from the sheer spectacle-for-spectacle's sake of the production, and without that distance to the reality of the film we run the risk of missing the point of the satire—like apparently most critics did. **MK**

▶
Verhoeven's characters, including Rico (Van Dien, right), Carmen, and Dizzy, were never meant to be "real," but this was missed by many critics and viewers alike. *Starship Troopers* is almost Brechtian in its epic quality "alien-ation."

Una coproducción hispano-franco-italiana. Una producción de José Luis Cuerda para Sogetel, Las Producciones del Escorpión, Les Films Alain Sarde y Lucky Red con la participación de Sogepaq S.A. y la colaboración de Canal + España.

abre los ojos

una película de Alejandro Amenábar

EDUARDO NORIEGA + PENELOPE CRUZ + CHETE LERA + FELE MARTINEZ + NAJWA NIMRI como "Nuria"

guión: ALEJANDRO AMENÁBAR + MATEO GIL montaje: MARIA ELENA SAINZ DE ROZAS sonido: GOLDSTEIN Y STEINBERG
música: ALEJANDRO AMENÁBAR + MARIANO MARIN director de arte: WOLFGANG BURMANN director de fotografía: HANS BURMANN
director de producción: EMILIANO OTEGUI productores ejecutivos: FERNANDO BOVAIRA + JOSÉ LUIS CUERDA
director: ALEJANDRO AMENÁBAR

Sogetel   CANAL+   Les Films Alain Sarde   LUCKY RED   EURIMAGES   Sogepaq

OPEN YOUR EYES 1997 (SPAIN · FRANCE · ITALY)

Director Alejandro Amenábar **Producers** José Luis Cuerda, Fernando Bovaira
Screenplay Alejandro Amenábar, Mateo Gil **Cinematography** Hans Burman
Music Alejandro Amenábar, Mariano Marín **Cast** Eduardo Noriega, Penélope Cruz,
Chete Lera, Najwa Nimri, Fele Martínez, Gerard Barray, Jorge de Juan, Ion Gabella

Abre Los Ojos or *Open Your Eyes* tells the story of César (Noriega) a
rich, handsome young man who is enjoying life to the fullest—
attracting women with his money and good looks. This often
irritates his best friend, Pelayo (Martínez), who realizes that he
can't compete with his friend's charming personality or striking
good looks. On the night of his 25th birthday, César meets the
gorgeously beautiful Sofia (Cruz) and thinks he has found his
perfect woman. He decides to use Sofia to help ward off his
date for the night, Nuria (Nimri), who confronts him the next
morning in a jealous, possessive rage. César tries to appease
her, and when he agrees to accept a ride from her, she drives
her car off the road, killing herself and permanently mangling
César's once handsome visage.

Awakening in a psychiatric prison for a murder that he
doesn't remember committing, and prompted to wear an
expressionless mask to hide his scarred face, César—with the
help of Antonio (Lera), a sympathetic psychiatrist—tries to
figure out what happened and why he keeps seeing images
of a man (Barray) on TV touting the benefits of cryogenics. As
he does so, César's life begins to unravel as reality and fantasy

◄
**The film was
nominated for
ten Goya Awards,
Spain's equivalent
of the Oscars.**

begin to blend together in a nightmarish fashion that may just drive him mad if he cannot remember a past that may or may not have ever happened.

Open Your Eyes touches on and passes through so many genres that it cannot be classified as any one single movie theme, although sci-fi-thriller would be pretty close to the target. However, the clever blurring of reality and illusion

"SOMETIMES YOU CAN'T WAKE FROM A NIGHTMARE EVEN IF YOU DO."

MOVIE TAGLINE

seamlessly shifts from melodrama to romance to film noir to science fiction as the limits of "personality" are explored.

Perhaps most impressive of all, director and cowriter Alejandro Amenábar effectively blends together many diverse genre elements using conventional narrative techniques such as flashbacks, dream sequences, and scenes in the "present." The way these techniques are used to piece the film together gives the audience the impression that they are unraveling the convoluted plot along with the protagonist. Amenábar went on to direct *The Others* (2001) starring Nicole Kidman, in one of the best horror movies. *Open Your Eyes* remains ambitious and disturbing while looking stunning, which is why it was famously given the Hollywood makeover in the Tom Cruise–Penelope Cruz vehicle *Vanilla Sky* (2001) directed by Cameron Crowe, in which Cruz played the same character, Sofia. **CK**

▶
Cesar (Noriega) in the games-playing sci-fi thriller that cleverly blurs reality and illusion.

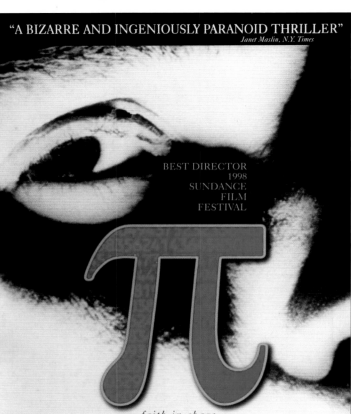

PI 1998 (U.S.)

Director Darren Aronofsky **Producer** Eric Watson **Screenplay** Darren Aronofsky
Cinematography Matthew Libatique **Music** Clint Mansell **Cast** Sean Gullette,
Mark Margolis, Ben Shenkman, Pamela Hart, Stephen Pearlman, Samia Shoaib,
Ajay Naidu, Kristyn Mae-Anne Lao, Espher Lao Nieves, Lauren Fox, Clint Mansell

The "Faith in Chaos" tagline gives a definite flavor of the
contradictions and conflicts depicted in this mathematic
number crunching–meets–end of millennium film. The
chaos is all focused on the struggles of the central character
Max Cohen (Gullette) as he looks for patterns in the random
numbers of the Stock Exchange while failing to communicate
with the people around him—his mentor Sol (Margolis), Lenny
the Hasidic Jew studying the Torah (Shenkman), the corporate
suits hounding him, and his neighbors.

Pi is a rightly acclaimed masterpiece of subjective cinema.
The opening titles—a montage of brain cells and mathematical
diagrams superimposed on the streaming digits of the infinite
number for pi—take the viewer directly into the protagonist's
mind. The story Max relates about looking into the sun when
he was a child also hint most strongly that this is a failure of
vision. *Pi* is a film with a single narrative point of view—Max's.
Everything (and all) the viewer sees is what he experiences.
Aronofsky uses a range of cinematic effects to enhance this
association with Max's state of mind. When Max walks the
streets, Aronofsky employs a Snorricam: a camera attached to

◄

**"Faith in Chaos"
reads *Pi*'s (or π)
poster tagline,
efficiently
conveying the
core themes of
number theory
and religion while
simultaneously
suggesting a sense
of mystery.**

the actor. This separates Max from his environment, depicting his isolation and alienation. The subtle changes in film speed strangely disorient the viewer. The plot is also punctuated by Max's migraines, each following a repeated pattern and each escalating in severity, from Max's twitching thumb to desperate scramble for drugs at onset, culminating in hallucination and final fade to white. Anyone who has ever suffered from

> # "LIKE THE HAND OF GOD REACHING DOWN AND PULLING OUT A CHUNK OF BRAIN." DARREN ARONOFSKY

migraines will recognize the experience, if not the actual set of symptoms; so convincingly does Aronofsky capture the attacks, these sequences become painful in themselves.

The subjectivity also confounds any sense of truth in the narrative: Is this a depiction of true events, hallucination, or Max's paranoia? Whatever the answer, and this is clearly left open to individual interpretation, the film conveys more atmosphere and emotion in its black-and-white cinematography than many a mainstream film. It is rich in imagery—from spiral shells to the pieces on Sol's Go board; metaphor—Max's room is so packed with computer equipment that he seems to become the conscious part of the machine; allusion—ants are the literal bugs in Max's program; and allegory—he is Icarus flying too close to the sun. *Pi* is all about mood and no more, but it is executed so proficiently that mood is all it needs to be. **BC**

► The number Max (Gullette) is searching for is 216 digits long: 216 is 6x6x6, and 666 is the "number of the beast" according to the *Book of Revelation*.

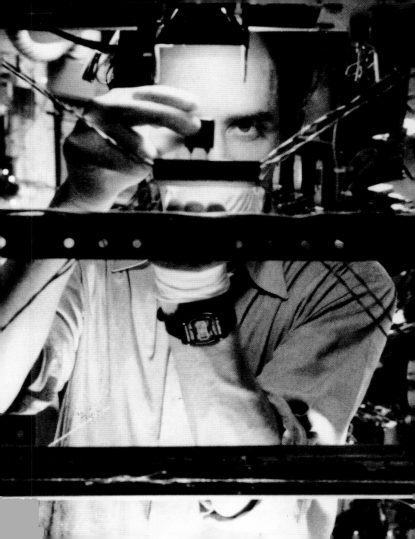

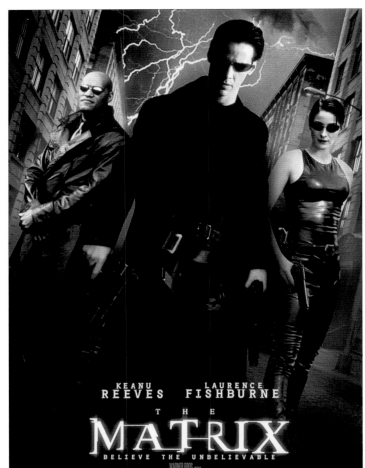

KEANU **LAURENCE**
REEVES **FISHBURNE**

THE
MATRIX
BELIEVE THE UNBELIEVABLE

WARNER BROS. PRESENTS

SILVER PICTURES PRODUCTION VILLAGE ROADSHOW PICTURES - GROUCHO II FILM PARTNERSHIP

KEANU REEVES LAURENCE FISHBURNE "THE MATRIX" CARRIE-ANNE MOSS HUGO WEAVING JOE PANTOLIANO MUSIC DON DAVIS EDITOR ZACH STAENBERG

OWEN PATERSON DIRECTOR OF BILL POPE PRODUCERS DAN CRACCHIOLO BARRIE OSBORNE ANDREW MASON ANDY WACHOWSKI LARRY WACHOWSKI ERWIN STOFF BRUCE BERMAN

PRODUCED JOEL SILVER WRITTEN AND DIRECTED THE WACHOWSKI BROTHERS

www.whatisthematrix.com

THE MATRIX 1999 (U.S. · AUSTRALIA)

Directors Andy and Larry Wachowski **Producer** Joel Silver **Screenplay** Andy and Larry Wachowski **Cinematography** Bill Pope **Music** Don Davis **Cast** Keanu Reeves, Laurence Fishburne, Carrie-Anne Moss, Hugo Weaving, Joe Pantoliano, Matt Doran, Belinda McClory, Gloria Foster, Marcus Chong, Julian Arahanga

Containing cultural references that span religious symbolism, literary references, and philosophical allusions, the Wachowski brothers' 1999 film *The Matrix* seems most indebted to Plato's *Allegory of the Cave* for its story and theme. A box-office blockbuster that had audiences raving over breathtaking action sequences and stunning visual effects, *The Matrix* is also a film that, like Plato's text, tells the story of those who are trapped in darkness, those who seek to keep them imprisoned, and those who search for ways to bring freedom and enlightenment to the prisoners. In *The Matrix*, Neo's (Reeves) path is like that of Plato's prisoner brought slowly and painfully to enlightenment; Neo too must overcome physical and psychological barriers that are obstacles to his true enlightenment.

Within the first few scenes of *The Matrix*, the world as Neo has known it is brought crashing down around him. His depressing apartment, his stultifying job at the corporation Metacortex, even his black market dealings in computer software are all part of The Matrix, a computer-generated replication of a world that no longer exists. Neo is, in reality, sleeping away his life in a pod-like apparatus, in which he is hooked up to a

◄

The monumental success of *The Matrix* spawned two popular (but not nearly as successful) sequels featuring the same main characters, animated films and videogames.

computer program that provides these dreams of a real life. The real world, instead, is now run by machines, which live off human energy harvested from vast pod farms—just one of the many memorable and bleak special-effects scenes. Only a few humans now live in the real world, a grim and at times terrifying reality in which they must constantly battle against the machines, and the machine's computer-

"UNFORTUNATELY, NO ONE CAN BE TOLD WHAT THE MATRIX IS. YOU HAVE TO SEE IT FOR YOURSELF." *MORPHEUS*

programmed agents, for survival. These few rebels seek to free the imprisoned and are also searching for "the One," a human about which a prophecy has been told, who will lead them to victory against the machines. The rebels' leader, Morpheus (Fishburne), believes that Neo may be this very person, and much of the film revolves around Neo's journey toward understanding what his role may or may not be in the approaching revolution against the machines.

The Matrix was a box-office sensation, largely because of its innovative "Bullet Time" sequences, which used time-freezing photographic technique for outstanding visual effect. This optical achievement gained such fame that it has been used, sometimes to parodical effect, in numerous other Hollywood movies and, ubiquitously in many crime, drama, and action television shows. **AK**

▶
A breakthrough in optical technology, the movie won (among others) an Oscar for Best Visual Effects.

GALAXY QUEST 1999 (U.S.)

Director Dean Parisot **Producers** Mark Johnson, Charles Newirth
Screenplay David Howard, Robert Gordon **Cinematography** Jerzy Zielinski
Music David Newman **Cast** Tim Allen, Sigourney Weaver, Alan Rickman, Tony
Shalhoub, Sam Rockwell, Daryl Mitchell, Robin Sachs, Enrico Colantoni, Patrick Breen

In DreamWorks' family-friendly film *Galaxy Quest*, the actors
from a 1970s science-fiction television show attempt to milk
the last of their fame by banding together for their "comeback"
through making appearances at sci-fi conventions and store
openings in costume and character. Self-centered star Jason
Nesmith (Allen) portrays heroic, womanizing Captain Taggart,
who infuriates coworkers with his inflated ego; Gwen DeMarco
(Weaver) plays the role of the bodacious space sexpot; and
Alexander Dane (Rickman) has never been able to live down
his role as a Spock-like, purple-headed alien.

The team is at each other's throats until a trio of "shiny-suited
oddballs" turn up at Jason's door. These oddballs are not staple
convention-goers in fancy dress (also much lampooned in *The
Simpsons* TV series) but real aliens known as the Thermians. The
great premise that mashes sci-fi with TV culture and genuine
laughs is that they have mistaken the show for fact and have
consequently modeled their entire culture around it. The
Thermians transport Jason and the rest of his unbelieving crew
to the Klatu Nebula to help fight the war against their nemesis
General Sarris (Sachs).

◄
**The film's homage
to *Star Trek*
extended to
the marketing
campaign,
which included
a promotional
website intended
to look like a
poorly-constructed
fan website.**

Directly spoofing the original *Star Trek* series—the film is literally littered with *Star Trek* TV and movie references and visual gags—Dean Parisot does an excellent job of reveling in the world of fandom. The movie portrays the ultimate fan as these Thermian aliens who have been dedicated viewers of the series from light-years away. Their attempt to recruit the *Galaxy Quest* actors to help transform their world directly mimics the

"I'M THE GUY IN THE EPISODE WHO DIES TO PROVE HOW SERIOUS THE SITUATION IS. I'VE GOTTA GET OUTTA HERE!" *GUY*

logic of *Galaxy Quest*'s earthbound fans and validates the reality that exists between film text and fan. Moreover, the aliens' interpretation of the show as a "historical document" is representative of some fans' incapacity to distinguish fact from fiction. Similar to what exists in the *Star Trek* world of fandom where dedicated fans are known as "Trekkies," Parisot is able to accurately portray this by paying tribute to—as well as spoofing—the very notion of fandom. Several of the genuine "geeky" fans (such as Brandon played by Justin Long) get to help the *Galaxy Quest* crew save the day. Nesmith has to convince Brandon it's not just a TV show, to which he responds: "Oh my God, I knew it. I knew it! I knew it!" There's even a knowing reference or two to Sigourney Weaver's previous incarnation in the sci-fi-horror franchise *Alien* as the hard-core "kick-ass" Ellen Ripley: "Ducts? Why is it always ducts?" **CK**

► The Thermians are aliens charmingly under the illusion that the *Galaxy Quest* TV broadcasts they have picked up in their solar system are real, factual "historical documents."

SIGNS 2002 (U.S.)

Director M. Night Shyamalan **Producers** M. Night Shyamalan, Frank Marshall, Sam Mercer **Screenplay** M. Night Shyamalan **Cinematography** Tak Fujimoto **Music** James Newton Howard **Cast** Mel Gibson, Joaquin Phoenix, Rory Culkin, Abigail Breslin, M. Night Shyamalan, Cherry Jones, Patricia Kalember, Ted Sutton

Signs was M. Night Shyamalan's second writer-director project after his genre breakthrough, *The Sixth Sense* (1999). Shyamalan's work had become strongly linked with major plot twists, and to an extent *Signs* participates in this game-playing with audience expectations. This time around, however, Shyamalan didn't just offer up a surprise ending, but also toyed with the limits and frameworks of genre, delivering an alien invasion tale in which very few aliens are ever seen, and in which the invasion itself occurs pretty much off-screen. Instead of spectacular, large-scale visions of U.S. cities being destroyed, Shyamalan focuses in on one family—the Hess clan—and a microcosm of a small-town, rural lives.

And the titular "signs" are not just the mysterious crop circles that appear around the world and presage the emergence of extraterrestrial intelligence; they are also the signs of faith and divine intervention as interpreted by the character of the former Reverend Graham Hess (Gibson). As such, *Signs* audaciously reworks the sci-fi-horror-thriller conventions of the alien invasion storyline by filtering these through an existential, even theological lens.

◄
The crop circles shown in *Signs* were created by the crew, as Shyamalan doesn't particularly like using CGI.

The film's relative departure from blockbuster norms may have irritated some moviegoers hoping for a more conventional sci-fi movie, but by working to produce a sense of awe and wonder at signs of transcendence, it can be argued that *Signs* participates in one tradition of arthouse-mainstream crossover science-fiction film, harking back to the ilk of *2001: A Space Odyssey* (1968), at least in terms of its basic themes.

"I TAKE A B-MOVIE STORY . . . AND TREAT IT AS IF IT'S AN A-MOVIE IN TERMS OF MY APPROACH." M. NIGHT SHYAMALAN

In form and content, *Signs* owes much more to Hitchcock, Romero, and Spielberg, and Shyamalan's tendency to cast himself in an acting role—going beyond the mere cameo or Hitchcockian walk-on—rears its head here, as he plays the character Ray Reddy, responsible for much of the suffering of the Hess family. This gives rise to moments of dialogue where the writer-director seems to be almost "breaking the frame" by commenting on his own narrative and visual construction.

The film has an out-of-time feel because of its rural setting, and its narrative imaginatively seeks to explain profound coincidences not as the work of a writer looking for a radical new twist, but rather as markers of divine potency and planning. Ultimately, *Signs* stands as an impressively ambitious auteurist project within mainstream, blockbuster parameters. It may yet prove to be Shyamalan's genuine masterpiece. **MH**

► An existential-turned-extra-terrestrial crisis: Mel Gibson as Rev. Graham Hess in *Signs*.

TIM ROBBINS   SAMANTHA MORTON

MICHAEL WINTERBOTTOM's **CODE 46**

How do you solve a crime when the last thing you want to know is the truth?

UNITED ARTISTS PRESENTS THE UK FILM COUNCIL AND BBC FILMS REVOLUTION FILMS PRODUCTION
MICHAEL WINTERBOTTOM FILM TIM ROBBINS SAMANTHA MORTON "CODE 46" CASTING WENDY BRAZINGTON
MUSIC THE FREE ASSOCIATION DESIGNER MARK TILDESLEY PHOTOGRAPHY ALWIN KÜCHLER EDITOR MARCEL ZYSKIND
PETER CHRISTELIS CO-PRODUCER NATALIE WARD ASSOCIATE PRODUCER ERICA ROMERO EXECUTIVE PRODUCERS ROBERT JONES AND DAVID M. THOMPSON
SCREENPLAY FRANK COTTRELL BOYCE PRODUCED BY ANDREW EATON DIRECTED BY MICHAEL WINTERBOTTOM

CODE 46 2003 (U.K.)

Director Michael Winterbottom **Producer** Andrew Eaton **Screenplay** Frank Cottrell Boyce **Cinematography** Alwin Kuchler, Marcel Zyskind **Music** Stephen Hilton, David Holmes **Cast** Tim Robbins, Samantha Morton, Togo Igawa, Nabil Elouahabi, Sarah Backhouse, Jonathan Ibbotson, Om Puri, Nina Fog, Emil Marwa

In English director Michael Winterbottom's futuristic drama, *Code 46*, a provocative love story is lived out in the not-too-distant future between William Geld (Robbins) and Maria Gonzales (Morton). In this future of genetic policing and tightly restricted travel, William is an insurance investigator on the hunt for forgers specializing in "papelles," the identity cards that are now required for travel between cities. Without a valid papelle, people are stuck living in squalor outside of the city and are deemed prisoners by the rest of society.

During his research, William discovers that a woman from Shanghai, Maria, is one of the top document forgers. Because William has been infected with the "empathy virus"—one of the futuristic elements of the film—he cannot bring himself to turn Maria in to the authorities, and instead develops a romantic relationship with her that turns into a deep-seated love affair. William eventually realizes that he is dabbling in dangerous territory. Besides betraying his job as well as his wife and child back in Seattle, he also neglects to think about how his one-night stand with Maria has violated Code 46, a law designed to prevent genetically similar people from having children.

◄

Frank Cottrell Boyce, the acclaimed British screenwriter who has penned six of Michael Winterbottom's films to date, created an exceptionally clever script.

Winterbottom's vision of the future is one in which people speak in a polyglot language combining English, French, and Spanish. For example, when William travels to Shanghai he speaks in Spanglish, "Pray for her un poco." Genetic engineering is a heavily regulated process where everyone's DNA is tracked, and there are codes against reproducing with others, depending on their genetic formulas. There are

"IF WE KNEW WHAT WOULD HAPPEN IN THE END, WOULD WE EVER BE ABLE TO TAKE THE FIRST STEP?" MARIA

plenty of high-tech gizmos such as credit card–sized video cell phones and touch-screen displays that control or access just about anything.

Despite Winterbottom's ability to portray a chilling future and to capture a wide array of urban territories including Dubai, Seattle, Shanghai, and Hong Kong, the film's slow pace can make it difficult for the average viewer. *Code 46* captures a classic premise, however—the enduring struggle for freedom. Despite its flaws, the picture delves deeply into issues of empathy and morality in a highly controlled world. Winterbottom's stab at science fiction is as mixed as his general oeuvre, following a harrowing docudrama of Afghan refugees trying to get into the U.K. in *In this World* (2002) and preceding the sexually explicit *9 Songs* (2004). As English film critic Philip French put it, "it tries to run the gamut from *Alphaville* to *Zardoz*." **CK**

► Samantha Morton in *Code 46*: a movie that is reminiscent of *Gattaca* (1997) in its portrayal of criminals defying a dystopian future that has rigid laws based on genetics.

PRIMER 2004 (U.S.)

Director Shane Carruth **Producer** Shane Carruth **Screenplay** Shane Carruth
Cinematography Shane Carruth **Music** Shane Carruth **Cast** Shane Carruth, David
Sullivan, Casey Gooden, Anand Upadhyaya, Carrie Crawford, Jay Butler, John Carruth,
Juan Tapia, Ashley Warren, Samantha Thomson, Chip Carruth, Ashok Upadhyaya

The concept of time travel is depicted so thoroughly in Shane
Carruth's debut feature that it seems like we are observing
people trapped in a self-inflicted experiment. Carruth presents
his unusual story in a manner somewhat similar to a Discovery
Channel documentary. The extremely low budget (about
$7,000) in this particular case actually allows Carruth to focus on
his characters and their interactions, backing everything with
solid research about physics.

There is a fair amount of tech talk right from the beginning.
Abe (Sullivan) and Aaron (Carruth) are two engineers with great
ambition who are, perhaps, too smart for their own good. We
meet them in the middle of their everyday routine. They inhabit
their own world and have their own habits and jargon, which
may seem confusing to someone peeking in from outside.
Then again, this is a perfect way for Carruth to suck you into
the story. While you are trying to grasp what's going on, you
are starting to get familiar with those characters. And when the
time-travel aspect finally kicks in, you might want to rewind
back to some scenes in the beginning, because the devil is in
the details…and so is science fiction.

◀
**Shane Carruth has
stated that, out of
80 minutes filmed
for the movie, only
two minutes were
cut to create the
final product.**

The idea of time travel has been used to various effect in sci-fi cinema, but Carruth exemplifies that its inherent dangers do not lie only in paradoxes, but also in the most complex and unpredictable variable—man himself. So, the world of possibilities soon becomes a nightmarish maze that only gets bigger and more elaborate with every action that Abe or Aaron take. Each of them is on their own personal moebius

"IT ASSUMES THE INTELLIGENCE AND INTEREST OF ITS AUDIENCE, A BRAVE MOVE THAT PAYS OFF BIG." TOM LONG

strip looking for an exit, trying not to run into themselves. With a number of different time lines Abe and Aaron also create their own doubles. By the end you may lose count of them, but the plot's internal logic remains intact, even if you still need additional viewings to comprehend it. The key word here is *paranoia*. You can't even trust yourself. Abe and Aaron discover that you are one person today, but a different one tomorrow—and they learn this the hard way. Imagine, then, what would happen if those different versions of the same person could interact. Seems like a pretty literal way of becoming your own worst enemy. Similar in vein to the sci fi–horror films of David Cronenberg, *Primer* definitely lacks those other movies' visceral punch, but on a cerebral level it works overtime. It functions like a fascinating puzzle that, when complete, provides a rather cynical but accurate outlook on human nature. **MC**

▶
Abe (Sullivan, left) and Aaron (Carruth, right) perform mad science in *Primer*.

ETERNAL SUNSHINE
OF THE SPOTLESS MIND 2004 (U.S.)

Director Michel Gondry **Producers** Anthony Bregman **Screenplay** Charlie
Kaufman, Michel Gondry, Pierre Bismuth **Cinematography** Ellen Kuras **Music** Jon
Brion **Cast** Jim Carrey, Kate Winslet, Elijah Wood, Thomas Jay Ryan, Mark Ruffalo,
Jane Adams, David Cross, Kirsten Dunst, Tom Wilkinson, Gerry Robert Byrne

Here is a prime example of how the merging of creative writers
and directors can result in a movie that is both pyschologically
captivating and emotionally complicated. The film tells a love
story between Joel Barish (Carrey) and Clementine Kruczynski
(Winslet) in a highly abstract and inventive way. Joel is a quiet,
cautious man who is not adept at expressing his feelings,
though his emotions certainly run deep, and Clementine is an
extremely extroverted, daring young woman who changes her
hair color as regularly as her moods.

  What is not realized until the end is that the majority of
the movie is a flashback, used to emphasize the dissipation
of Joel and Clementine's relationship. This effect is achieved
by implementing the science-fiction technique of "memory
erasure." After a nasty breakup, Clementine hires the New
York firm Lacuna to erase her memories of the relationship.
Upon discovering this, Joel too, decides to undergo the same
erasure procedure despite still being in love with Clementine.
The film, which takes place mostly within Joel's mind, follows

◄
The "memory
fading" techniques
used throughout
represent the
symbolic nature of
the disappearance
of memory, but
ask the question:
At what point does
love overcome
man's erasure tools
and mechanisms?

his memories of Clementine backward in time as each recent memory is replaced. But once the process starts, Joel realizes he doesn't really want to forget Clementine, so he starts inserting her into parts of his memory where she doesn't belong.

Meanwhile Stan (Ruffalo), the technician in charge of the procedure, and his girlfriend Mary (Dunst) get stoned, drink beer, and dance on their client's bed. Another employee,

> ## "MAYBE YOU CAN FIND YOURSELF A NICE ANTIQUE ROCKING CHAIR TO DIE IN." *CLEMENTINE KRUCZYNSKI*

Patrick (Wood), Stan's assistant, confesses to having stolen Clementine's panties and then leaves so that he can continue with his quest to seduce her. The scenes in which these individuals appear help to maintain the movie's pace and to give the audience space from the protagonists as well as create a more complicated plot.

A number of cinematic techniques are utilized during the portrayal of Clementine and Joel's memories. The picture quality and sound resolution of the memories purposefully deteriorate, and subtle details from a scene will fade from view. Moreover, there are several instances where characters simply vanish from the scene—while Clementine is seated in the car with Joel, her figure suddenly fades away, and when Joel and Clementine are running through Grand Central terminal the people around them start to disappear. **CK**

►
Joel (Carrey) and Clementine (Winslet) wake up in bed on a snowy beach in one of the "memory erasure" scenes.

I, ROBOT 2004 (U.S. · GERMANY)

Director Alex Proyas **Producers** John Davis, Topher Dow, Wyck Godfrey
Screenplay Jeff Vintar, Akiva Goldsman (from the novel written by Isaac Asimov)
Cinematography Simon Duggan **Music** Marco Beltrami **Cast** Will Smith, Bridget
Moynahan, Alan Tudyk, James Cromwell, Bruce Greenwood, David Haysom

Set in 2035, *I, Robot* previews a time when robots handle all of
life's most mundane chores—from cooking and cleaning to
balancing checkbooks and walking dogs. Humans are now
free to enjoy life without the normal everyday stresses. Best of
all, robots do not commit crimes. However, techno-phobic cop
Detective Del Spooner (Smith) does not trust these machines,
and his fears become a reality when Dr. Alfred Lanning
(Cromwell) is found dead after apparently having jumped to his
death out of his office window. Spooner's personal connection
with Lanning leaves him assured that the man was not one to
take his own life, and he suspects that Sonny (voice-over by
Alan Tudyk), a very specialized robot who claims to feel real
emotions, is, in fact, the killer who has managed to find his way
around the Three Laws of Robotics.

◄

**The movie
initially went into
development as an
original screenplay
entitled *Hardware*,
before being
converted into
an "inspired by"
adaptation of Isaac
Asimov's novel.**

These Laws—made famous in the robot "Foundation" trilogy
by science-fiction author Isaac Asimov—state that (1) a robot
may not injure a human being; (2) a robot must obey orders
given it by humans; (3) a robot must protect its own existence
as long as such protection does not conflict with the First or
Second Law. Dr. Susan Calvin (Moynahan), a robo-psychologist

who works for U.S. Robotics, and CEO Lawrence Robertson (Greenwood) are suspicious of Spooner's motives for blaming a robot, and skeptical of his conclusions. But that doesn't stop Dr. Calvin from aiding Spooner's investigation and developing a slightly flirtatious relationship with him in the process.

Director Alex Proyas uses some of the best computer-generated special effects to date in this film in the way that he

"CAN A ROBOT WRITE A SYMPHONY? CAN A ROBOT TURN A CANVAS INTO A MASTERPIECE?" *SPOONER* "CAN YOU?" *SONNY*

is able to blend dozens—sometimes hundreds or thousands—of robots with the live actors. When Smith and Moynahan are interacting with Sonny, he truly appears to be a real person who just happens to look a bit robotic.

In a remarkable battle scene, robots are battling robots alongside humans battling robots, and the pain inflicted on the "good" robots is felt by the audience. There is also a mesmerizing and hugely enjoyable CGI car chase set in a tunnel. Moreover, cars drive sideways, appliances are voice-activated, and gasoline is almost a thing of the past.

► **Del Spooner (Smith) anxiously searches for one particular robot hiding among the masses.**

I, Robot is a murder mystery set around robots and it addresses serious moral questions, but it isn't always successful and does borrow heavily from other science-fiction films. Overall, however, the entertainment quotient and Will Smith's box office draw deliver more than their share of adventure. **CK**

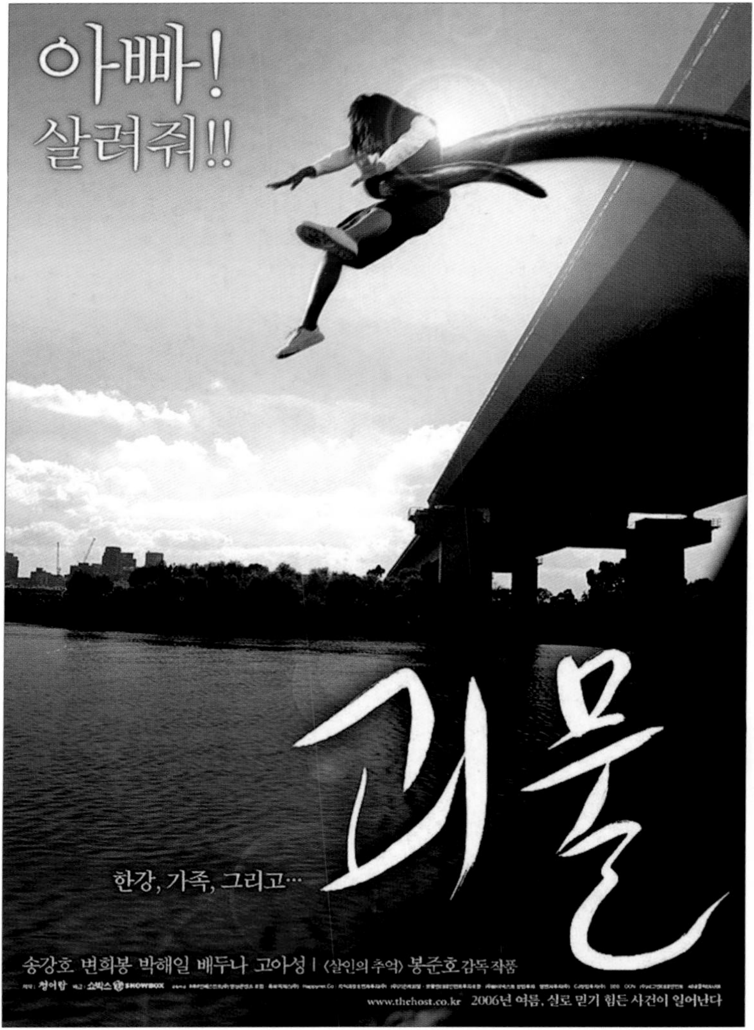
아빠!
살려줘!!
괴물
한강, 가족, 그리고…
송강호 변희봉 박해일 배두나 고아성 | 〈살인의 추억〉 봉준호 감독 작품
청어람 쇼박스 SHOWBOX
www.thehost.co.kr 2006년 여름, 실로 믿기 힘든 사건이 일어난다

THE HOST 2006 (SOUTH KOREA)

Director Joon-ho Bong **Producer** Yong-bae Choi **Screenplay** Chul-hyun Baek, Joon-ho Bong, Won-jun Ha **Cinematography** Hyung-ku Kim **Music** Byung-woo Lee **Cast** Kang-ho Song, Hie-bong Byeon, Hae-il Park, Du-na Bae, Ah-sung Ko, David Joseph Anselmo, Martin E. Cayce, Cristen Cho, Brian Lee, Clinton Morgan, Dal-su Oh

After *Memories of Murder* (2003), a film that brilliantly re-examined the serial-killer genre, South Korean director Joon-ho Bong decided to take on the monster movie. He really enjoys breaking the rules of the genres he is working in, and it shows on screen. Although *The Host* (a.k.a. *Gwoemul*) succeeds on different occasions in offering the expected thrills, one can justifiably argue that its real richness lies in Bong's audacious aesthetic choices and the film's wild mood swings.

Once the origins of the giant monster are established, it is not long before it starts attacking people. Contrary to all expectations, however, it does so in broad daylight, during a sunny and quiet afternoon. Even if part of the action takes place in subterranean settings (sewers, to be exact) inherited from the gothic tradition, *The Host*'s world is first and foremost a grounded and realistic one. This bias is quite clever and enables the film to focus on something other than the conventional suspense linked to the creature's appearance. In fact, Bong provides the viewers with a constantly shifting mix of horror, (slapstick) comedy, and melodrama. Park Gang-Du (Song), a dimwitted but ultimately heroic man working in a nearby snack

◄

The film scooped Asian Film Awards for Best Actor, Best Cinematographer, Best Film, and Best Visual Effects. It is also reputedly the most watched film in South Korean movie history.

bar, sees his young daughter taken away by the indescribable creature coming out of the Han River, and will do anything to find her with the help of his family. Central to the picture is thus a strong desire to reconstruct familial unity, but equally important is the theme of problematic communication both within this entity and with the outside world—as the final sequence demonstrates.

"I DON'T KNOW WHY, BUT I LOVE GENRE MOVIES AS MUCH AS I HATE THEM." JOON-HO BONG

As entertaining as it is, *The Host* nonetheless manifests strong socially conscious morals. Although he asked an American company, The Orphanage, to create the digital special effects for his movie, Bong overtly criticizes the U.S. government for interference in Korea's internal affairs and contempt for the preservation of the environment as the monster originates from chemical products poured into the river by a Korean scientist (unwillingly following the orders of his unscrupulous American superior). *The Host* also foregrounds the disillusion of a whole generation (that of the director), in particular via Gang-Du's qualified but unemployed younger brother. Society is seen as being as monstrous as the creature that it has generated, only much more absurd; whereas the monster simply kills to survive, the authorities are forced to use an even more harmful product so that the threat can be eradicated. **FL**

► **Du-na Bae shows great guts and determination in this fast-paced science-fiction monster delight.**

"★★★★ CHILLINGLY REAL, ELECTRIFYING, THRILLING AND NAIL-BITING"
PETER BRADSHAW, THE GUARDIAN

"TOP FLIGHT THRILLER...
THERE'S BARELY A PAUSE FOR BREATH"
HOLLYWOOD REPORTER

THE YEAR
2027:
THE LAST DAYS OF
THE HUMAN RACE

NO CHILD HAS BEEN
BORN FOR 18 YEARS

HE MUST PROTECT
OUR ONLY HOPE

Clive Owen
Julianne Moore
Michael Caine

Children
of men

a film by Alfonso Cuarón

www.uip.co.uk www.childrenofmen.co.uk

eat

VIDEO CALL 81661 FOR CLIP STREAMED DIRECT TO YOUR MOBILE NOW

AT CINEMAS NATIONWIDE SEPTEMBER 22

CHILDREN OF MEN 2006 (U.K. · U.S. · JAPAN)

Director Alfonso Cuarón **Producers** Marc Abraham, Eric Newman, Hilary Shor, Iain Smith, Tony Smith **Screenplay** Alfonso Cuarón, Timothy J. Sexton, David Arata, Mark Fergus, Hawk Ostby **Cinematography** Emmanuel Lubezki **Music** John Tavener **Cast** Clive Owen, Julianne Moore, Michael Caine, Clare-Hope Ashitey

Like many science-fiction films, *Children of Men* believes in individual action—activism even—as an antidote against the out-of-control corporate capitalism that has polluted the environment and poisoned humanity in search of profit. But unlike many others it rejects simplistic answers. There are no absolutist, utopian solutions, and yet no sheer dystopic nihilism either. Nor is *Children of Men* just a rant. Instead, the film celebrates humans just for being the unpredictable, life-loving, and meaning-seeking creatures they are.

London, 2027. It's been 18 years since the last baby was born into a world that is in apocalyptic disarray. Refugees, mobs, and crowds of disenfranchised fill the streets as official representatives of society hide in golden cages, denying them access to the world's collected wealth and issuing ever more draconian restriction orders; it is a battle of the many who have nothing (not even children or a home any more) against the few who do. And then a single baby arrives. Theo Faron (Owen) is approached by his former girlfriend, activist Julian (Moore) to escort a pregnant young woman, Kee (Ashitey), out of the country, where she can safely deliver her child. Helped by old

◄

Based on the novel *The Children of Men* by P. D. James, the movie picked up Oscar nominations for Best Writing, Best Cinematography, and Best Editing.

hippie Jasper (Caine), and hunted down by militias, the police, and army, Theo succeeds, but at the cost of his own life.

Children of Men is a bravura piece of filmmaking. The first two minutes match those of 1958's *Touch of Evil* (a virtuoso tracking shot ending with a bomb explosion the protagonist narrowly escapes), and there are further parallels in the way themes of xenophobia and government corruption are mixed with

"EVERY TIME ONE OF OUR POLITICIANS IS IN TROUBLE, A BOMB EXPLODES."

JASPER

dazzling action scenes. Occasionally, *Children of Men* appears to take on too much—each scene conjures up allegorical or political overtones, from the food and energy crisis and the war on terror, via immigration camps and popular uprisings, to religious metaphors (Theo means "God"). But these never stand in the way of a fast-paced, twisting plot that keeps viewers captivated. After all, everything is connected in this world, so it only makes sense to portray it as such.

"Keep her close" is Theo's final advice to Kee and her child. For director Alfonso Cuarón, *Children of Men* pleads for a world that downscales. Any organization that exceeds direct, interpersonal contact (nation-states, multinationals, the media) is considered suspicious. At the same time, as the sounds of laughing children with which the film closes testify, *Children of Men* really asks, do we love humanity enough to save it? **EM**

▶
Faron (Owen) and Kee (Ashitey) walk the guantlet of a dystopian future. Kee's name is a homophone for "chi" (or "chee"), meaning the energy or force of life itself.

INDEX

INDEX

CONTRIBUTORS

(AB) Aleksandar Becanovic is a Montenegrin writer and film critic.

(AK) Amy Kushner lectures at the University of Wisconsin-Parkside.

(AS) Adam Simon writes on film out of Santa Monica, California and Melbourne, Australia.

(BC) Brigid Cherry lectures in film and television at The University of London and researches horror film audiences, science-fiction fan cultures.

(CK) Casey Kent is a student at the U.S.C. in Los Angeles.

(CV) Constantine Verevis is a film scholar at Monash University.

(DF) Dan Hassler-Forest teaches at Amsterdam University, where he is writing on superheroes in films.

(DO) Dejan Ognjanovic writes reviews for www.kfccinema.com and www.beyondhollywood.com, and contributed essays to the BFI's *100 European Horror Films*.

(EM) Ernest Mathijs is Director of Cinema Studies at the University of British Columbia. His books include *The Cinema of David Cronenberg: From Baron of Blood to Cultural Hero*.

(FL) Frank Lafond teaches Film Studies in Lille (France). He has written a book on Jacques Tourneur and edited one on George A. Romero.

(GC) Guy Crucianelli is a writer whose work has appeared in *Senses of Cinema* and *Brightlights Film Journal*.

(IR) Ivo Ritzer is Editor-in-Chief of the German art magazine *Ikonen*.

(JA) Jerold J. Abrams writes in the philosophy of film and popular culture.

(JM) Jay McRoy's latest book is *Nightmare Japan: Contemporary Japanese Horror Cinema* (2008).

(KS) Kevin L. Stoehr is an editor and writer (*Nihilism in Film and Television*).

(LB) Linda Badley is a film scholar at Middle Tennessee State, and author of *Film, Horror, and the Body Fantastic*, and *Writing Horror and the Body*.

(MA) Michael Atkinson has written *Ghosts in the Machine: Speculating on the Dark Heart of Pop Cinema*.

(MC) Matthew Coniam is a freelance writer and author of *Pre-Code Horror*.

(MCv) Miloš Cvetković writes film reviews for the internet magazine *POPBOKS*. He has been published in magazines specialising in science-fiction: *Znak Sagite* and *Emitor*.

(MH) Matt Hills is author of books such as *Fan Cultures* and *The Pleasures of Horror*.

(MK) Mikel Koven is a film scholar at Worcester University (U.K.). He has written *Blaxploitation Film*, *La Dolce Morte: Vernacular Cinema and the Italian Giallo Film*, and *Film, Folklore and Urban Legends*.

(MM) Marty McKee moderates the Sci-Fi, Horror, & Fantastic Cinema discussion board at Mobius Home Video Forum (www.mhvf.net).

(MS) Michael Sevastakis has written extensively on film and authored several books on the horror film and the films of Russ Meyer.

(NT) Nathaniel Thompson is the author of the three *DVD Delirium* books, and has overseen the release of numerous cult films on DVD. www.mondo-digital.com.

(PH) Peter Hutchings lectures in Film at Northumbria University, U.K.

(PM) Philippe Met is a film scholar at the University of Pennsylvania, and writes on crime and horror cinema.

(RH) Reynold Humphries has written *The American Horror Film: An Introduction*, and *The Hollywood Horror Film, 1931-1941*.

(RH) Russ Hunter is researching Italian genre cinema as a PhD, at the University of Wales, Aberystwyth.

(SB) Shai Biderman is a doctoral candidate in Philosophy at Boston University, and researches the philosophy of culture, film, and books.

(SH) Steffen Hantke has published essays and reviews on contemporary literature, film, and culture in journals and anthologies.

(SMS) Steven M. Sanders is editor of *The Philosophy of Science Fiction Film*, co-editor of *The Philosophy of TV Noir*, and a contributor to *Film Noir: An Encyclopedic Reference to the American Style*.

(WD) William J. Devlin is a film tutor at Bridgewater State College, MA. His fields of interest include Philosophy of Science, theories of truth, Nietzsche and Existentialism.

(WW) William Wilson is a film writer who graduated from The College of William & Mary.

PICTURE CREDITS

Many of the images in this book are from the archives of The Kobal Collection, which owes its existence to the vision, courage, talent and energy of the men and women who created the movie industry and whose legacies live on through the films they made, the studios they built, and the publicity photographs they took. Kobal collects, preserves, organizes, and makes these photographs available. Quintessence wishes to thank all the film distribution and production companies and apologizes in advance for any omissions or neglect, and will be pleased to make any necessary changes in future editions.

2 UFA/Kobal **5** Universal/Kobal **6** Lucasfilm/20th Century Fox/Kobal **8** Melies/Kobal **11** Melies/Kobal **12** Det Danske Filminstitut/Nordisk Film A/S **15** Det Danske Filminstitut/Nordisk Film A/S **16** Mezhrabpom/Kobal **19** Mezhrabpom/Kobal **20** Films Diamant/Hollywood Select Video, P. O. Box 3107, La Jolla, CA 92038-3107 and www.lifeisamovie.com **23** Films Diamant/Kobal **24** UFA/Kobal **27** AKG Images **28** Universal/Kobal **31** Universal/Kobal **32** Rex Features **35** London Films/United Artists/Kobal **36** 20th Century Fox/Kobal **39** 20th Century Fox/Kobal **40** RKO/Kobal **43** RKO/Kobal **44** Rex Features **47** Paramount/Kobal **48** 20th Century Fox/Kobal **51** 20th Century Fox/Kobal **52** Universal/Kobal **55** Allied Artists/Kobal **56** Rex Features **59** Paramount/Kobal **60** Walt Disney/Kobal **63** Walt Disney/Kobal **64** Rex Features **67** Allstar **68** Warner Bros./Kobal **71** Warner Bros./Kobal **72** Rex Features **75** MGM/Kobal **76** Allied Artists/Kobal **79** Allied Artists/Kobal **80** Universal/Kobal **83** Universal/Kobal **84** 20th Century Fox/Kobal **87** 20th Century Fox/Kobal **88** MGM/Kobal **91** Rex Features **92** Goskino/Kobal **95** RIA Novosti **96** Argos Films **99** Argos/Kobal **100** Paramount/Kobal **103** Paramount/Kobal **104** Chaumiane/Film Studio/Kobal **107** Chaumiane/Film Studio/Kobal **108** Embassy/Kobal **111** Embassy/Kobal **112** Rex Features **115** Allstar **116** 20th Century Fox/Kobal **119** 20th Century Fox/Kobal **120** Paramount/Kobal **123** Paramount/Kobal **124** Terryho ponožky/Ateliery Bonton Zlin **127** Terryho ponožky/Ateliery Bonton Zlin **128** Hammer/Kobal **131** Hammer/Kobal **132** Allstar **135** MGM/Kobal **136** Rex Features **139** 20th Century Fox/Kobal **140** Warner Bros./Kobal **143** Warner Bros./Kobal **144** American Zoetrope/Warner Bros./Kobal **147** American Zoetrope/Warner Bros./Kobal **148** Universal/Kobal **151** Universal/Kobal **152** Universal/Kobal **155** Universal/Kobal **156** Terryho ponožky/Mosfilm **159** Mosfilm/Kobal **160** Films Armorial, Les/Kobal **163** Films Armorial, Les/Kobal **164** United Artists/Kobal **167** United Artists/Kobal **168** MGM/Ronald Grant Archive **171** MGM/Kobal **172** MGM/Kobal **175** Allstar **176** Jack H. Harris Enterprises/Kobal **179** Jack H. Harris Enterprises/Kobal **180** MGM/Kobal **183** MGM/Kobal **184** Rex Features **187** EMI/Kobal **188** Rex Features **191** Columbia/Kobal **192** Lucasfilm/20th Century Fox/Kobal **195** Lucasfilm/20th Century Fox/Kobal **196** 20th Century Fox/Kobal **199** 20th Century Fox/Kobal **200** Mosfilm/Kobal **203** Mosfilm/Kobal **204** Rex Features **207** Warner Bros./Kobal **208** LucasFilm/Ronald Grant Archive **211** Lucasfilm/20th Century Fox/Kobal **212** Universal/Kobal **215** Universal/Kobal **216** Avco Embassy/Kobal **219** Avco Embassy/Kobal **220** Warner Bros./Kobal **223** Warner Bros./Kobal **224** Rex Features **227** Film Plan International/Kobal **228** Ladd Co./Warner Bros./Kobal **231** Ladd Co./Warner Bros./Kobal **232** Allstar **235** Universal/Kobal **236** Paramount/Kobal **239** Paramount/Kobal **240** Universal/Kobal **243** Universal/Kobal **244** Walt Disney/Kobal **247** Walt Disney/Kobal **248** Le Films du Loup/Kobal **251** Films Du Loup/Kobal **252** LucasFilm/Ronald Grant Archive **255** Lucasfilm/20th Century Fox/Kobal **256** Universal/Kobal **259** Universal/Kobal **260** Courtesy of the Academy of Motion Picture Arts and Sciences/A-Train Films/Cinecom C **263** A-Train Films/Cinecom C/Kobal **264** Universal/Kobal **267** Allstar **268** Umbrella/Rosenblum/Virgin Films/Kobal **271** Umbrella/Rosenblum/Virgin Films/Kobal **272** Rex Features **275** Edge City/Universal/Kobal **276** Columbia Pictures/Ronald Grant Archive **279** Columbia/Kobal **280** Orion/Kobal **283** Orion/Kobal **284** Amblin/Universal/Kobal **287** Amblin/Universal/Kobal **288** Universal/Embassy/Kobal **291** Universal/Embassy/Kobal **292** Cinepro/Mr. Yellowbeard Productions Limited & Company **295** Allstar **296** 20th Century Fox/Kobal **299** 20th Century Fox/Kobal **300** Paramount/Kobal **303** Allstar **304** Amercent Films/Ronald Grant Archive **307** 20th Century Fox/Rosenthal, Zade/Kobal **308** Rex Features **311** Orion/Kobal **312** Akira/Kobal **315** Akira/Kobal **316** Arenafilm/Kobal **319** Arenafilm/John Maynard Productions **320** 20th Century Fox/Kobal **323** 20th Century Fox/Kobal **324** JHV/Ronald Grant Archive **327** K2 Spirit/SEN/Kobal **328** Allstar **331** Carolco/Tri-Star/Kobal **332** Carolco/Kobal **335** Carolco/Kobal **336** Amblin/Universal/Kobal **339** Amblin/Universal/Kobal **340** Allstar **343** Manga Entertainment/Kobal **344** Polygram/Kobal **347** Polygram/Caruso, Phillip/Kobal **348** Rex Features **351** 20th Century Fox/Barius, Claudette/Kobal **352** © 1997 GAUMONT. Musée Gaumont Collection **355** Columbia/Tri-Star/Kobal **356** Columbia/Kobal **359** Columbia/Michaels, Darren/Kobal **360** Columbia/Kobal **363** Columbia/Kobal **364** Sogetel/Le Films Alain Sarde/Kobal **367** Rex Features **368** TriStar Pictures/Ronald Grant Archive **372** Artisan Ent./Kobal **375** Harvest/Truth & Soul/Libatique, Matthew/Kobal **376** Allstar **379** Dreamworks LLC/Close, Murray/Kobal **380** Rex Features **383** Warner Bros./Kobal **384** Touchstone/Blinding Edge/Kobal **387** Touchstone/Blinding Edge/Kobal **388** BBC/Revolution Films/Kobal **391** BBC/Revolution Films/Lee, Sarah/Kobal **392** Focus Features/Kobal **395** Focus Features/Lee, David/Kobal **396** 20th Century Fox/Kobal **399** 20th Century Fox/Digital Domain/Kobal **400** Allstar **403** Thinkfilm/Kobal **404** Universal Pictures/Ronald Grant Archive **407** Universal/UIP/Kobal **408** Allstar **411** Chungeorahm Film/Kobal

ACKNOWLEDGMENTS

Quintessence would like to thank the following people for their help in the preparation of this book: Dave Kent, Angela Levin, and Phil Moad at the Kobal Collection, Stephen Atkinson at Rex Features, Paul McFegan at ALLSTAR, the Ronald Grant Archive, David Price-Hughes at AKG, Ralph Gibson at RIA Novosti, David Budsky, Jan Vnoucek, Pavel Rajčan, Terryho Ponožky (www.terryposters. com), Mogens Dester, Stine Nielsen, Christine Bayly, Hollywood Select Video, and David Foster.

General Editor Steven Jay Schneider would like to thank all of the contributors, along with everyone at Quintessence, especially Jane, Helena, and Chrissy.

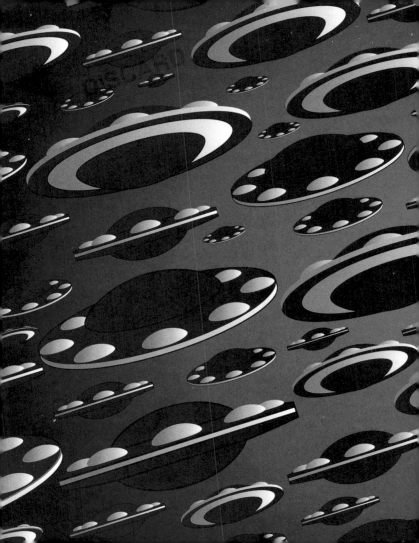